To:

From:

Message:

A Gift of Grace and Gratitude

Copyright © 2019 by Christian Art Publishers,
PO Box 1599, Vereeniging, 1930, RSA

© 2019
First edition 2019

Designed by Christian Art Publishers
Cover designed by Christian Art Publishers

Scripture quotations are taken from the *Holy Bible*, New Living Translation®,
copyright © 1996, 2004, 2007, 2013, 2015 by Tyndale House Foundation.
Used by permission of Tyndale House Publishers, Inc., Carol Stream, Illinois 60188.
All rights reserved.

Printed in China

ISBN 978-1-4321-3079-4

19   20   21   22   23   24   25   26   27   28   -   10   9   8   7   6   5   4   3   2   1

A gift of
GRACE
and GRATITUDE

CHRISTIAN ART
PUBLISHERS

The LORD is my
Strength
and my shield;
my heart trusts in Him,
and He helps me.
My heart leaps for joy,
and with my song
I praise Him.

PSALM 28:7

Introduction

Hello Dear Readers,

As I began working on this book about grace and gratitude, I realized anew that grace is not only about salvation or forgiveness. Literally everything we have in our lives is by God's grace. Everything. That realization filled my heart with gratitude. So, yes, the two go together.

My prayer for you is that your understanding of God's moment-by-moment grace to you will fill your heart with gratitude too. Gratitude that spills over into everything you do!

Blessings,

Carolyn

January

Are You Hungry?

Everyone has sinned; we all fall short
of God's glorious standard. Yet God,
in His grace, freely makes us right in His sight.
He did this through Christ Jesus when
He freed us from the penalty for our sins.
ROMANS 3:23-24

You're a sinner. Have you admitted that? Let's say you do admit it. How does it make you feel? Ashamed? Guilty? Guilt is no fun. It's consuming and affects your attitudes, relationships and self-image. Are you hungry to find a way to end the guilt and the sense of failure that goes with it? Well, there is a way and it's not difficult. You only need to accept God's forgiveness, which is given through His grace.

God isn't surprised that you disobey or do selfish, mean things. He knows you can't help it. It's in your human DNA. But, the situation isn't hopeless because He has a plan that He set in place simply because He loves you. It's a simple plan (for you) though it cost Him the ultimate sacrifice. God doesn't want you to feel guilt. He wants you to have a personal relationship with Him. So, God forgives your sin by His grace; which means He forgives you though you do not deserve it, will never deserve it, and can do nothing to deserve it. He sent His Son, Jesus, to die for your sins and in that single action He set the table of grace. Are you hungry? Come to the table.

Where are you in the process of taking
a seat at God's table of grace? How can you
pull out a chair for someone else to have a seat?

What Do You Want?

"I will give you a new heart, and I will put a
new spirit in you. I will take out your stony,
stubborn heart and give you a tender, responsive heart."
EZEKIEL 36:26

Losing weight is hard work. It takes discipline. You have to make good food choices and unfortunately that means you can't always have what you want. You must choose what you need. If you're disciplined things go well. If not, you give in to the craving for cookies and push away the carrots. Yep, that won't get you to your goal.

That want vs. need thing applies in several areas of life. For example, do you sometimes ask God for what you want forgetting that He knows what you need? When He gives you what He knows you need rather than what you want, are you disappointed?

It's because of God's grace that He gives you what you need. His love for you is deeper and more sacrificial than you can comprehend. He loves you too much to give you what you want in the immediacy of the moment.

He sees the bigger picture of your whole life and He knows what you need, that will help your faith in Him grow deeper. He gives you what you need – a new heart and spirit that are tuned to Him. That's God's grace. He gives more than you deserve; more than you could dream.

When has God given you what you
needed instead of what you asked for?
How did that impact your faith in Him?

JAN
3

Forgiven and Forgotten

If we confess our sins to Him,
He is faithful and just to forgive us our sins
and to cleanse us from all wickedness.
1 JOHN 1:9

You understand forgiveness, right? When someone hurts you and apologizes, you forgive her. But be honest, total forgiveness is hard. You "say" you forgive and you even try with all your heart to mean it. Maybe you're even successful in forgiving, but forgetting … well, that's another story. The memory of the wrong done is always there in the back of your mind so it's never really forgotten.

Grasping the difficulty of your own struggle to forgive and forget serves to give you an even greater appreciation of God's total forgiveness and "forgetfulness" of your sin. It's amazing – God promises that no matter what you've done or how many times you promise to never do that thing again – but, of course, you do it again anyway – if you confess it, He will forgive. He doesn't only forgive you; He wipes the slate clean. Your sin is gone; never to be mentioned again. That's God's forgiving grace.

Shouldn't you be able to offer grace to one who has wronged you? It's probably not possible to do that without God's help. So, ask Him to help you forgive your friend and not hold her offense in a file for later use.

Is there some offense you have forgiven but haven't been able to forget? What would happen if you intentionally did something nice for the offender? Bought her a coffee? Or just said hello? What could you do?

Growing through Pain

Dear brothers and sisters, when troubles of any kind
come your way, consider it an opportunity for great joy.
JAMES 1:2

You're supposed to cheer when the medical report is bad or when a spouse walks away or a job is lost or a child rebels? That's not what this verse is saying at all. Of course, it's hard to be thankful when you're going through a painful situation. All you know is you hurt and you want the hurt to stop. But, even in the pain, God's grace is there.

As hard as it is, your faith grows stronger through times of pain and suffering because as other things you depend on are pulled away, your dependence on God grows stronger. It hurts, but it's not without purpose.

God's goal is not for your days to be easy but for your faith in Him to be the most important thing to you. In the big picture, that's what matters most.

It's because of His grace that God's love reaches through your pain helping your trust in Him grow deeper as you see Him holding you tight and helping you persevere.

Don't beg God to take your problems away. Recognize that you can make it because of Him! Thank Him for His grace that grows your trust in Him and makes you more like Christ.

What problems are you struggling with today?
Are you fighting against them – refusing to "consider
them an opportunity for joy?" What lessons do you
feel God may want to teach you through them?

Be Thankful

Now, just as you accepted Christ Jesus as your Lord,
you must continue to follow Him. Let your roots grow
down into Him, and let your lives be built on Him.
Then your faith will grow strong in the truth you were
taught, and you will overflow with thankfulness.

COLOSSIANS 2:6-7

Go back to the beginning … to that day when you accepted Jesus as Savior. Do you recall how, as you recognized your sinful hopelessness, you were overwhelmed with gratitude for His grace in providing salvation from your complete lostness and starting you on your way to life and a relationship with Him? As your faith grew, there were, no doubt, difficult times, struggles and maybe even questions. The journey to really knowing Jesus takes you through deep waters. Growing strong faith means being intentional about sticking close to Him in tough times and even thanking Him for the struggles.

Be grateful for the lessons you're learning even when it's hard. Be thankful for the faith you're developing. Thank God for the truth you're learning. As you learn to appreciate the journey and the benefits it brings, your heart will swell with gratitude for Jesus' plans for your life. Don't settle for "easy" when the difficult can give you so much more.

What does your life look like with its roots grown down
deep in Jesus? In what areas have you seen growth?

Pay It Forward

Let your conversation be gracious
and attractive so that you will have
the right response for everyone.
COLOSSIANS 4:6

The experience of God's grace should not – no, must not – stop with you. God encourages you to pay grace forward. That's so others can begin to know His grace. Your grace to them may be the doorway that opens their hearts to Him.

How do you pay grace forward? Well, it's getting harder and harder in our world but it should not be so difficult. Simply – be kind. Don't allow your conversation to be filled with judgmental criticism of others. Our society has become polarized so that we are not accepting of others' beliefs or opinions. You don't have to agree with them but you can respond with kindness and love. Remember what our elders used to say? "If you can't say something nice. Don't say anything at all." Good advice.

Go against the grain of society and speak words of encouragement and kindness to others – retail workers, waitresses, medical workers. Show grace to others as God has shown grace to you! Give friends the benefit of the doubt when they disappoint you. Be forgiving of those who hurt you. Simply put – offer grace to others as it has been offered to you. It's the Jesus thing to do.

How can you pay grace forward? Start with baby steps if you need to. With whom can you begin? What's a tangible way you can pay grace forward?

Don't Give Up

For the LORD God is our sun and our shield.
He gives us grace and glory. The LORD will withhold
no good thing from those who do what is right.
PSALM 84:11

God willingly gives His grace. There is ample evidence of His grace poured out on all. However, there's one thing that pleases His heart more than anything else … your obedience to His commands and truths. To the best of your ability, with a submitted heart, obey the truth you know. Your obedience shows that your true desire is to please God and grow in your life with Him.

God offers His table of grace set with a feast so magnificent that the table sags beneath its weight. Of course, He wants to give to you and bless you more than you can imagine. But, there are seasons when you can't sense His presence in your life, times when your spiritual growth feels stymied. Why does that happen? Does God withdraw from you because you struggle to obey Him?

Remember, Child of God, that He loves you. He sees your heart's desire to obey Him and to grow deeper in love with Him. He doesn't withdraw … He teaches by grace and in love. If you have obedience struggles, don't give up on yourself. God doesn't give up on you!

Have you experienced a time when God seemed
distant? How long until you began to feel reconnected
to Him? What did you learn from the experience?

Share What You've Got

God will generously provide all you need.
Then you will always have everything you need
and plenty left over to share with others.
2 CORINTHIANS 9:8

Is your response to this verse something like, "No, God has not generously given me all I need!" Does it feel like your prayers go unanswered or even unnoticed? It's hard to have any kind of perspective of God's love and grace when you're struggling so much with these kinds of thoughts.

Here's the truth – God actually does give you everything you need to live and serve Him. He said He would and He does. That's His grace in action. You can trust Him. He might not give you everything you want but you have what you need to do the work He has for you.

Notice the last part of this verse. It promises that God will give you what you need. But He doesn't stop there. He gives you even more than you need. That extra is not for you to save for a later date. It's not for you. He gives you more so that you can share it with others. God showers you with His grace, over and above what you need so that it will spill over from you to those around you. God's grace is given to you and through you.

Can you think of a time when God's care for you
was so generous that it spilled over to others? How
did it make you feel to be able to share with others?

Saying Grace

Give thanks to the LORD, for He is good!
His faithful love endures forever.
1 CHRONICLES 16:34

One of the most wonderful times in life is when you can enjoy the blessing of sitting down to a delicious meal with your loved ones! You join hands and say grace before you dive into the meal. How cool that you say grace for God's grace.

Thankfulness … gratitude for God's grace-filled gifts is important because it recognizes His generosity to you. Saying the words "thank you" is easy. Sometimes it's hard to actually feel the gratitude.

Gratitude is realizing that you wouldn't have any of what you are enjoying without God's grace. Gratitude flows from a humble heart. You can't be thankful if you feel that you actually deserve what God has given you. You may say the right words and even feel thankfulness on some level, but sincere heartfelt gratitude for being given what you do not deserve will be missing.

So, put away the arrogance that you deserve any of God's grace and confess that you are the undeserving recipient of God's generosity. Humble your heart and let it fill with true gratitude for God's grace, blessings and faithful love. Be thankful.

Do you regularly thank God for His generosity to you? What are you most thankful for? Does your gratitude truly come from a heart that recognizes you are not worthy of any of God's blessings? How can you help those around you be grateful to Him, too?

Side by Side

Look after each other so that none of you fails to receive
the grace of God. Watch out that no poisonous root of
bitterness grows up to trouble you, corrupting many.
HEBREWS 12:15

News flash – God's generous grace is not only all about you! Look around you – at the people you know and those you don't. God's plan is that people should live in community. That means that you help one another, love one another, forgive one another, encourage one another and show grace to one another.

Invite others to share God's grace with you by simply sharing grace with them. How do you do that? In this social media driven world hatefulness, criticism and a judgmental spirit characterize too many peoples' attitudes. People are unwilling to allow others to hold different beliefs or even to disagree with them without reacting in a cruel way. None of that behavior can be characterized as "looking after" one another as this verse instructs.

No, grace that you share is kind, loving, understanding and peaceful. This behavior doesn't mean that you approve of or even accept others' opinions. It simply means that you respond to them with grace. It may very well be that some people will only become aware of God's grace by how they experience grace from you. Look after one another with grace.

There are, no doubt, people in your world who hold
differing opinions and beliefs from you. How have you
shown them grace? How can you interact with them
today in a way that extends God's grace to them?

Baby Steps

Like newborn babies, you must crave pure
spiritual milk so that you will grow into a full
experience of salvation. Cry out for this nourishment.
1 PETER 2:2

Cravings can come out of nowhere. The thing with cravings is they continually niggle at your mind like a constant "Let's eat this!" or, "Let's do that!" Cravings wear you down. That's why it's interesting that Peter described the desire to grow spiritually to a craving. It should be something you long for. It should be constantly crying out for your attention.

You have to start somewhere. So, you accept Jesus and begin your personal relationship with Him. You start as a baby Christian. There's a lot to learn on the journey to become more like Jesus. Just as you mature and grow physically, your spirit also matures and grows through your study of God's Word and as you stay close to Him. By God's grace, He walks with you through this process.

His grace provides the lessons for you to learn and grow. Each step takes you deeper with Him. Some of the more "mature" meals won't taste good. They may be bitter and hard to swallow. But remember that they are helping you become more like Christ. Don't ever be satisfied with where you are. Keep seeking, learning and growing. God's grace will take you deeper.

Take an honest assessment of your desires. Do you crave reading God's Word? Do you constantly long to know Him more intimately? If not, maybe it's time to evaluate where your time and energy goes and ask God to fill your heart with the desire to know Him better.

The Rubber Meets the Road

Make allowance for each other's faults,
and forgive anyone who offends you. Remember,
the Lord forgave you, so you must forgive others.
COLOSSIANS 3:13

The rubber meets the road with the reality of how you treat people. No doubt, some people get on your nerves and it's difficult to be patient or forgiving with them. Then there are people who know exactly how to push you to your limit – and they do it as often as they can.

Stop and think about how God makes allowances for you. Do you always do what God wants? Of course not. Does God forgive you over and over? Yes. That's His grace in action.

Now think about that person who constantly criticizes, judges, complains and demands her own way. The person who wears on your patience. What's the best thing you can do? Forgive her and move on. Extend grace to her just as God extends grace to you. Can you do that in your own strength? Probably not. Ask God's help. When you're ready to explode, He will remind you of all the things He has forgiven you for in just this one day. Or perhaps He will remind you that the person who is getting on your nerves is dealing with some pretty heavy stuff herself. You are the recipient of God's undeserved grace, extend that same gift to those around you.

Name the person who is the one constantly frustrating and hurting you. How have you handled that relationship in the past? How can you do better? List some tangible ways to improve the relationship.

Why Is Grace Needed?

If we claim we have not sinned,
we are calling God a liar and showing
that His word has no place in our hearts.

1 JOHN 1:10

How do you feel about your status as a sinner? Do you say things like, "My sin is no worse than anyone else's sins." "I'm justified in the big picture by this or that verse for what I've done, even if people are hurt in the immediate." Life gets complicated when you try to justify your behavior against what Scripture says is right or wrong.

No one enjoys admitting when they do something wrong. So, they'll minimize their sin with words like, "Well, at least I didn't do this or that." Or, "Yeah, I did that, but look at what so and so did! It's a lot worse!"

Scripture tells us that we are all sinners. So you can't avoid the truth that you sin. Face it. Admit it. Confess it. Repent from it. Even if you deny your sin to other people, you can't hide it from God. Your sin doesn't surprise God. He knows you need forgiving. God's provision to forgive your sin is proof of His grace that comes from His great love for you.

Don't deny your sin. Confess, repent, ask forgiveness. But then, don't forget to thank God for His amazing grace.

Are you able to be honest with yourself regarding your sin?
Why is it hard for you to admit and confess your sin
to yourself and to God? Take some time right now
and evaluate your life. What do you need to confess?

The Cost of Grace

From His abundance we have all received
one gracious blessing after another. For the law
was given through Moses, but God's unfailing
love and faithfulness came through Jesus Christ.
JOHN 1:16-17

Grace is sometimes defined as the undeserved favor of God seen through His generous blessings. The word has even become an acronym for "**G**od's **R**iches **A**t **C**hrist's **E**xpense." Have you gotten so jaded in your heart that you've come to take it for granted?

Satan wants you to ignore the reality of God's grace. He squirms his way into your attitude about it by encouraging you to feel apathetic about God's blessings. He may even cause you to feel as though you actually deserve the good things God gives you. He will keep your life so chaotic that you don't often think about God or His grace at all. That's amazing isn't it … in fact, it's quite an insult to God to feel that His grace is not important enough to even think about.

God's grace to you cost Him dearly. It was not free for Him. God's grace comes through the horrific sacrifice of His Son, Jesus. God and Jesus were willing to make the sacrifice because of their love for you. God gave His best so that He can offer you grace. Don't take it lightly. Don't take His best … His grace for granted.

What kind of response do you hope for when you give someone an incredible gift? Sincere gratitude, right? Have you responded with sincere gratitude to God for His incredible gift of grace? What would you like to say to Him right now?

Grace in Words

Some people make cutting remarks,
but the words of the wise bring healing.
PROVERBS 12:18

Words have tremendous power. Hopefully, you say the right kind of words – words of kindness, love, grace and compassion. Here's a little test … can you recall a time when hurtful, mean, unkind words were spoken to you? No doubt you can. Those kinds of words stick with you for years.

Now, can you recall a time when something kind and encouraging was said to you? Hopefully you can, but the kind words may not be the first things that come into your mind.

One of the things God asks of you, as the recipient of His grace, is to let grace spill out to those around you. Jesus said that the second greatest commandment is to love others as you love yourself.

One of the ways to share God's grace is through the words you speak. There's a tension in learning how to live your faith and stay true to your beliefs but still speak words of grace to those with whom you disagree. Words of grace to those who don't believe in God or the truths of the Bible will keep the communication open so they can learn of God's love by the way you treat them.

Do you have an idea as to what your reputation is among those who know you? Are you thought of as kind or mean? Encouraging or critical? How can you monitor your words to see if you're speaking words of grace to others?

Gratitude Blocker

*Not that I was ever in need, for I have learned
how to be content with whatever I have.*
PHILIPPIANS 4:11

Contentment. It's an elusive emotion in our world these days. Everything in our culture cries out, "You should want more!" "You deserve more!" "Don't settle!" We strive for bigger houses, more complex toys, faster cars, better jobs, bigger salaries, more power … more, more, more. That makes contentment nearly impossible to own.

One result of that lack of contentment is a lack of gratitude. It's hard to be grateful for what you have if you are always wanting more than what you have. It's like having an itch that always needs to be scratched.

There's a constant drive to have more. That feeling undermines anything you're doing. You're never satisfied. That problem goes even deeper when you begin to believe that you actually deserve more than what God has given you. Then it's not just dissatisfaction with your life; it is also frustration with God.

To find real contentment you must be humbly grateful for the life God has given you and the blessings He bestows on you. Don't compare your life with others. Don't get sucked in by the hunger for more and more and more. Find contentment in what you have.

Do you fight the battle of discontentment? Take stock of what God has given you. Has He been generous to you? How does that affect your discontentment? Does it help you be grateful for what you have?

Passing Grace Along

Don't just pretend to love others.
Really love them. Hate what is wrong.
Hold tightly to what is good.
ROMANS 12:9

Do you have a special group of friends with whom you have a close relationship? Some make you laugh. Some listen to you, pray for you, share life with you.

Your special group of friends gives you a place to belong; a place to know you're cared for; a place to be useful to others. They give you security in having a sense of belonging. They are your people.

Some people don't have a "group." There are many reasons for that. Everything from being new to an employer, church, city – it takes time to develop a community. If you look around at church or work, you may notice a woman standing on the edge of your circle of friends. She's alone. She doesn't feel she belongs because she doesn't know anyone. Why should you care? Because God tells you to. Don't just say the "Christian" words about loving others. Pass along God's grace to those who are strangers; those who are difficult to love; those who are different, by really loving them.

Don't be exclusive – be inclusive. Grace makes room.

How can you put this challenge into action? How can you really love others? Those who are on the fringe? Those who are different? Their first experience of God's loving grace may come through you.

All or Nothing

God saved you by His grace when
you believed. And you can't take
credit for this; it is a gift from God.
EPHESIANS 2:8

Sin breaks your relationship with God. The only thing that can repair it is salvation. Grace is forgiveness of your ongoing sins. You are completely undeserving of this forgiveness. It doesn't matter how good you think you are.

There's no room for ego when it comes to accepting God's grace. You can't take credit for anything God gives you or does for you. You had no part in His grace-filled forgiveness. Come to God with humility. Be careful not to say you're sorry for your sin if you don't honestly mean it. Your pride gets in the way of fully receiving and grasping God's great love and sacrificial grace.

So come to God in this way: Let go of pride. You probably can't do this on your own. It's hard to just decide to be humble. Satan will fight you by continuing to tell you how much you deserve and how God slights you. Ask God to humble your heart and help you focus on how amazing His grace is and how much He loves you. Ask Him to help you be truly repentant for your sin. Give Him full and complete credit for your salvation. It's all because of His grace!

Do an honest self-evaluation of your own humility. Do you justify your sins? Do you feel entitled to the blessings and life you have? Do you recognize Jesus' total sacrifice for you? What do you want to say to Him right now?

A Healthy Spirit

You know the generous grace of our Lord
Jesus Christ. Though He was rich, yet for your sakes He
became poor, so that by His poverty He could make you rich.
2 CORINTHIANS 8:9

Nutritious food sustains the body and keeps it healthy. Without it your muscles cannot stay strong; your body cannot do what it's supposed to do; your organs can't function; you lose strength; you get fuzzy brained. If you eat only junk, well, your body will function like it's being fed junk and you will find yourself weak, overweight and unhealthy.

Compare those facts with how you feed your spirit. What you put in plays a big role in determining what comes out. If you feed your spirit an attitude of criticism, negativity, unhappiness and self-centeredness you can hardly expect to grow an attitude of Christlikeness and humble obedience to God. If however, you feed your spirit on God's Word, daily times of prayer to Him, an attitude of submission and humility, then God, by His grace will help you grow in faith and grace received from Him and shared with those around you.

Grace sustains your spirit. It doesn't just maintain your heart, it grows it to trust more deeply and love more sincerely. Knowing God more deeply and becoming more Christlike in your attitude, heart and actions comes only through a constant feeding of God's grace.

How regular is your Bible reading time? How much time do
you spend meditating and praying? Compare that with time on
social media or doing any of the multitude of things that occupy
your day. Do you need to restructure your priorities?

Party Time!

> You prepare a feast for me in the presence
> of my enemies. You honor me by anointing my
> head with oil. My cup overflows with blessings.
>
> PSALM 23:5

Those times when it feels like everyone is out to get you. You feel like you have few supporters. Lies are told about you. Misunderstandings damage relationships. Projects fail. Hurts abound. Yes, enemies everywhere and you sense no way to escape! Do you cry out, "God. Come on. I'm with You. I believe. I trust You. So … come on!"

This verse in Psalm 23 has an exciting nugget hidden in it. Enemy attacks on you don't surprise God. Remember He even said that you would experience problems – simply because you choose to follow Him. So, nothing that's happening to you is a surprise to Him.

In His grace, God strengthens you and sticks with you through those enemy attacks. But that's not all! Here's the hidden nugget! God plans a feast for you while your enemies have to stand around watching. And, they can do nothing to stop the party! He may not deliver you from the problems or even punish your enemies. But, He celebrates you and reminds you of His presence while your enemies can do nothing but watch. It's your party, thrown by God! He plans a celebration for you in the middle of the attacks! That's grace in action!

Can you think of times you have sensed God preparing
a feast for you while you were still in the middle of
a hard time? How did you see His presence
and know His encouragement?

Just Keeping Rules

If you are trying to make yourselves right with
God by keeping the law, you have been cut off
from Christ! You have fallen away from God's grace.
GALATIANS 5:4

Do you like the structure of having rules? Some people like boundaries that rules give them to decide what's right and what's not. Rules give them lines to live between and they insist that others live within those same boundaries.

The Bible certainly lays out some definitive guidelines as to what a life lived in obedience to God looks like. But there is a significant difference between the rules for living laid out in the Old Testament and the guidelines for obeying God as outlined in the New Testament. What's different? Grace. Jesus came. He taught. He loved. He died. He rose again. And … grace became a part of a relationship with God. If you're just living your life by a set of rules and not in a relationship with Christ … you're not experiencing God's grace.

Knowing Jesus as Savior is important to knowing God. Yes, there are still commands to obey. But don't get so caught up in obeying rules that you forget that one of Jesus' commands is to love others. Find the balance of loving others and living in obedience. Don't get so caught up in rules that you miss the love part of relating to God and others. That's where the grace comes in.

OK. Time to self-evaluate … do you have difficulty relating to folks who don't live by the rules you value most? How are you doing at valuing the person if you don't value the lifestyle? Are you good at loving others?

Worship Thankfully

Let all that I am praise the LORD; with my
whole heart, I will praise His holy name.
PSALM 103:1

Worshipping God is what believers should want to do. Maybe you do want that – so you gather with others who love Him as you do, at your local church or in a small group or maybe in your home with just a couple of friends and you worship Him for His love and grace. Worship is voluntary, personal, active and interactive. However, have you ever considered this … it's impossible to actually worship God if thankfulness is not a part of your worship.

It's true. Gratitude. Thankfulness. Acceptance. Submission. All of those go together. If you're resisting His will, disappointed at His choices, angry at Him for any reason, stubbornly refusing to submit to Him, jealous of others, feeling slighted or entitled … thankfulness is not flowing from your heart and neither is real worship. Real thankfulness is evidence of submission to God and trust in Him. It shows a willingness to not only accept whatever God brings into your life but to trust Him enough to be truly thankful for it.

Stop resisting. Accept His guidance and His will. Be satisfied with where He's taking you and … be thankful.

Admitting that you are angry with God or resisting His plan is difficult. You know that isn't the right attitude. Are you resisting Him? Are you willing to confess your attitude and ask His help in humbling your heart?

Come Boldly

Let us come boldly to the throne of our
gracious God. There we will receive His mercy,
and we will find grace to help us when we need it most.
HEBREWS 4:16

You've probably heard the mandate that "children should be seen and not heard." Or perhaps you recall a time when folks said that children should not speak unless spoken to and should keep quiet and wait for an invitation to speak, especially to an adult in a position of authority.

Think about this – there isn't anyone more authoritative than God and guess what – He wants you to talk with Him! Because of His grace, you are invited … even encouraged to come boldly and bravely to Him. That means you can come with no fear.

Whatever you want to say to Him – He can take it. He wants your courageous honesty. Tell Him what you're feeling and thinking. He encourages you to keep a conversation going with Him.

You see, God's grace doesn't stop with your salvation. Because He loves you He wants to be the center of your daily life. He wants to hear how you feel about the way your life is going. He cares about what you're thinking. He cares about how you're feeling. He cares about how you're growing. God doesn't save you then forget about you. His grace goes on and on.

Come boldly to the Lord right now. Boldly tell Him how
you are feeling. Create an attitude of honesty with Him
as you worship Him and celebrate His grace in your life.

Learning Process

The grace of God has been revealed, bringing salvation
to all people. And we are instructed to turn from godless
living and sinful pleasures. We should live in this evil world
with wisdom, righteousness, and devotion to God.

TITUS 2:11-12

Hopefully someone in your young life taught you how to live as a kind, decent, law-abiding, God-obeying person versus what's selfish or downright, wrong. These life lessons are a learning process that comes with maturity and often with making mistakes – but learning from them so you don't continue making the same bad choices over and over. It confirms that life is a journey.

The spiritual life is a journey too, and there are deep spiritual lessons to learn as to how to obey God, how to learn to discern His guidance, how to share His light and love with those around you, how to love others … well … how to be more and more like Jesus. After all, that's the goal.

God's grace, revealed in you, will help you learn and grow in your spiritual walk. As His grace grows in your heart and you become more and more open to it, you will begin to see ungodly choices for what they are and turn away from them.

Stay close to God and allow His grace to mold your heart into becoming more and more like Jesus.

As you look back on your spiritual journey what have you learned? What lessons has God taught you? Are you surprised by any of them?

Grace For All

"This is how God loved the world: He gave
His one and only Son, so that everyone who
believes in Him will not perish but have eternal life."
JOHN 3:16

The world has become more and more polarized into "us" and "them." The "us" and "them" folks have a difficult time getting along. A lot of venom is tossed back and forth. It can be tempting to think that God's grace is reserved for your own group – whether you are an "us" or a "them" and that others are hopeless unless they come to your side. However, Scripture tells us that Jesus died to offer God's grace to anyone who chooses to believe and that He is patiently waiting for all to come to Him.

Can you appreciate that God loves someone who doesn't yet love Him? He loves those whose beliefs are diametrically opposed to yours? Are you able to have a respectful conversation with someone who holds different ideas than you do? If you can't, how will you build a relationship so that you can show God's love and be an example of His grace?

Ask God to help you be willing to love across the "us" and "them" lines. Be willing to allow God to make you flexible enough that you can be sent to be a bridge between the two groups. God's love and grace is for all.

Do you have "us" and "them" lines in your circle of acquaintances? How can you be the bridge between the two groups? What are some practical ways you can bridge the gaps?

Pay It Forward

"Do to others as you would like them to do to you."
LUKE 6:31

Someone hurts you – intentionally or unknowingly. Or, a friend repeatedly takes advantage of you. These things happen. But, what's your reaction? Do you firmly call out the person who is treating you badly? Do you make public her offense so all your friends are on your side? Do you long to make her pay for what she's done – whatever that means and to whatever extent you consider due payment? Yeah, that might feel good for a moment but here's an interesting thought – at the same time you're experiencing these feelings toward your offender, are you, with great relief, thanking God for His grace in forgiving you for your own constant and repeated failures?

That creates an interesting scenario, doesn't it? You are the recipient of grace, which is forgiveness that's completely undeserved. Shouldn't you, as a child of God, be willing to pass that grace along to the one who has hurt or offended you?

Extend grace as you have received grace. What a novel idea! You want God's grace. You want others to extend grace to you. Do the same for them. Pay it forward.

Stop holding a grudge ... to whom do you need to extend grace? What can be your first step in doing so?

He Understands

Since He Himself has gone through suffering
and testing, He is able to help us when we are being tested.
HEBREWS 2:18

Surely God could have come up with a different way to make salvation available. After all, He's God. There had to be a way that didn't involve sending His only Son to earth. So why did He choose the plan that involved Jesus becoming human, leaving heaven, suffering, dying and coming back to life?

There's a good reason for His plan – it makes salvation personal for you. In Jesus' short time of ministry, He experienced bullies trying to push Him around. He faced criticism, even from religious leaders. He was hit with disbelief that caused Him grief. He had physical pain and virtually every other situation and emotion that any human will face in life. That's why He can help you with any of the things you experience in relationships, at work, in ministry – because He knows what it's like. He gets it. He understands because He experienced it, too. He is not some person who shoves advice at you about a situation He Himself has never faced.

In Christ's human life you have the fullness of God's grace. He didn't just provide salvation, He made sure you would know that He understands all you face. That's how much He loves you!

What situation do you struggle with and wonder if God
really gets the details of it? What experience did Jesus
have that might have similar emotions attached?

What Really Matters

*May God give you more and more grace and peace as you
grow in your knowledge of God and Jesus our Lord.*
2 PETER 1:2

Why is life sometimes so hard? Hopefully you didn't buy in to some speaker's philosophy that once you gave your heart to Christ, He would smooth out the rough spots in your life and perhaps even generously reward you financially. If you did, you probably found out pretty quickly that life doesn't work that way. Why not? Does God want you to suffer?

The reality goes deeper than whether or not life is tough. The hard truth is that the bumpy times in life are, in fact, the times when your faith grows the most. As all other crutches are knocked away you realize there is no one to lean on except God Himself. When you turn to Him and find that He is there for you … Boom … your faith grows stronger, a step at a time.

God knows these growth times are painful so He offers more and more grace to help you through them. Isn't that cool?

God cares about your struggles and pain. He doesn't want you to hurt but He does want you to grow because that's what matters most. Lean on Him and His peace and grace will see you through.

Looking back on your life, where can you see that
your faith and trust in God has grown through pain?
How does that make you feel about future hard times?

The Need for Grace

*If we claim we have no sin, we are only
fooling ourselves and not living in the truth.*
1 JOHN 1:8

Sin means failure to obey, rebellion, disappointment. No one enjoys admitting they have done wrong. You know how a child will claim, "Wasn't me! I didn't do it! It was my brother or sister!" Similarly, pride makes us justify, blame others or even totally deny our failures. You can do all that and maybe even convince people that you're in the right but you won't convince God that you aren't a sinner. He sees. He knows.

But, there's an important fact about sin; if you weren't a sinner, there would be no need for God's grace. It is the very fact of your sin that cries out for God's grace. Only a broken vessel needs mending. An unbroken vessel is just fine.

When you can understand sin and grace in this way, it makes admitting and confessing a little easier – in fact, a necessity because you see how one fulfills the other. You'll see the grace in grace. God knows you're going to sin regardless of how hard you try not to. He knows and He's right there, ready with the solution – grace that flows from love.

So, accept your brokenness. Confess and repent. Receive His grace that mends your broken places in love.

Confession is sort of like washing the stain out of a favorite white shirt.
It cleans it. It makes the shirt useable again. What do you need to confess
today? Confess and clean your heart. Accept the grace in God's grace.

No Matter What

Give thanks for everything to God the Father
in the name of our Lord Jesus Christ.
EPHESIANS 5:20

A young girl's mother encouraged her to say "thank you" to an adult who had given her a small gift. The little girl did not want to oblige. The mother encouraged more firmly and the child resisted more strongly. The situation escalated until the child was in clear danger of punishment. Just then the son of the other adult stepped in. He placed one hand on the girl's upper lip and the other on her lower lip. As he puppeted her lips he squeaked, "thank you!" The frustrated mother dissolved into laughter and the girl was not punished. (You can bet it was talked about later though).

Saying "thank you" is an important lesson to be learned. There is no "thank you" more important than the thank you to God. Thanks rolls from your lips when He does what you want. But, what about when He does things His way? Are you disappointed? Do you feel He isn't paying attention to your desires or how you hope your life will go?

Thankfulness is evidence of your submission to God's wisdom and His plan for your life. Giving thanks in the hard times, even through disappointment shows that you trust Him – no matter what.

Saying "thanks" in the hard times is difficult, but shows true humility before God. What hard times do you need to thank Him for? How has He seen you through hard times in the past?

The Grace of Keeping Quiet

Too much talk leads to sin.
Be sensible and keep your mouth shut.
PROVERBS 10:19

Words can cause immense damage to another person's spirit. That's probably why God often warns us in Scripture to be careful with our words. Think about it – as a Christian, you should want to share God's love with others. You want to help others know of His grace. You may even teach a Bible study, join in prayer groups or share your faith on a personal level. That's all great. It's wonderful that you want the world to know about God!

However, if people around you feel that you do not control your words then your efforts at sharing God's love will be severely impacted. If they hear you gossiping about other people, saying unkind and possibly even untrue things about others, your reputation is damaged. Speaking critical, judgmental words not only makes you unpleasant to be around but also serves to cause people to not want to listen to you.

Be careful with your words. Don't be word lazy. Realize that each thing you choose to say may be heard by those with whom you are trying to witness. Those negative words will be heard and remembered a long time. Speak words flavored with grace.

How are you doing at controlling your words? Are you critical? Do you share gossip? Are you quick to talk about others? Do you try to be humorous at the expense of other people?

February

No Room for Pride

He gives grace generously. As the Scriptures say,
"God opposes the proud but gives grace to the humble."
JAMES 4:6

God has blessed you with talents, abilities, wisdom, intelligence and passion. Of course, He does that for every person. While you may have the same talents and abilities that others have, God has given you what you need to do whatever work He has for you. As you use those things and develop them so that you get better and better at what you're doing, there may be a temptation to become proud of yourself.

Yes, you've worked to improve your abilities, but the initial talent or gift was given to you by God. Even the progress you make in developing them is made possible by Him.

The point is that you have no grounds to have pride in any of it. In fact, there is very good reason to give all the credit to God and to be humble in your assessment of yourself.

God is not pleased with pride. He wants you to humbly recognize that all you have and all you can do is because of His grace in your life. Acknowledge that and He will give you more and more opportunities to serve Him and more and more grace to do it well.

Have you been harboring some pride about things that are only
yours because of God's grace? Do you need to confess that,
ask His forgiveness and humbly give Him all credit?

Groundhog Day

*The faithful love of the LORD never ends! His mercies never cease.
Great is His faithfulness; His mercies begin afresh each morning.*
LAMENTATIONS 3:22-23

In the old movie, *Groundhog Day*, the character played by Bill Murray continually lives the same day over and over. Everything is always the same until he sees what's happening and he begins to change his behavior, which then brings a better outcome to the day.

How many times have you wished for a "Do Over" button? You know what it's like – you're going through your day, just living your life, interacting with people, working, being a mom or a wife and all of a sudden you realize that you're not doing such a good job. Wouldn't it be nice to have a redo and be given a chance to do better?

God knows that living for Him is a journey that has a daily learning process. By His grace He gives you a restart every single morning. Each day is a fresh blank plate filled with His forgiveness and mercy. You have a new opportunity to learn, grow, serve and obey.

God doesn't carry over the sins of yesterday. Once confessed, they are forgiven and forgotten. You have new opportunities to obey Him and show His love to those around you.

If you could have a do over for yesterday,
what would you hope to do better? How do
you see God's mercies new to you each day?

Share What You Know

How can they call on Him to save them unless they believe in Him? And how can they believe in Him if they have never heard about Him? And how can they hear about Him unless someone tells them? And how will anyone go and tell them without being sent? That is why the Scriptures say, "How beautiful are the feet of messengers who bring good news!"

ROMANS 10:14-15

God didn't save you just for you. Of course, He loves you and Jesus definitely came, lived and died for your salvation. But God has a bigger plan than just your presence in eternity. You probably know the familiar verse, John 3:16 that states, "For God so loved the whole world ..." It's pretty clear that God's desire is for everyone to know how much He loves them. Everyone. But, these verses in Romans ask how people will be saved if no one tells them about God's love? You were saved by God's grace and it follows that anyone who accepts Christ when you share your faith, is also saved by God's grace.

Nothing else can bring salvation, just His grace. But before God's grace can save these folks, He asks you to do your part in telling them about His love. Now, not everyone is a preacher or speaker. But, you can share God's love with others by the way you help them, speak to them and live your life in front of them. Show them God's grace by your life of grace. Your life may open the door for them to meet God.

How do you share your faith with those around you? Who do you have in your life who does not know Christ so that you can show His love by the way you live your life?

Making Good Choices

Trust in the LORD with all your heart; do not depend
on your own understanding. Seek His will in all you do,
and He will show you which path to take.
PROVERBS 3:5-6

God's grace is more than your salvation. For example, life is filled with choices. Many times each day you choose what to do; where to go; words to speak; work to do; attitudes to foster … choices that affect the outcome of your day as well as the feelings and experience of others. Your life is not lived in a vacuum. Your words, actions and behaviors touch a lot of lives each day – family, friends or people you bump into along the way – store clerks, waitresses or waiters, civil servants, other drivers or even people you pass on the sidewalk.

Some choices you make without thinking. Some you consider for a moment and some you agonize over. Where does God's guidance come into play? If you ask Him for guidance in a specific instance and submit to His leading, He will guide you.

But what about the hundreds of daily choices you make without thinking? Those are guided by your daily practice of reading His Word, praying and submitting your heart to His Spirit's leading. He will, by His grace, guide your words and actions so that those around you will be blessed from your presence.

Are you facing some big choices right now?
Have you sought God's guidance? When have
you sensed His leading in the past? How does that
experience affect your trust in His leading now?

God's Word

Your word is a lamp to guide
my feet and a light for my path.
PSALM 119:105

How can you obey someone if you don't know what's expected? It's hard to be part of a team if you don't know what the team stands for. That's the benefit of God's Word. As you study it, you learn what it means to be a follower of God.

The Bible is an amazing evidence of God's grace. It's the inspired Word of God; His personal Word to you. The Bible is sometimes called a love letter from God. He wants you to know about Him.

In the Bible God shares stories of how He has interacted with mankind since the beginning of time. By reading those stories you learn of His character and His love. You see His care for His people and His guidance in their lives. You see His insistence of obedience to His commands. You read of His desire for all mankind to know His love so that He can have a personal relationship with each person.

Be careful not to take the gift of God's Word lightly. It is an amazing evidence of His grace-filled love for you. He gave it because He wants you to know Him and His love for you.

How often do you read God's Word? How often do you
actually study it? Do you have a hunger to know His Word?
How does it make you feel when you read it?

Just Ask

If you need wisdom, ask our generous
God, and He will give it to you.
He will not rebuke you for asking.
JAMES 1:5

This world gets more and more confusing. It's a challenge to take a stand for God and His Word, and to do so in a way that conveys love to those around you. God shows His grace to you by His giving you wisdom. So you ask, "God, how do I state my beliefs in Your Word in a way that is not off-putting to those who disagree?" "How do I stand strong for You and still draw others to You?" "How do I know if my opinions and beliefs are simply MY opinions and beliefs and not actually in keeping with Your Word?" "Help me to always speak showing grace … not law."

How do you get answers to these questions? Ask. Just ask Him for wisdom and He will give it. The key is that you must be willing to listen to Him and to follow the wisdom He gives you.

God gives wisdom to you, not just for you, but so that you can make good choices which will benefit you and those around you as you give an honest reflection of God's love and care to them. His wisdom comes to you because of His grace. Just ask.

How do you need God's wisdom to help you?
Where do you struggle with decisions or behaviors?
Have you asked Him for help? Has He given it?

A Constant Help

"When the Father sends the Advocate as My representative –
that is, the Holy Spirit – He will teach you everything
and will remind you of everything I have told you."
JOHN 14:26

When you're learning a new job, training is important. Hopefully that goes well but even so the first time you work solo can be a bit anxiety inducing. It's helpful if your trainer is close by to answer questions and give guidance as needed. Her presence takes the pressure off and helps your learning continue.

You have a "spiritual trainer" who is always with you! He never leaves you to learn on your own. God graciously gave the gift of His Spirit to live in your heart and be with you each day, teaching and guiding. He reminds you to take life seriously and to apply yourself to the situations you face.

The Spirit acts as your conscience and prods you when you're getting off track or heading in the wrong direction. He is like a friend who helps you notice when someone around you needs help or attention.

Since the Spirit is always with you He is constantly guiding you and helping you learn to be more like Christ. You never need to feel that you are alone in the struggles of life. God has provided His Spirit for you and He is a solid evidence of God's grace and love for you!

How are you aware of the Holy Spirit's presence in
your life? When was a specific time that He directed you?
How does that affect your feelings about Him?

Keep On Keeping On

Those who trust in the LORD will find new strength.
They will soar high on wings like eagles. They will run
and not grow weary. They will walk and not faint.
ISAIAH 40:31

"I can't take any more. I can't do any more. I'm lost. I'm scared. I'm tired."

Have you experienced days, weeks or even years when whatever is going on in your life is oppressive? Making your way through difficulties takes emotional and mental energy. It takes perseverance and intentionality. It's tiring. Some days it feels as though each foot weighs a hundred pounds. Getting up each day, dressing and getting out of the house takes all your energy. Some days you can't even do it.

Yes, it's hard. But in the midst of your struggles, remember that you have the "ear" of the God of the universe and He has power over everything. If you ask He will help you rise above the trouble or walk with you through it. However, you must be willing to give up your own agenda in the problem.

God may not choose to fix the problem as you want Him to. He may let the troubling situation continue, as difficult as it is, but you will never be alone. He will send friends to walk with you. He will help you. He will strengthen you. He will not let you give up. This is His grace in action.

What's wearing you down? Have you asked God for help? How has He helped? Through friends? In your spirit? With physical and emotional endurance?

The Temptation Battle

The temptations in your life are no different from what others experience. And God is faithful. He will not allow the temptation to be more than you can stand. When you are tempted, He will show you a way out so that you can endure.

1 CORINTHIANS 10:13

You don't hear about Satan very much, but you should. He's crafty and persistent in attempting to pull you away from God. How does he do it? He knows your weaknesses and how to tempt you to give in to them. Just because you say no to a temptation one time doesn't mean it's over. Satan will come back at you again and again, in different ways to get you to give in. He wants to pull you away from God by making you feel like a failure. You will face temptation. Never doubt that. But, you don't have to fight against Satan's barrage of temptation by yourself. In fact … you can't.

As soon as you realize that you're facing temptation, call on God to help you. He will! You're His child and He loves you! He won't let Satan have the victory over you. Don't try to do it on your own. Don't think you can give in just a little and then fight back the temptation. If you give Satan an inch, he will take a mile!

God will show you a way through the temptation. Satan has no power against God. This direction and faithfulness is another evidence of God's loving grace.

Do you know where your weaknesses lie? The places where Satan will attack you with temptation? Do you call on God to help you fight the battle?

One of *Those* Days

God is working in you, giving you the
desire and the power to do what pleases Him.
PHILIPPIANS 2:13

There may be nights when you wearily plop your head on the pillow and think, "Whew, I sure blew it today. My anger or selfishness or pride ... let's just say that not much Jesus showed in my life today."

There are days when you keep Jesus covered up by your own agenda. While you shouldn't dismiss those days as something you can't change you also shouldn't give up on yourself. Here's why – because you care. You care that your life didn't reflect Jesus' love this day. You care that your obedience to God's teachings was not visible in your behavior.

You care and that means God's grace is still working to teach your heart to be less self-focused. He's still working to break down walls that years of hurt have built. He helps you recall Scripture verses you read years ago that speak to you today.

When you have "one of those days" don't settle for that being the best you that you can be. Recognize that God is still working in you. He's giving you the desire to be better – to be more like Jesus. His power, supplied through His grace will help you do just that!

How has God worked in your heart lately? What has
He taught you? Is there a verse that He continually
brings to mind to remind you to obey Him?

Joy vs. Happiness

Always be joyful. Never stop praying.
Be thankful in all circumstances, for this is
God's will for you who belong to Christ Jesus.
1 THESSALONIANS 5:16-18

Joyfulness and happiness are not the same emotion. Happiness happens because of some external situation. Happiness is short-lived and fleeting. Joyfulness comes from within and, interestingly enough, thankfulness is rolled into joy.

It's possible to be joyful even when you aren't happy. How can that be? Life sometimes is tough. Hard things happen. Your heart hurts. The future looks bleak. There isn't any reason to be happy. However, you can still have an attitude of joy in your heart. Look at the progression in these verses – joy is built on the foundation of prayer and thankfulness. That thankfulness happens because you know that God is in control of your life and you trust Him. You trust that He knows what's happening today and He knows the future. He has it all under control.

So, you stay in conversation with Him and tell Him honestly how you're feeling, what you fear, how life is going and even what you want Him to do about things. Then you can be genuinely thankful – not for the pain of the moment – but because you know He is in control. He has a plan and He won't let you down.

How do you blur joy and happiness together in your life?
What kind of problems does that cause for you? Can you say that
you honestly trust God with your today and tomorrow? Why?

Bungee Grace

Encourage each other and build each other
up, just as you are already doing.
1 THESSALONIANS 5:11

Have you ever bungee jumped? Taking a deep breath and leaping off a tower with just a harness around your ankles shows you have a lot of trust that the harness will hold and that it is exactly the right length to keep you from crashing into the rocks or whatever is rushing to meet you headfirst. Just as it seems you're about to crash, the elastic bands reach their limit and you're pulled up into the air, safe until the next (shorter) bounce down.

God's grace sometimes plays out like bungee jumping. When you reach the point where you cannot face the situation you've been dealt and you're tensing up for the crash landing, His grace bounces you back up to safety.

Sometimes that rescue comes through the people He has put around you. Friends who grab you and pull you to safety through their prayers and encouragement are God's grace in the moment. A friend's presence in a hard time is sometimes just the comfort you need for a surge of strength and hope.

Thank God for His grace seen in friends and pay attention to times when you can be His grace to someone else.

Who are your friends who often come to your
rescue? How do they help you? When have you
been able to be God's grace to someone else?

Remember Thanks

Enter His gates with thanksgiving;
go into His courts with praise.
PSALM 100:4

Sometimes children need to be reminded to say a simple "thank you." It may not come to their minds to be thankful without some gentle prodding. It's one of the important responsibilities of parents to help their children learn the respect of appreciating the kindness of others.

It's also important for you to have real thankfulness to God for the blessings He gives you. Gratitude can be smothered under the attitude that you actually deserve all God gives you, or perhaps even more than He gives you. The danger is that as you become numb to His blessings, your gratitude shrinks.

Gratitude that easily flows from your heart reflects a true appreciation of God's grace and love for you. It recognizes that God generously and sacrificially blesses you. He guides and protects and teaches you, all because of His love and grace.

If you're more like the child who doesn't easily remember to be thankful than the one who always remembers, ask God to place a reminder in your heart to be truly grateful for all His blessings.

Remember, in your prayer time to not only ask God for things but to thank Him for all He does.

For which of God's blessings are you most thankful?
Does your prayer time include more requests for what you
want God to do than it does thanks for what He does for you?

Don't Worry; Be Thankful

Don't worry about anything; instead, pray about everything.
Tell God what you need, and thank Him for all He has
done. Then you will experience God's peace, which
exceeds anything we can understand. His peace will guard
your hearts and minds as you live in Christ Jesus.
PHILIPPIANS 4:6-7

One of the first things parents teach their children who have just learned to talk is to say "thank you" when someone does something kind for them or gives them something. It's a basic act of kindness and respect for others to express gratitude. However, it doesn't always come easily to children … or to adults for that matter.

These two verses offer a beautiful invitation to stop worrying about stuff and just give your worries to God. Simple, right? But look at those seven little words tucked in the invitation … thank Him for all He has done. Say thanks to God for everything He has done for you; the hard things and the wonderful things. Don't take anything for granted because everything has a purpose in your life and your spiritual growth. Be careful about asking God to do more and more without giving thanks.

Notice the pattern here: Don't worry. Pray. Thank Him. Peace. That's a pretty wonderful progression. So, recognize His grace in wanting your prayers. Thank Him for all He gives and does. Receive His peace that is more amazing than anything you can imagine.

When life is going well, do you remember to thank God for His blessings or have you become too used to receiving them? When life is difficult, do you thank Him for those hard times too and all you learn through them?

Forgiving Others

"For you will be treated as you treat others.
The standard you use in judging is the standard
by which you will be judged."
MATTHEW 7:2

Go back to basics. God, by His grace, forgives your sin. His grace gives salvation. His grace forgives you for your selfish disobedience of His commands. His grace is never-ending. You gladly receive God's grace-filled forgiveness each day even knowing you really don't deserve it. Of course, you would never tell Him that you don't want it.

Now remember that you do not live in this world alone. People are part of your every day life. People who disappoint. People who make mistakes. People who are sometimes unkind. So how good are you at paying God's forgiveness and grace forward?

When a friend or family member disappoints you or hurts you, do you simply cut them out of your life or are you willing to forgive them and give them another chance? Do you make quick judgments about others based on your perceptions of their behavior? How would you feel if God treated your sins with the same level of forgiveness and grace that you offer others? What if His forgiveness were as conditional as yours? The grace you offer to others may be what brings them into God's family. Love enough to forgive and offer grace just as you are loved.

How aware are you of God's daily forgiveness?
Is there someone you need to forgive and
offer grace to? How willing are you to do that?

Where's Your Hope?

Show me the right path, O LORD; point out the
road for me to follow. Lead me by Your truth
and teach me, for You are the God who saves
me. All day long I put my hope in You.
PSALM 25:4-5

Life gets confusing when there are so many choices. Which one is best? Which choice leads to a better future? Which one takes you where God wants you to be?

Here's the cool thing … God doesn't save you by His grace then leaves you to find your way through life on your own. Remember, He loves you, so He sticks with you and guides you through every day of this chaotic life. Now it would be easiest if He would write instructions in the sky, right? Of course, He doesn't do that. However when you come to a fork in the road where several choices look appealing, He will show you which way to go. He will teach you. He doesn't write instructions in the sky but He has already written His guidance and directions in His Word.

So, yes, God will guide and direct you. That is His continuing grace in action. You must do your part by staying close to Him. Read His Word to see how He dealt with His people. As you read their stories you learn of God's character and trustworthiness. Read how He guided, directed and protected the people in the Bible. He will do the same for you.

How has God guided you in the past?
Have you received His guidance
through Scripture or in other ways?

More and More Grace

Though we are overwhelmed
by our sins, You forgive them all.
PSALM 65:3

There's an expression that goes, "That's the straw that broke the camel's back." It refers to that one thing that pushes you over your limit of endurance – so that you can't stand any more bad behavior or one more time of backtalk from your kids or one more frustration. You get the idea. Perhaps there have been people with whom you reach a limit of endurance. When that happens, you may have absolutely no patience with that person. You may even take measures to avoid being with her or him.

Thanks be to God, He doesn't reach that point with you. You may have times of knowing that you have disappointed Him over and over. You know that you continually commit the same sins. But, by His grace, God forgives you every single time! You may become overwhelmed by your sins and your failures to the point that you may not be able to forgive yourself. You may not understand how the perfect God could possibly not lose patience with you – how could "this time" not be the straw that breaks the camel's back.

But, it never happens. His grace keeps giving and giving and giving again. He never stops forgiving.

Think about some of the forgiveness for which
you are most grateful. Tell God about your gratitude.

But, God …

> Now all glory to God, who is able, through
> His mighty power at work within us, to accomplish
> infinitely more than we might ask or think.
> EPHESIANS 3:20

Some people achieve impressive things in their lives. They do so much to help others. They are dedicated to serving God and accomplishing amazing things for His Kingdom. If you hold your life up to comparison with theirs, it may begin to look like your life is rather mundane. It can feel like you're not really accomplishing anything of value.

But, God, … those two little words make all the difference. But God knows exactly what He's doing with your life! He has a plan for every person's life. He gives specific talents and abilities to each person and has specific work for each person to do.

No job is small. No job is big. Each job is His. Each job matters to His Kingdom. Whether you're a full time mom of toddlers, CEO of a mission organization, a waitress, a minister, a professional musician or a factory worker, God puts you where He wants you to be. He will accomplish His work through your heart's willing service.

Accomplish more than you can ask or think! Sharing His love with even just one person is the most important thing you can do. Just be willing.

Sometimes we don't want to admit what we're good at because it seems like we're being pride-filled. But right now, just admit what God has gifted you to do. What are you good at and how do you use those gifts for Him?

Loving the Unlovable

Hatred stirs up quarrels,
but love makes up for all offenses.
PROVERBS 10:12

Some people have a knack for stirring up trouble. They say the wrong thing at the wrong time. They know which of your buttons to push, how often to push them and how long to hold them down. Those kinds of people are no fun to be around. They seem to enjoy keeping trouble stirred up; even pitting friends against friends or family members against family members.

How do you handle people who behave like this? Do you lose patience with this behavior? Does it make you want to stay away from this troublemaker? Do you encourage others to stay away from her, too? Do you and your friends gang up on her with negative comments and possibly even gossip?

What if you treated her with grace? How would that change things? It's not easy to love an unlovable person, but your love could just be the thing that spurs her to change her behavior. Of course you don't want to enable bad behavior or allow yourself to be taken advantage of but you can try offering grace and see what happens. God covers your behavior with grace so … give it a try!

Who do you need to handle with grace?
How can you take the first steps to do that?

Practical Grace

"I was hungry, and you fed Me. I was thirsty, and you gave
Me a drink. I was a stranger, and you invited Me into your home.
I was naked, and you gave Me clothing. I was sick,
and you cared for Me. I was in prison, and you visited Me."
MATTHEW 25:35-36

It's important to share the grace of God's love with others. Of course it is. Everyone should have the opportunity to hear about His love. We're instructed in God's Word to share our faith with others and it's an instruction we need to take quite seriously.

But does it show God's love if you tell a hungry, cold, sick person about Him then keep on walking? Are they to think that your thoughts are, "Good luck with finding food, clothing, medicine?"

There are practical ways to show the grace of God's love; ways that put your faith into action; ways that show your true concern for others' wellbeing. It makes sense that it is impractical to expect someone who is cold or hungry or sick to listen to you talk about how much God loves them without doing anything to help. Why not put these verses into action and meet the practical needs of people as a visible show of your love and concern for them.

Remember that faith without works is dead. Share your faith but also help them in practical, life-affirming ways.

Are there some ways of meeting peoples' practical
needs that you could join in? What are they?
Have you ever thought about a practical ministry
you could get started? What's the first step?

Forever and Ever

Thank God! He gives us victory over sin
and death through our Lord Jesus Christ.
1 CORINTHIANS 15:57

No one gets out of this life alive. No matter how well you take care of yourself by eating healthy foods, exercising, peaceful mindfulness … you are going to age and eventually you pass from this life.

Of course, it's very sad when you must say goodbye to a loved one who passes. But the grace of God is seen in the truth that death isn't the end for a believer. God promises more. Thank God! He has victory over death because of Jesus Christ. When you accept Jesus as Savior that victory becomes yours!

It is by God's grace that you can anticipate the heavenly reunion with your loved ones in the presence of your Savior. So, even as you grieve those you have lost or even face your own death, you can hold on to the promised eternal life in heaven and reunion with loved ones. Even more amazing will be the joy of being in the presence of Jesus … forever!

This is the ultimate blessing of God's grace. Wouldn't grace seem a little anticlimactic if it ended here? Praise God for eternity!

Do you have the assurance of victory over death? How does that impact your sense of urgency to share the message of God's love with others?

Cut to the Quick

The word of God is alive and powerful. It is sharper than the sharpest two-edged sword, cutting between soul and spirit, between joint and marrow. It exposes our innermost thoughts and desires.
HEBREWS 4:12

The expression, "Cut to the quick" refers to a physically deep cut or hurt. It is also used to speak of a deep emotional wound.

The Word of God goes deep into your soul and reveals your true obedience to God. If you care about obeying Him and if you read His Word with an open heart and mind, the Bible will teach you how to live for God and become more like Christ in your heart, attitude and behavior.

A Christian who desires to obey God's Word can never say she doesn't know how. She can't fool herself into thinking she's doing just fine because God, by His grace, tells you all you need to know in His Word. Its truth reveals your innermost thoughts if you're willing to listen to it.

Do you hunger to read God's Word? Do you love the understanding you gain from reading it? Do you give as much time to reading His Word as you do to other things in your day?

Ask God to give you a hunger for His Word and to open your heart to allow it to go deep into your soul, revealing your own true thoughts and teaching you to be like Him.

Do you hunger to know God's Word? What are your habits for reading it? What has the truth of His Word revealed to you about your own attitudes?

Strength and Power

He gives power to the weak
and strength to the powerless.
ISAIAH 40:29

What an amazing statement this is. Imagine Jesus standing right in front of you and speaking these words, "Don't worry about the challenges in your life. I know some days are hard. I know sometimes you barely have strength to face a new day. I will give you the strength you need to get out of bed and face the day. I will put sunlight into the days that seem filled with darkness. I can do that and I promise I will. You will have the strength to do the work before you. You will have My help dealing with challenging relationships. My strength will help you discern good choices. My strength will give you hope that the days ahead will be better."

The Bible tells you that these things are true. Jesus cares so much about what you're facing. He knows that there are seasons in life when you feel weak and powerless. Scripture is filled with His promises to give you what you need in those times in order to get through them.

When you feel weak and powerless, cry out to Jesus and ask for His help. Then be still and notice when His help comes.

When have you felt weak and powerless?
How did you see God's strength come to help you?

Scaredy Faith

"Don't be afraid, for I am with you. Don't be discouraged,
for I am your God. I will strengthen you and help you.
I will hold you up with My victorious right hand."
ISAIAH 41:10

What scares you? What wiggles around in the back of your mind bumping up against the truth that God loves you and can be trusted? Are you afraid of change? Do you obsess over the wellbeing of your loved ones? Do you fear what lessons you may need to learn and how God might allow those to be taught?

Does your fear sometimes overpower your trust? When it does, do you hold things back from God. Do you say, "OK, I'll trust You with this but not with that?" Then you're not completely submitted to Him, are you?

When your trust in God is half-hearted then your relationship with Him is impacted. You don't feel connected with Him and you may wonder if He's paying attention at all. That, of course, leads to discouragement and questioning what this faith thing is all about.

Now you probably keep your doubts hidden because you don't want others to know your struggles. But, God knows … and what does He do? He loves you and in grace takes you step by step to learn to trust Him and not be afraid. It's a journey of grace.

What scares you? With what kinds of things
do you have the most difficulty trusting God?
How can you learn to trust Him more?

A New Life

We died and were buried with Christ by baptism. And just as
Christ was raised from the dead by the glorious power
of the Father, now we also may live new lives.
ROMANS 6:4

A new life … does that sound appealing to you? A do-over. A new start. Would you like to be able to go back and make a few corrections in your life? You know, change some choices you've made … correct a few blunders … fix some relationship choices?

There are probably things that you would do different now that you can look back at how your choices and actions have affected your life and others' lives, too. Hindsight is wonderful but you can't really go backward to change things, can you?

The only way you can go is forward. You can't change the past. However, by God's grace, when you accept Jesus as Savior, you are born into a new life with Him as your teacher and guide. So, you have an opportunity from that moment on to do better. You can make amends as much as possible with any who your behavior has hurt. You can give others the opportunity to see that your behavior has changed because Jesus is changing your heart.

God's grace gives you this opportunity. Your submitted and humble heart allows a new life to grow from your new heart.

If you had the opportunity, what would you change from your past? As you think about choices you've made or the way you've treated others in the past, can you see things Jesus has taught you and ways your behavior has improved as you know Him more?

Party in Your Spirit

*Let everything that breathes sing
praises to the LORD! Praise the LORD!*
PSALM 150:6

Perhaps you've seen a young child who is eagerly waiting to open his birthday gifts. The anticipation nearly makes him wild. When it's finally time for him to rip the paper off and see what his gift is, he goes for it with gusto. Then he sees that this gift is exactly what he had hoped for and his celebration is loud and happy and it pulls everyone in. He celebrates with his whole body and spirit! Such fun!

Wouldn't it be fun if we celebrated God's blessings with that much energy? We seldom do. Either we've become so used to His blessings that we've come to expect them or we've become so politically correct that we can't allow ourselves to actually celebrate.

What does Psalms say? Sing praises! Celebrate! Be filled with gratitude for your blessings! Have a party in your spirit! God gives and gives and gives. His blessings are constant and steady. Don't get apathetic about them.

Let celebration praise spill out of your heart and splash on all those around you! That will encourage those around you to celebrate God, too! Your joy just might encourage them to see His goodness in their own lives!

When was a time you were so blessed by God
that you wanted to shout it to the world? Did
you? How do you celebrate His blessings?

A Party for You

"There is joy in the presence of God's
angels when even one sinner repents."
LUKE 15:10

Have you been the guest of honor at a birthday party? A wedding or baby shower? A retirement party? It's pretty wonderful when your friends and family gather to celebrate you because they want you to know how much you mean to them. They want to share the celebration with you. That's what loved ones do.

Well think about this – even the angels in heaven celebrate you! When you accepted Jesus because you knew it was a better way of life than what you had, the angels had a party in heaven! That should make you feel pretty special.

You're not just one of a multitude. You're not invisible to God or His angels. They noticed when you followed Jesus and that caused a party in your honor!

What's your response to their joy? Hopefully it fills you with joy because you … *you* matter that much to God. You can know that He will take care of you, guide you when you ask and generally help you be a better person as you learn to be more like Christ.

Your repentance was not a once and done … it was the beginning of a new life.

Do you believe you are so special to God that the
angels celebrate you? What's your response to that?

God, You and Your People

"Where two or three gather together as
My followers, I am there among them."
MATTHEW 18:20

The hot term in churches these days is "small groups". You need a small group to connect with because they become your "people." The ones you share your life with. You share prayer requests with each other. You study Scripture together. You serve together. A good small group becomes your intimate friends who know the good, the bad and the ugly of you and they love you as you love them.

God made a promise to you about these kinds of friends. When you get together with them to pray; to study; to care … He is right there with you. There's strength in numbers. It's no accident that God put people in your life.

While He knows that He is enough for you, He also knows that you need physical people around you. He celebrates that with you by making His presence known with you and your people.

Thank God for the people He has placed in your life. Those who celebrate with you. Those who cry with you. Those who pray with you. Those who pray for you. Those who hold you accountable. They are your people and His gift to you.

Who are your people? How do you share
together? How do you encourage each other?
How do these friends help you grow?

The End Is the Beginning

The Lord Himself will come down from heaven with a commanding shout, with the voice of the archangel, and with the trumpet call of God. First, the believers who have died will rise from their graves. Then, together with them, we who are still alive and remain on the earth will be caught up in the clouds to meet the Lord in the air. Then we will be with the Lord forever.

1 THESSALONIANS 4:16-17

There's that special feeling when you know you have gotten just the right gift for someone you love. You have no doubt that your loved one is going to be super excited about the gift. It's going to land right in her sweet spot! It doesn't matter what the gift cost you. It doesn't matter how difficult it was to get. You can hardly wait for her to open it. You are filled with anticipation to see the excitement in her face. What a fun thing!

Maybe God feels that same way about His final gift of grace – bringing you to heaven with Him. He must be so excited to show you the glory of where you will spend forever. He's been busy preparing your eternal home in His beautiful heaven. He knows that you will be so excited to be there and to be in the presence of Jesus. The promise of eternity with Him and being reunited with loved ones is further proof of just how very much God loves you! Leaving this earth isn't the end of life as some people say. It's the beginning of forever!

Do you believe in the promise of heaven? Does death still frighten you? What about heaven are you most looking forward to?

March

Part of the Family

You are no longer a slave but
God's own child. And since you are
His child, God has made you His heir.
GALATIANS 4:7

Think about the vast differences between a slave and a child. A slave has no freedom and is at the mercy of her owner. She doesn't get to choose what she wants to do or when. She has no freedom to go where she wants or to choose to work or not work. Her time is not her own. Her opinions do not matter. There are no options for her to make her own choices. There is no one who cares what she thinks or what she wants. Do you see how narrow the life of a slave is?

Then there is the position of being a family member. Adoption is a wonderful thing. It makes a child who is alone a member of a family. She becomes a part of that family, no longer an outsider or a visitor. She has the same rights, privileges and blessings as a biological child. She also has extended family, a heritage and the promise of inheritance as any child. She belongs.

That's what God's grace has given you – you no longer have to be a slave to your sinfulness. You have been adopted into God's family and all that is His is now yours, too!

What does it mean specifically to you that you are a child
of God ... a member of His family? How does it change
your view of yourself and of your whole life?

Credit Where It's Due

Whatever I am now, it is all because God poured out His special favor on me – and not without results. For I have worked harder than any of the other apostles; yet it was not I but God who was working through me by His grace.
1 CORINTHIANS 15:10

The Apostle Paul gave credit where credit was due. He knew his life was blessed. He knew he was doing amazing work for God. But he also knew, and readily admitted that no part of his life was of his own doing. It was all by God's amazing grace working in his heart, changing his focus, directing his steps and presenting opportunities. Paul was wise enough to embrace those opportunities and do the work God gave him – even when it was difficult and unpopular.

Sometimes God may put opportunities before you that are difficult and even painful. However, you can trust that if you will do what He asks, He will give you the strength, perseverance and power to do it. He will be beside you each step of the way.

Do you take credit for your work or your position in this world (even in your own mind)? Or, are you as open as Paul to give credit where it's due? Credit for the work you do. Credit for the wisdom, intelligence, compassion, creativity and strength you have.

All that you are and all that you do is by God's grace. Acknowledge that. Without Him you are nothing.

Be honest with yourself … do you struggle a bit with pride in your own accomplishments and position? What would you like to say to God about that right now?

Your Choice

Give your burdens to the LORD,
and He will take care of you. He will
not permit the godly to slip and fall.
PSALM 55:22

Who do you trust to take care of you? Who is the person you go to when your fear wakes you in the middle of the night, unrelentingly reminding you of what "could" happen and what "might" happen? What's your response to these kinds of attacks? Because that's what it is, you know, a Satanic attack on your faith and your relationship with God. Satan is trying to make you fall away from God by making you doubt His care.

Physical falls are so dangerous for people. For older folks, it's often a fall that begins their health descent. Even for young folks, falls are physically damaging and hard to recover from. A spiritual fall can be just as damaging to your relationship with God.

Don't let Satan win. When worry starts to consume you ask God to take the worry from your heart and remind you that He has promised to keep you on your feet. His grace will hold you close and keep you from doubting His care and provision.

You have a choice – trust in God's care or allow your fear to pull you away from Him and be miserable in your fear and worry. Seems like an easy choice, right?

What worries are you struggling with? Have you asked God to help you? How have you sensed Him keeping you from falling?

Be at Peace

Since we have been made right in God's
sight by faith, we have peace with God because
of what Jesus Christ our Lord has done for us.
ROMANS 5:1

When you bump into someone who has previously disappointed you or hurt you, is your first thought of the memory of that hurt or disappointment; even if it has been years since that experience? You do your best to forgive but forgetting the hurt is hard to do. Your relationship with that person is impacted because you'll never fully trust her again. The relationship is broken.

When God looks at you, all He sees is good. He doesn't see your multitude of failures or your repeated sins. He looks at you and sees a child He loves so very much and for whom He would do anything.

Even if you feel you have disappointed Him by your failure to obey Him, your relationship with Him is not broken. Jesus paid the price that washed you clean so that God sees you with only love in His eyes. That's grace in action. You get to have peace with God because of Jesus' work. You can't do anything to earn that peace. It's all because of God's grace-filled forgiveness.

Don't fret about what God thinks of you. Take a deep breath and be at peace. You're good … because Jesus is good.

God's forgiveness of your sin is complete. Nothing
is held aside to haunt you later. Is there someone
you need to forgive; even if she hasn't asked
forgiveness? How are you going to handle that?

Celebrate Weakness

Three different times I begged the Lord to take it away.
Each time He said, "My grace is all you need. My power
works best in weakness." So now I am glad to boast about my
weaknesses, so that the power of Christ can work through me.
2 CORINTHIANS 12:8-9

"God, this is too hard to deal with, please take it away," you pray. Paul prayed for that, too. After all if God loves you as much as He says He does, then He wouldn't want you to hurt so surely He would take away the illness or the crisis and make your life easier, right?

Not necessarily. Of course God loves you. That's a given. But it may be BECAUSE of His love that He doesn't take your problem away. It must be hard for Him to leave you hurting, but He does because of His grace that longs for you to be more than you are. He wants greater things for you than the person you are right now. He knows that through your pain, He will be glorified and your faith will grow stronger as you experience His presence and His care.

More people will see His love and care by how you respond to the crisis in your life. If you submit to His plan, trust His love and cele-brate ... even in your pain ... He will be glorified.

Allow Christ to work through your situation and honor Him with your attitude and praise!

What situation or illness are you still dealing with even though
you've asked God to remove it? What has your response
been to Him not taking it away? How have you seen God
glorified through the situation and your response to it?

Good Night!

In peace I will lie down and sleep,
for You alone, O LORD, will keep me safe.
PSALM 4:8

Peace is a sweet gift of God's grace. Where do you find peace in this chaotic time in our world filled with wars? Violence fills our world. Social media has made bullying too easy from the high levels of government to young people. Financial stresses, job loss, broken relationships – there are a multitude of stresses with a definite loss of peace.

Peace is possible but it can be found only through trusting God. That means that when your thoughts go to any of those things that make you feel stressed or afraid your first action should be to cry out to God for peace. Tell Him what's frightening you and ask Him for His comfort. Give the problem to Him and trust Him to handle it. Granted, you may need to do that over and over – not because He fails to handle it but because you continue to grab it back and worry about it.

What is more refreshing than lying down in the darkness and peacefully sleeping because you know that the God of the universe is guarding you and will get you through the problems – either by solving them or walking through them with you. Sleep well!

What has been keeping you awake at night?
Have you given it to God? How has He helped you?

Doing God's Work

God has given each of you a gift
from His great variety of spiritual gifts.
Use them well to serve one another.
1 PETER 4:10

You are who you are because of God's grace. There's no place for pride in your skills or what you accomplish in life. It's all by God's grace.

He planned who He wanted you to be and what He wanted you to do. He equipped you to do what He wants you to do. He did that for every person, just as He did for the Apostle Paul.

You may have obediently worked to develop and perfect your skills and talents but even the ability to do that is only by God's grace. So how should you feel about your talents, skills and careers?

You should feel thankful! Thank God for the skills He's given you. Thank Him for the interests He has given you. Thank Him for the opportunities He gives you to do His work. Thank Him that you matter to Him as much as any other of His people. Thank Him that the work He has given you to do is valuable to His Kingdom.

What a privilege to be a part of God's work on this earth and to do it in just the way He has equipped you to do. God's plan is perfect!

What work has God given you to do? How has He prepared you for that work? Have you thanked Him for His plan for you?

Growing Pains

We can rejoice, too, when we run into problems and trials,
for we know that they help us develop endurance.
And endurance develops strength of character, and
character strengthens our confident hope of salvation.
ROMANS 5:3-4

When you're trying to strengthen your body or even just a particular muscle group, you exercise them, right? You stretch and do strength training with weights over and over until your muscles cry out for relief. That's the only way to develop your muscles' strength. For most people it's not fun but the end result is their goal.

Faith muscles are developed in much the same way. The "workout" that your faith gets when you encounter problems and trials develops your faith – grows it deeper and stronger. At least it does if you turn to God for help and depend on Him to get you through them. Each time you turn to God instead of any other answer you are tempted to try and see His help, your faith grows a bit.

God cares about your journey to know Him more deeply. He sees that your faith steps grow your endurance to face problems and that endurance develops your character as a believer who trusts Him. His grace allows the trials that start this process – not because He wants you to hurt but because He wants you to grow. So accept your trials, learn from them and thank Him for the process.

What spiritual growing pains have you felt?
How can you see your faith maturing?

The Gift of Friendship

The heartfelt counsel of a friend
is as sweet as perfume and incense.
PROVERBS 27:9

If you have a good friend, you have an incredible gift. One of God's most gracious gifts is friends because they make life so much richer. Having at least one friend you can be vulnerable with, who will share your struggles, not judge you for them, and who will celebrate your victories, not be jealous of them is a true gift from God. A friend you can trust with your deepest struggles who won't criticize you but will work with you as you explore life and find your way. A friend who doesn't spout, "You shoulds …" but waits for you to ask advice.

A friend who shares your faith in God and will challenge you to stay close to Him and grow in your faith, even as you go through hard things, is a true gift.

It's also a gift to be that kind of friend to someone. Look around you at the people God has put in your life. Value those with whom you can be honest and vulnerable. Value those to whom you can be a loving, honest friend. Grow together in your faith. Encourage, love, challenge, laugh and enjoy!

Who is a friend with whom you can be honest and vulnerable? Have you told this friend how much she means to you? Why not do that today?

Rest

Jesus said, "Come to Me, all of you who are weary and carry heavy burdens, and I will give you rest."
MATTHEW 11:28

Rest is not the same as a good night of sleep. It doesn't happen just because you take a day off work or go on a vacation. Rest is deeper than those. Rest happens down deep in your soul. It's the freedom from worry and anxiety. It means your heart isn't tied up in knots of concern.

There's always plenty to worry about. If you have children, the worry (ahem, *concern*) never stops. Concern swirls around getting or keeping a job, making financial ends meet, health, relationships and even (or especially) world situations. There's always something to keep your heart at least flirting with angst.

How does Jesus give rest? Because of His grace-filled love, He takes your worries and you'll have rest because you know you can trust Him to handle things. Does that mean He will bring a wandering child home, heal a relationship, fix your finances …? No. He doesn't say He will fix anything – except the worry in your heart. He will give you peace by staying close and reminding you that nothing surprises Him.

You might not see resolution today or tomorrow but you can trust that God knows what's happening.

What do you need rest from? Have you given this concern to God? Have you experienced His rest?

God's Grace Disciplines

Joyful are those You discipline, LORD,
those You teach with Your instructions.
PSALM 94:12

Remember being disciplined by your parents? It was no fun, was it? How did they discipline you? Were you grounded or did you lose privileges? Sometimes parents give extra chores as punishment or discipline. Whatever your discipline was, it wasn't fun … it wasn't meant to be, that's why it's discipline.

Discipline has a purpose which is to help you understand what you did wrong that made the discipline necessary and to help you focus so that you don't repeat that behavior. Discipline is actually meant to be instructional. Understanding that makes discipline more bearable.

God's discipline is also meant to be instructional. It's actually His grace in action that chooses to discipline you. It's because of His love, which seeks to encourage you to learn more fully how to live for Him. His discipline will help you learn to love others as He does. It will help you choose to seek God's guidance as you learn to obey what Scripture teaches.

As you experience the discipline God gives you will see the good that comes from it. You'll see your faith growing stronger so you will be able to joyfully celebrate His discipline.

When was a time you knew God's discipline? What did you learn from it? Are you grateful for His care that disciplines you?

The What's Next?

You will show me the way of life,
granting me the joy of Your presence and
the pleasures of living with You forever.
PSALM 16:11

Sometimes it feels like you're free-floating in life. You have your plans laid out and you know where you're going and what you're going to do. But then everything comes crashing down. Nothing goes as planned. You're left with no plans and no clue about what direction to head. What do you do?

By God's grace, you are not really free-floating. He has a plan and has been waiting for you to let go of control and trust His guidance about the "what's next?" for you.

Be still long enough for Him to guide and direct. Pay attention to opportunities He brings to you and rely on the Holy Spirit to guide your steps. He has a plan and He will reveal it to you. You'll be a part of growing God's Kingdom as you follow His direction and obey Him.

His plan may simply be for you to be a voice of kindness for those you work with or to be a friend to someone in your neighborhood. It may not be for a high-powered career. That's okay. The power is in being the person God wants in the place God wants! There's nothing better in the world than that!

When have your own plans crashed and burned?
How did God redirect your life? How do you
see your role in growing His Kingdom?

God Is Always the Same

Whatever is good and perfect is a gift coming down to
us from God our Father, who created all the lights in the
heavens. He never changes or casts a shifting shadow.
JAMES 1:17

Things in life are constantly changing. It's not easy to find something
you can count on – something that will always be exactly the same.
The character of life today seems to be change. It can be unsettling.
When you experience a multitude of changes it can seem that they
are never going to stop so you're constantly waiting for the other shoe
to drop. Is there anything or anyone who remains constant, who never
changes?

You know there is ... God. He is the same yesterday, today and
tomorrow. His character never wavers. His love is constant. His forgiveness is steady. His guidance is real. God gives you wonderful
blessings every day. You can depend on Him that His generosity of
blessings will always be there for you. God's grace will always be a
constant in your life because He is always the God you read about in
the Bible.

The way you have seen Him in the past is the way He will be now
and in the future. He is your Father. He doesn't get frustrated with your
disobedience and turn away. He doesn't give up on you. He loves you
now and He always will.

What part of God's character do you most appreciate never
changing? How do you depend on that unchanging character?

Each Day Is a Gift

This is the day the LORD has made.
We will rejoice and be glad in it.
PSALM 118:24

Some people live as if they will live forever. They take their days for granted, doing what they want with little concern for other people or doing their part to further God's Kingdom. They may have fun but in the big picture of life, they are simply wasting time … spending their time foolishly.

God, in His grace, gives you each day. Some are good, filled with people you love and things you love to do. Thank God for those days! Some are tough, filled with people who make life difficult or situations that are painful. Those days are from God too.

Every day is an opportunity to learn more about living for God. It is an opportunity to show love and kindness to others. Is it okay to laugh and have fun? Of course. Does God mind if you spend a few hours playing a sport, reading a book or working in your garden? No!

He just wants you to remember that each day you have is a gift from Him. Give Him credit for His generosity. Thank Him for His blessings. Do the work He has for you to do. Enjoy each and every day God gives you!

How can you acknowledge that each day
is a gift from God? With what activity do
you spend the majority of your days?

No Excuses

The law applies to those to whom it was given, for its purpose is to keep people from having excuses, and to show that the entire world is guilty before God. For no one can ever be made right with God by doing what the law commands. The law simply shows us how sinful we are.
ROMANS 3:19-20

You have no excuse for excuses about whether or not you obey God. He made sure of that by giving His Word, which so clearly outlines what sin is and what God's goal for His children is – to know Him, to obey Him, to serve Him, to love others unselfishly and fully.

Scripture is a mirror that shows you the truth of the person you are compared to the person God wants you to be. There are no excuses for your behavior or justification of your choices to excuse your sins. God makes it clear that every person is a sinner. No one can honestly claim to be sin-free.

But ... grace. God's grace made a way for your sins to be forgiven so that you can have a personal relationship with God ... be called His child ... have the blessing of His Spirit living in you ... have the assurance of heaven forever.

Don't waste energy trying to justify your sins. Instead, receive Christ and His forgiveness. Embrace the grace of salvation and the blessings He showers down on you daily.

Are there certain sins you sometimes
try to justify? Does that seem fair in your own mind?
What do you read in Scripture about justifying your sin?

Getting Along
with Others

Let the peace that comes from Christ rule in your
hearts. For as members of one body you are called
to live in peace. And always be thankful.

COLOSSIANS 3:15

Some people are hard to get along with – even some who share your faith in Jesus – and those are the ones you're told to be at peace with!

There are at least a couple of roadblocks to living in peace with others. One is … some people are just difficult and no matter how hard you try there are bumpy spots in your relationship. They know how to push your buttons or they don't even care that you have buttons!

Another roadblock is … you. Be honest now, sometimes you are selfish and self-centered. Your attitude is all about you and you don't want to be kind or giving or focused on what others need or want.

How do you live in peace with others? Jesus. Ask for His help. Keep your heart focused on loving Him and reflecting Him. Ask Him to help you be less annoyed by others and less focused on self. He will help you see that others are dealing with their own troubles in life and that plays into how they behave. He will help you live in peace. Be thankful for that – it's a gift straight from His grace.

What causes bumps in your efforts to live in
peace? Situations? People? Have you asked
God for help? What has He shown you?

God Speaks

The LORD came and called as before,
"Samuel! Samuel!" And Samuel replied,
"Speak, Your servant is listening."
1 SAMUEL 3:10

You probably know this story in 1 Samuel where God audibly spoke to a young boy … not once, not twice but three times until Samuel responded. Why is it important to you? Because it shows that God will do whatever is necessary to get your attention.

Sometimes He speaks through the words of Scripture. A verse or phrase literally jumps out and sticks in your mind. You can't stop thinking about it so you know it's something God wants you to pay attention to.

Sometimes He speaks through another person's counsel or something they say that, again, seems to light a fire in your heart. It keeps rolling through your mind. God is saying, "Pay attention to this."

Often He speaks through nudges in your heart that continually move you toward something or away from something. You know it's Him so you follow the nudge.

Have you ever heard God speak? Have you heard a voice so clearly that you expected to turn around and see someone in the room with you? It happens. God, in His grace, wants to communicate with you. He will pursue you until you hear Him! That's love. Real love.

God wants to communicate with you. How has He done that?
When was the last time you knew, without a doubt, that God was
speaking? Did you follow His guidance? How did it turn out?

A Part of the Body

As a result of your ministry, they will give glory to God. For your generosity to them and to all believers will prove that you are obedient to the Good News of Christ. And they will pray for you with deep affection because of the overflowing grace God has given to you. Thank God for this gift too wonderful for words!
2 CORINTHIANS 9:13-15

You can't do everything. Try as you might, regardless of how devoted you are to God and His Kingdom, you can't do everything. God knew that, and in His grace, He made you a member of His family so you don't have to do it all. You have a family working together to do His work. You have your role in helping others learn of Him and other people have different roles. All are necessary.

Sometimes your role is to pray for another's ministry. By doing that you have a part in their service to God! Sometimes your role is to give financially so that their work in sharing His love can grow. By doing that you have a part in their ministry. Sometimes your role is to go – have a physical role in another's ministry.

In the same way, others pray for you and your specific ministry. Sometimes they give finances to help you. Other times they will join in with you to physically do the work.

Thank God that you are a part of His family and that you are able to share in the bigger picture of His work because of your association with others.

What do you see as your specific work for God? How have you been able to share in others' ministries? By praying, giving or working?

Singing a Thankful Song

But let all who take refuge in You rejoice; let them sing
joyful praises forever. Spread Your protection over them
that all who love Your name may be filled with joy.
PSALM 5:11

God protects you every day, probably in ways you don't even recognize or notice. Perhaps you have come to take His protection so for granted that you don't think about the accidents that are averted or the missteps that are protected. Do you expect His protection because you've always known it, even recognizing that some people around the world struggle with longing for protection from danger every day of their lives?

Take a few minutes and reflect on the safety you have enjoyed in your life. Or, perhaps you've seen God's obvious protection rescue you over the years. His care for you through His protection gives you the opportunity to sing joy-filled praises to Him. Take that opportunity and show your thankfulness for His protection. Let the whole world know. Give Him the credit that He is due. Your thankfulness in praise will increase your awareness of His constant protection, which will increase your praise.

Your songs of joy will be a witness to all around you that God is working and that you recognize His protection. Remember that your gratitude to Him is as much as a witness as any other words you can speak about God's love.

Have you seen God's protection in your life?
How? Did you privately thank Him?
How did you publicly give Him credit?

Leave Your Worries with God

Give all your worries and cares to God, for He cares about you.
1 PETER 5:7

What keeps you awake at night? When you're lying in the darkness at 3:00 A.M. what runs through your mind over and over? Sure you may talk with God about it but you are too filled with angst to leave it with Him. How can you stop being consumed with worry?

Simple. Give your worries to God, who, in His grace, and because of His love will take care of them. He promises that. God doesn't want you to lose sleep by worrying. But, why is it so hard to give Him your problems and not grab them back in the darkness of night?

Maybe you're impatient. God doesn't act as quickly as you'd like and waiting is very difficult. Then there's always the possibility that God will not actually solve the situation but will walk with you through it and comfort you in the suffering it brings.

Perhaps you grab back your concerns because you don't completely trust God to handle them. You tell Him what to do – you have a wonderful plan for Him to follow. However, God has His own plan and it is the best in the long run. Trust Him and realize His great love for you.

What runs through your mind at 3:00 A.M. when you can't sleep? Have you given it to God but grabbed it back? Why do you struggle to leave it with Him?

By His Grace

"Be strong and courageous! Do not
be afraid or discouraged. For the LORD
your God is with you wherever you go."
JOSHUA 1:9

When you know beyond the shadow of a doubt that your protection is with you, it's easy to be brave and even to take measured risks. Nothing can get at you. You don't feel like you're facing the world alone.

You're never alone. God is with you wherever you go. That's why you're told over and over in Scripture to not be afraid. Sure you'll have problems in life. There will be times when you are attacked BECAUSE of your faith in God. It may happen but you won't be facing it alone because God is with you always. He is strengthening you and giving you courage to face whatever happens.

When tough situations develop, call out to God for strength and help. Let those around you see that your help comes from God. Your dependence and trust in Him will be a witness to others that He is real in your life and that you know His presence and protection are constant.

It is by His grace you have a relationship with Him. It is by His grace that He is always with you. It is by His grace that His strength and protection are yours.

Are you facing something today that frightens you?
How do you see God's presence with you?
How do you need His strength today?

Forgiving Others

Be kind to each other, tenderhearted, forgiving one
another, just as God through Christ has forgiven you.
EPHESIANS 4:32

God, in His infinite grace, forgives your sins – over and over – day after day – and you are undoubtedly grateful for that kindness. Are you grateful enough to carry it forward? Are you willing to forgive people who hurt you? It's not easy when a friend or loved one deliberately hurts you and if she does it over and over … forgiveness may be out of your realm of possibility. Except … you need forgiveness over and over.

Granted, there is a difference between allowing someone to take advantage of you and forgiving another's behavior. If you need to cut ties with an abuser, then do so. But in the normal ebb and flow of life, when you're hurt or offended, give your offender the benefit of the doubt. Try to see what's going on in her life that may play into her behavior. Care about what she's dealing with in her life. Approach her with kindness and a tender heart to talk through what's happened.

Be willing to forgive and be reconciled because of God's love. If you can't do that on your own, ask Him to flow His love through you. He will. Let grace beget grace.

Forgiving is hard, isn't it? Sometimes it takes an act of your will to choose forgiveness over hurt or anger. Do you need to forgive someone? Who and why? Have you tried unsuccessfully? Have you asked God's help?

It's Up to You

Letting the Spirit control your
mind leads to life and peace.
ROMANS 8:6

You have a choice to make – choosing to allow the Holy Spirit to control your thoughts or letting the original you control them. You have been saved because of God's grace. By His grace His Holy Spirit lives in your heart helping you follow His commands and molding your heart to be like Jesus. But, you can throw roadblocks up to that by where you allow your mind to go.

You know when your thoughts wander into things that aren't helpful in obeying God. You can choose to turn away from those thoughts or to dwell on them. If you let unclean, unkind, selfish thoughts stay in your mind, turning them over and over – imagining what could be or might have been – you're letting the old you … the you before God … control your mind. That's not good.

The Holy Spirit can chase away those thoughts and fill your mind with ideas, thoughts, memories or hopes that honor God and lead to life. Thoughts that will move your heart toward becoming more like Jesus. This possibility is God's gift to you. It's His grace to you.

Old you thoughts are a constant temptation.
How is this a struggle for you? Where do the old you
thoughts tempt you the most? How do you battle this?

Gift of Grace

"Father, if You are willing, please take
this cup of suffering away from Me.
Yet I want Your will to be done, not Mine."
LUKE 22:42

Jesus prayed this just before He was arrested in the Garden of Geth-semane. It's a prayer of total submission to His Father. He recognized that God's plan is best and He was willing to submit to it for God's glory and your salvation.

An interesting phrase in this prayer is "if You are willing." Jesus knew that God could stop everything that was coming. He could whisk Jesus back to heaven to avoid the suffering that was ahead. Do you think God wanted to do that? Didn't He want to protect His beloved Son from the horror? Maybe, but He didn't. He left Jesus to face per-secution and death … because He loves you.

Jesus also said, "I want Your will to be done, not Mine." He knew what was ahead. He was part of setting the plan in motion but He was willing to go through the agony … because of His love for you.

God's grace is an unspeakable, undeniable, unmatchable gift by both God, the Father and God, the Son. Don't take it lightly. Let His gift of grace impact every part of your life. Let it change you.

How has God's gift of grace changed you?
How does it impact you every day
in your thoughts and behavior?

God's Creation

In the beginning God created
the heavens and the earth.
GENESIS 1:1

Did God have to make the heavens and the earth? Of course not. God doesn't HAVE to do anything. However, creation was the beginning of His grace to mankind. He set His plan in motion by creating a beautiful world, filled with something for everyone to enjoy.

Some people connect with Him through the steady waves of massive oceans that show the rhythm of the universe. Others find awe and reverence from majestic, beautiful mountains. The heavens reflect His vastness in the grandness of His power. Still others love the comfort of a gentle stream meandering through a forest or meadow. There is something for everyone in God's creation.

Why did He make the earth and the heavens? For you. Nature itself shouts of His power and creativity, His love and gentleness. Spending time out in the part of nature you love will help you connect with God in a fresh way. He made it for you because He wants you to worship Him. His creation helps you see His power and majesty as well as His gentleness and love.

God's grace began with creating a world that you get to enjoy and that will encourage your worship.

How does nature encourage you to worship God?
How can you intentionally get out into nature where
you can see God's creative power and love?

Made in His Image

God created human beings in His own image.
In the image of God He created them;
male and female He created them.
GENESIS 1:27

God's grace is evident in this very fact … He made you in His image. He didn't make you to be less than you are. He made you to think with intelligence, care, love, serve others, and be creative just as He is.

Because God loves mankind, He made humans to be like Him because He knew that's the best life experience you could have. He could have created people who can't think for themselves or who aren't intelligent enough to make a decision. He could have made sure that you are dependent on Him for every movement, thought, action, success or failure by not giving you the freedom to make your own choices.

However He did give mankind the freedom of choice and the intelligence and heart to make good choices. He also gave you the opportunity to learn about His love and care and to choose to know Him and follow Him.

God's grace is shown in that you are made in His image. What a blessing that is! And you can know Him as your Savior! Praise God!

How does it make you feel to know you are made in God's image? How does thinking about this truth impact your choices or behavior?

Grateful Submission

> I plead with you to give your bodies to God
> because of all He has done for you. Let them be a
> living and holy sacrifice – the kind He will find
> acceptable. This is truly the way to worship Him.
> ROMANS 12:1

Some people feel that submitting their will to God makes them like a marionette with God pulling the strings to direct their every movement. They fear they will have no freedom to make choices in their lives if they submit to Jesus. That's not true. You always have freedom to choose your actions and your thoughts.

God hopes that you will have such a deep gratitude for His love and grace that you willingly give your life to Him. This only happens when you come to the realization that God wants only what is best for you because He loves you so deeply. His best plan will not always be what you feel is best for you or even what you hope for. But, when you understand His great wisdom and that He sees the whole of your life – not just the immediate, then you know that His plan will always be for your good. His plan always moves you deeper into becoming like Jesus and honoring Him with your life. That's what really matters.

So, accepting His plan for good fills your heart with such deep gratitude that you gladly submit to Him and anticipate the good that is to come.

Submitting to God is not always easy. With what area of your life do you most struggle with submission? Do you feel that you can trust God with ALL of your life?

Sharing with Jesus

In His kindness God called you to share in
His eternal glory by means of Christ Jesus. So after
you have suffered a little while, He will restore, support,
and strengthen you, and He will place you on a firm
foundation. All power to Him forever! Amen.

1 PETER 5:10-11

You share life with Jesus. God's plan is to mold your heart to be more like Jesus' heart – caring, loving, strong, obedient, worshipping and honoring God. That's a wonderful thing and is beautiful evidence of God's grace in your life. However, sharing life with Jesus also means sharing in His suffering. Whoa … did you just think, "Wait. I didn't sign up for that?" While it certainly isn't fun, it is a part of reality. There may be times when you're persecuted or at least mistreated, made fun of, dismissed or ignored because of your faith. For some, there could come a time when they are imprisoned or worse, simply because they choose to live for Jesus.

Whatever you face because of your faith, God promises that it is only for a time. Then, by His grace, He will rescue you. He will restore you to good health or good standing – whatever is needed. He will strengthen you emotionally, spiritually and physically. He will plant your feet on the firm foundation of His love. Suffering with or for Jesus is a privilege that is part of sharing His eternity in heaven. By God's grace you suffer … and win.

Have you been persecuted or suffered for
your faith? How? Did you persevere by
honoring God? Has He lifted you from the trial?
How did your faith grow stronger because of it?

Jesus, Your Mediator

There is one God and one Mediator who can reconcile
God and humanity – the Man Christ Jesus. He gave
His life to purchase freedom for everyone.
1 TIMOTHY 2:5-6

A mediator is a go-between, an arbitrator or negotiator. In sports terms it might be a referee or an umpire. So, someone who pleads your case to a higher power. Or, someone who is a bridge between two parties who disagree. Or someone who makes sure the rules are obeyed and the game is fair. Jesus is all those things for you.

God Almighty is the all-powerful Creator who insists on your purity to be in His presence. No sinfulness can be in His pure presence. He demands obedience to His laws and statutes. He wants your total submission and worship. But you can't do that … not all the time. Some of it you can't ever do on your own. So, God, in His grace made Jesus your Mediator. Because of Him, you can have a personal relationship with God since His mediation wipes clean your sin. God sees you through the purity of Jesus.

Even more than that, Jesus pleads your case before God. He reconciles or makes right the differences between the Creator and the created. The entirety of your relationship with God is made possible by the mediation of Jesus. Thank Him. Thank Him every day.

Have you ever needed a mediator in life? Why? How does
Jesus' mediation between you and God make you feel?

The Armor of God

Put on all of God's armor so that you will be able to stand firm against all strategies of the devil. For we are not fighting against flesh-and-blood enemies, but against evil rulers and authorities of the unseen world, against mighty powers in this dark world, and against evil spirits in the heavenly places.
EPHESIANS 6:11-12

Whew! This spiritual life is not easy. There really is an evil, dark side to life. The devil is a reality and he will do whatever he can to pull you away from living for God. The more determined you are to stay close to God, the harder he will work to trip you up. He's sneaky and he's persistent. He knows your weaknesses and he will continually attack them hoping that he can wear you down and you will finally give in. Then he has you.

EXCEPT … the devil didn't plan on the protection God provides for you. In His grace, God has provided armor for you to put on to protect you against the devil's attacks. Read Ephesians 6 to learn about the armor of God's righteousness, shoes of peace, shield of faith, helmet of salvation, and sword of the Spirit. Each piece is necessary for your full protection. God knows how the devil will attack you and He covered you completely with the armor mentioned in Ephesians 6. If you pay attention to each piece, you will be protected. God provided it for you. Use it.

Do you know where your weaknesses are? The devil does. Pay attention and use what God has provided for your protection. How do you put on the armor of God?

Love in Grace

Anyone who does not love does
not know God, for God is love.
1 JOHN 4:8

God's love doesn't exclude anyone. Scripture records Him reaching out to prostitutes, tax collectors, and thieves. He believed none were too far gone to come to Him. He wasn't afraid to get His hands dirty either. He touched lepers. He made mud to put on a blind man's eyes. He raised a smelly dead man back to life. Jesus didn't sit in a fine temple and wait for people to come to Him. He went where they were and spent His energy teaching, healing and helping all people.

Loving as God loves demands a broader reach than just staying close to those who are most like you. You might be asked to get outside of your comfy church and go to places that make you uncomfortable. It might mean spending time with people who are very different from you. Will it be hard? Sometimes. Will the people always want you there? Probably not. Will some listen? Yes. Will some be angry? Possibly. Should that stop you? No.

God's love is for everyone. His grace of salvation is for everyone. All deserve a chance to hear. Some will first see His love in how you treat them … then they will listen to what you say.

This topic may be hard for you because it's uncomfortable.
Has God asked you to reach out to others in a situation that
makes you uncomfortable? How? Did you do it? How did it go?

April

The Fruit of the Spirit

The Holy Spirit produces this kind of fruit in our lives: love, joy, peace, patience, kindness, goodness, faithfulness, gentleness, and self-control. There is no law against these things!
GALATIANS 5:22-23

The Holy Spirit living in your heart is a gift of God's grace. His presence in your heart helps you obey God. He challenges you when you aren't obeying Him. He teaches you and guides you as your heart learns to be more and more like Jesus.

The fruit of the Spirit, listed in these verses in Galatians are the characteristics your heart needs to develop in order for you to be like Jesus. These qualities will certainly help you live in peace with those around you and your relationships will be much more peaceful, healthy and filled with joy.

The process of developing these qualities is a journey. You're not perfect so it's not possible to consistently show every single one of them. But don't get discouraged – that's why God, in His grace, gave you the Holy Spirit. The Spirit will help you as you learn to keep these qualities in the forefront of your heart and mind. He will remind you of each of them in whatever situations you face. He will convict your heart when you aren't showing them. He is your teacher and guide. He is a gift from God.

How does the Spirit help you with the fruit of the Spirit? Is one quality harder for you than the others? Which one? Why?

What's Your Fiery Furnace?

"Look!" Nebuchadnezzar shouted.
"I see four men, unbound, walking around
in the fire unharmed! And the fourth looks like a god!"
DANIEL 3:25

Shadrach, Meshach and Abednego were punished by the king for refusing to bow down to his statue. They refused to bow down to anyone or anything but God Himself. The king ordered them to be thrown into a fiery furnace. He thought they would cave and decide to bow down to his statue. They didn't. They said their God would protect them no matter what. So into the furnace they went and the king ordered it to be made super hot! Then he sat down to watch them burn.

To his surprise, they didn't burn. They walked around in the fire and a 4th man was with them. When he had them pulled out the king was shocked that they weren't hurt and didn't even smell like smoke! The 4th man in the fire was an angel of God. The Lord protected His three servants.

You see, God doesn't always stop the fire from burning. He doesn't always keep you out of the heat. But He never, never lets you go through it alone. His grace steps into your fiery furnace with you – whatever it may be. He honors your obedience to Him. He protects you in the fire.

What "fiery furnace" are you struggling through? Have you asked God to take it away? Have you asked Him to keep you safe? Have you sensed His presence in the fire?

A Thankful Heart

Let us come to Him with thanksgiving.
Let us sing psalms of praise to Him.
PSALM 95:2

Thanksgiving is more than just a day noted on the calendar. It is a necessary part of your relationship with God. If you are truly, deeply grateful for something, it shows! Heartfelt gratitude explodes from your heart. Have you ever felt that thankful? When you stop and think about all that God does for you every single day does it fill your heart with gratitude? A grateful heart realizes that all you have comes to you from the grace-filled heart of God.

Take a few minutes and list the blessings He gives you every single day. Don't forget to begin with gratitude for your salvation and His constant forgiveness of your sins.

How many times a day do you think to thank Him for safety, your home, your job, your friends, your family, your health? What about the Bible, Christian mentors and teachers? Do you thank Him for books to read, music to enjoy, the ability to exercise?

Let thanksgiving spring from your heart every day. It brings joy to your spirit and inspires those around you to notice all God does for them. It pleases the Lord to hear your thanksgiving for all He does for you.

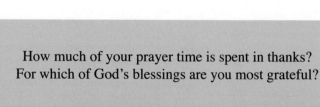

How much of your prayer time is spent in thanks?
For which of God's blessings are you most grateful?

Righteous Living

Now you are free from your slavery to sin,
and you have become slaves to righteous living.
ROMANS 6:18

Before you accepted Jesus as Savior, you couldn't stop sinning. Sin held you in its grasp like a slave-master. You thought you were free – most people do, but you weren't really. The power of sin over the old you led to behaviors and choices that did not honor God. Not all the time, of course. Some very good people choose not to believe in God or obey Him. Sin is choices that do not honor God. Sin doesn't obey His commands. Sin is making something or someone else more important in your heart than God.

Your freedom from that slavery came through God's grace making you His child. Now, you are a slave to righteous living. So … you're still a slave. Is that a bad thing? No, because the Master ruling your heart now is God. His mastery is filled with love and the desire for the very best life for you. He guides your heart to obey His commands, which means you honor Him, worship Him, love Him. You also love others, forgive them, serve them, put them before yourself. This "slavery" makes a better life for you and all those with whom you come into contact.

How has your life changed since accepting Jesus? Have you seen a change in your priorities? How are your choices different? Have these changes made a better life for you and those around you?

Three Standards

The LORD has told you what is good, and this
is what He requires of you: to do what is right,
to love mercy, and to walk humbly with your God.
MICAH 6:8

The Christian life is not a life of rules. You don't have to deny yourself pleasures, fun or laughter. Following God's commands actually opens your life to a better experience because He wants only good for you. In His loving grace He tells you what that means:

Do what's right – obey laws, treat others with respect and kindness, be focused on others, not yourself, and most importantly, make God number one in your heart.

Love mercy. Mercy means you care about others. You have compassion on them for what they're dealing with. You share in their sorrow and give of your time and money to help them through their problems.

Walk humbly with God. This may be the most difficult to consistently obey. It means that you submit to God's will for your life. You're not in control – He is. Sometimes it's hard to know what He wants. You have to be quiet and still in order to hear His voice. Sometimes it's hard to obey because it's not what you want to do. But you humbly recognize that He is in charge and that's a good thing … because He loves you and wants the best for you.

Do you feel like you're "following rules" to obey
God? How have you seen that His standards …
His commands … make your life better?

Be the Best You

In His grace, God has given us different gifts for doing certain things well. So if God has given you the ability to prophesy, speak out with as much faith as God has given you. If your gift is serving others, serve them well. If you are a teacher, teach well. If your gift is to encourage others, be encouraging. If it is giving, give generously. If God has given you leadership ability, take the responsibility seriously. And if you have a gift for showing kindness to others, do it gladly.
ROMANS 12:6-8

These verses say it all. God, in His grace, has given you a job to do and has given you what you need to do it. He doesn't call you to something then not equip you to do it. What's your gift?

Don't spend time comparing yourself to someone else? Don't fall into the trap of feeling your skills or jobs are less than anyone else's. That's not true. Every job has value because God chose it for you. All the pieces of what He has ordained are necessary to His Kingdom work.

Whatever God has made you good at – do it with joy. Celebrate what He has entrusted to you. Don't worry about others' work or if they are carrying their load or doing their job well. Be the best you that you can be and do your work well!

What has God gifted you to do? This list in Romans 12 doesn't list all gifts and talents so maybe yours isn't there. How do you serve God? Are you happy with that or do you find yourself longing to do someone else's job? Why?

Winning Grace

"I have told you all this so that you may have peace in Me.
Here on earth you will have many trials and sorrows.
But take heart, because I have overcome the world."
JOHN 16:33

"The bad guys are winning!" It feels that way, doesn't it? The evening news is one horrific story after another, from all over the world! People are suffering … dying … losing everything. Even Christians are being persecuted. Why doesn't God do something?

It is terrible and perhaps for the moment the bad guys ARE winning in some areas. They may win a battle or two but the war isn't over. God knows what's going on and He already knows who comes out on top … He does.

Jesus' words in John 16:33 recognize that there are going to be hard times; even for His followers, or especially for His followers. As time winds down to the end Jesus will become less popular in the world and therefore, so will His followers. That's already happening. Some of it is pure evil. Some is the anger of nature. All of it breaks your heart.

But Jesus, in His comforting grace, says to hang on to Him. Remember that God wins in the end. Take peace in the fact that when the final chapter is written, God comes out on top … and so do you, His child.

These are hard times in the world and things will probably get even harder. What do you struggle with the most? What do you pray about? How do you pray?

Hard Things

> You intended to harm me, but God intended
> it all for good. He brought me to this position so
> I could save the lives of many people.
> GENESIS 50:20

Joseph was Dad's favorite; his brothers couldn't stand it; they sold him into slavery and told Dad he died. Joseph became a slave in Egypt; was sent to prison but ended up as the second-in-command of the country. Then his brothers had to ask him for food, except they didn't know they were asking their long lost brother. They were terrified when they found out because Joseph could have thrown them into prison … or worse.

But he didn't. Why? Because Joseph understood that living for God means sometimes you go through hard things. One minute you're Dad's favorite and the next you're a slave. Did he question God? Maybe. Did he give up on God? Not at all. Joseph had the opportunity to get revenge on his brothers, but he didn't do it. Verse 20 is his response to their fear: "You intended to harm me, but God intended it all for good." God took Joseph to the place where he could do good and save a lot of lives.

Sometimes you have to go through the really hard stuff in life in order to get to the good place where God's grace wants you to be.

What hard things has life thrown at you? How have you responded? When you got the chance for revenge on your enemies, did you take it?

God's Protecting Grace

> So at last the king gave orders for Daniel to be arrested and thrown into the den of lions. The king said to him, "May your God, whom you serve so faithfully, rescue you."
> DANIEL 6:16

Even a king who didn't serve God recognized God's power. King Nebuchadnezzar was tricked into making a law that people could only pray to him. Daniel was a friend of his but because Daniel prayed to God, the king had to enforce the law. He had to have Daniel thrown into a pit of hungry lions. It wouldn't be a pleasant death. He gave the order but then told Daniel that he hoped Daniel's God could save him.

Daniel prayed to God every day … publicly … so his enemies knew they could get him in trouble with that. Daniel was God's man and God took him through a scary night in order to make the king proclaim God's greatness to the kingdom.

God shut the lions' mouths. They didn't even sniff Daniel. So the next morning when the king came to see what was left of his friend, he found Daniel safe and sound. That's when he proclaimed, "Everyone should tremble with fear before Daniel's God because He has rescued Daniel from the power of lions!"

The path of God will never lead you to a place where the grace of God will not protect you. Trust Him.

When was a time you were afraid?
Did you see God's protection? How?

Full-Time Job

*Whatever you do or say, do it as a representative of the
Lord Jesus, giving thanks through Him to God the Father.*
COLOSSIANS 3:17

Being a Christian is a full-time job. It's not something you put on at 8:00 A.M. and take off at 5:00 P.M. It's your essence. It defines you. Every word you speak becomes a reflection of what you think of God. Scary, huh? Every word. Everything you do reflects how important He is to you. There's no time off. There's never a time you are not a child of God.

Make your words and actions count. Be careful that all you say and do brings honor to His name. Are you kind? Do you speak with respect? Do you try to make others laugh at someone else's expense? Are you thoughtful? Do you serve others, even when it's not particularly attractive? Do you share Jesus and His love? Can others see Him in your life?

Are thanks and gratitude visible in you? Are you thankful for all you have without feeling that you deserve what you've been given? Are you grateful for every experience in life, even the painful ones? Are you thankful for what you learn from those hard things? Your thankfulness is a witness to your humility before God in recognizing that His way is always best.

How are you doing at your full-time child of God position?
Are you consistent in how you represent Him? How do
your words and deeds reflect His importance to you?

God Is Close

The LORD is close to the brokenhearted;
He rescues those whose spirits are crushed.
PSALM 34:18

There is a saying that states: "The will of God will never take you where the grace of God cannot keep you."

God is close to you regardless of what you're facing. No one makes it through life without experiencing pain. Losing a loved one to death is a pain that most people experience. It breaks your heart because it's so final. Your heart longs to see that person again, to have a talk or get one more hug. Broken hearts also come from broken relationships. When someone walks away from you but you still care, it hurts to the depths of your soul. Hearts are broken every day in a multitude of ways. When your heart is broken and your spirit is crushed it's hard to get up each day and keep going. It's hard to hope that things will get better.

But you will make it through the pain because God stays close to you. His grace holds you up when you think you're going to crumble. It gives you the strength to keep moving forward. It gives you hope that tomorrow will be better and the next day better still. God's grace keeps Him close to you always.

Have you had a broken heart?
What made it break? How did you sense
God's closeness through your pain?

Locked In Thoughts

You will keep in perfect peace
all who trust in You, all whose thoughts
are fixed on You! Trust in the LORD always,
for the LORD God is the eternal Rock.
ISAIAH 26:3-4

Are your thoughts firmly locked in on God? Locked in so that you can think of nothing else – every thought you have comes through the filter of who God is and what He means to you. Every choice you make is made through that same filter of what it means to obey God and what He wants you to do. With thoughts fixed on God you long to obey Him so you seek to know Him and His Word.

Having a mind fixed on God is not as easy as you would hope because everything in this world pulls against it – culture, friends, family, career … and especially Satan. It becomes almost a moment-by-moment choice to fix your mind on God and resist every thought or idea that pulls you away from Him.

The blessing of setting your mind on God is a great example of His grace – it is peace – something everyone longs to have. Peace is not something you can attain on your own. It's a gift of God's grace that comes through locking your mind on Him. That will grow your trust in Him as you see His constant presence and steadiness. Then peace.

How often during your day do you think about God and what He wants for you? Which of His commands does He often remind you of? Do you have peace in your heart? How's your trust level?

No Holding Back

Since He did not spare even His own Son but gave
Him up for us all, won't He also give us everything else?
ROMANS 8:32

There are no "sort of" children in God's Kingdom. He didn't sacrifice His only Son for some people but not for others. Think about this – God didn't hold back anything. He could have, at any moment, sent an army of angels to rescue Jesus. He could have stopped any of the horrific persecution Jesus faced. But He didn't. He let it all happen, knowing how terrible it was going to be. He gave up His Son for all mankind.

He's already given His most precious gift so it makes perfect sense that He gives you everything else. There is nothing more precious than His Son and the salvation that the gift of Jesus provides. God's not going to start holding things back now.

Get ready because His blessings and challenges and lessons and love are flowing at you. God loves you so much that He never tires of giving you things – good things that make you smile. Beautiful things that make you sigh. Hard things that teach you lessons. Painful things that pull you closer to Him. Wonderful things that bond you together with the rest of the family. All are gifts from God's heart of grace.

God holds nothing back from you. Have you thanked Him for His generosity? What blessing are you most thankful for? What blessing has been the hardest? What lesson did you learn through it?

Peaceful Rest

The LORD is my shepherd; I have all that I need.
He lets me rest in green meadows; He leads me beside
peaceful streams. He renews my strength.
PSALM 23:1-3

What does a shepherd do for his flock? He makes sure they have all they need. He leads them to fields where they have all the food they need. He makes sure they have water to drink. He gets them to a safe place at night and guards them while they sleep. They do have all they need – food, water, rest in safety.

Jesus is your Shepherd and He cares for you just as carefully as a shepherd cares for his flock of sheep. You have all you need and everything comes from the grace of Jesus.

One of the sweetest blessings of grace is rest. You may overlook it when considering your blessings because it's not as obvious as food or a home or a job. But rest makes all God's other blessings more enjoyable. The ability to lie down at night, close your eyes and know that your Shepherd is keeping watch over you allows you to rest in peace. Your anxiety doesn't keep you awake because you know you can trust God. He loves you, so even if there is danger lurking around, He protects your heart and sticks right beside you through the night.

What keeps you awake at night? Does knowing that your
Shepherd is watching out for you help you rest? Have
you thanked God for allowing you peaceful rest?

The Grace of Hope

We have heard of your faith in Christ Jesus and your love for all of God's people, which come from your confident hope of what God has reserved for you in heaven. You have had this expectation ever since you first heard the truth of the Good News.

COLOSSIANS 1:4-5

There are two words in this passage that stand out. Don't miss them. They are … confident hope. Paul and Timothy wrote to the Colossians and noted their faith in Jesus. They commented on the Colossians love for all God's people. And, they said those things were based on the confident hope of heaven.

Confidence. There seems to be very little anymore that you can really be confident about. Things can change overnight – from your health to finances, jobs, and relationships. Things in our world change quickly too, with wars and governments in upheaval. Having confidence that what God says is true and will always be true is a blessing of grace.

What you read in God's Word was true yesterday, is true today and will be true tomorrow. Don't let false interpretations sway you from what God says is true. His Holy Spirit will convict your heart if your belief begins to wander from His truth.

Believe God's Word, let it be alive in your heart so your faith grows deeper and deeper. Thank Him for the confident hope you have because of what it teaches you. Love God's people with all your heart – after all, they are family!

Are the three things Paul mentions about the Colossians apparent in your life? Do you trust God's Word so completely that your hope of heaven is confident? How are you doing at loving God's people … all of them?

The Grace of Protection

*At the end of the ten days, Daniel and his three friends
looked healthier and better nourished than the young men
who had been eating the food assigned by the king.*
DANIEL 1:15

How serious are you about honoring God? Do you trust that He will protect you if your obedience angers people who could hurt you? Daniel certainly did.

Daniel and his friends were captive slaves in a training program to serve the king. They were recognized as the cream of the crop of the boys in training so they were privileged to be able to eat the king's food. Really good food. But, Daniel refused the king's food because it was offered to idols before it came to him. He felt he would be dishonoring God by eating it. So he asked that he and his friends be given only vegetables and water for ten days. The guard was scared that if they weren't healthy at the end of the test, the king would kill him! Daniel and his friends might be killed too! God honored Daniel's desire to honor Him and they were healthier than all the other boys.

God, in His grace, protected Daniel and his friends for honoring Him. He protects you for honoring Him too. He may not remove you from danger but will comfort you in it. In any case, you can be assured that He will honor you for your devotion to Him.

Honoring God may sometimes make
you unpopular with others. How does Daniel's
story encourage you to make that choice?

God's Constant Love

> I am convinced that nothing can ever separate us from God's love. Neither death nor life, neither angels nor demons, neither our fears for today nor our worries about tomorrow – not even the powers of hell can separate us from God's love.
>
> ROMANS 8:38

You chose to accept Jesus as your Savior. You made that decision from your freedom to choose. God did not force you to choose it. When you made that choice you were adopted into God's family. You are His child and have all the benefits of being a member of His family.

Of course, your adoption didn't stop Satan from trying to reclaim your heart. In fact, it probably kicked up his efforts to pull you away from believing in God's grace and love. He will continue to try harder than ever to make you doubt God's goodness and care. But, even if you start to doubt or question His love, God doesn't change. You have the assurance of His love. Nothing can defeat it. No power is strong enough. No devil is smart enough. No fear is big enough. God's love always wins.

Hang on to that truth when you feel discouraged. Hold on tight when you're afraid. Don't let go when problems come; when your health fails; when your heart hurts. None of those things mean God's love has left you. God's love is steady, constant and strong. Always. No matter what.

Have you questioned or doubted God's love? Have there been times when it felt as though He left you? How did you handle that? How does the assurance that His love is constant and steady make you feel?

Giving What
You've Been Given

God will provide and increase your resources
and then produce a great harvest of generosity in you.
2 CORINTHIANS 9:10

You've been blessed by God's generosity. He has held nothing back from you; beginning with His gift of allowing His Son to be tortured and murdered as payment for your sin. Seriously, if He never gave you another thing, wouldn't that have been enough? But He didn't stop there. Whatever else is in your life is because of His generosity. What do you value the most? Family? From God. Friends? From God. Church? From God. Home, career, health, safety, ministry, talents? From God. All of them. His generosity is His grace and love in action.

What should your reaction to God's generosity be? Gratitude, for sure. Heartfelt, humble I-don't-deserve-any-of-this gratitude that comes from a woman on her knees, taken down by the magnitude of His generosity.

A second reaction must be a pay-it-forward generosity to others. God has put people together in this life. We must pay attention to one another and help those in need. There are people in your neighborhood, town, state, country and world who are truly suffering because they don't have enough to survive. If you do, then help them. Share your money. Share your time. Share your heart.

How do you share your blessings with others? Do you give financially? Do you give your time? To what organizations or ministries? Are there individuals you help? Could you do more?

Receiving Grace

Salvation is not a reward for the good things we
have done, so none of us can boast about it.
EPHESIANS 2:9

Some people thrive on, "Hey World, look at me! Notice what I've accomplished. See how great I am! Pat me on the back! Sing my praises!" To them life is all about them! They give no one else credit for their accomplishments. They even feel that they actually deserve all they have because of how hard they've worked and how important they are. They may even proudly proclaim, "Hey, God, You sure are lucky to have me on Your team!"

Arrogance does not honor God. Since you care about honoring and obeying God, your attitude should be one of humility beginning with your salvation. You get no credit for that. Grace was extended to you. It's not something you can go get. It's not something you can develop. It's not something you can work on. All you can do is receive God's grace. That means you can take absolutely no credit for your salvation or the means by which you received it.

God, in His grace, saved you when you believed in Him. He didn't have to. He wanted to. He didn't do it for Himself. He did it because He loves you. Salvation is an undeserved gift from the heart of God.

Time for an honest evaluation of your own heart … are you truly grateful for salvation? Has a little arrogance slipped into your attitude that tempts you to feel you deserve all God gives you? What are you going to do about it?

Celebration!

*David danced before the LORD with all his might,
wearing a priestly garment.*
2 SAMUEL 6:14

David's praise for God exploded out from his heart. His joy and gratitude made him dance for all he was worth. David had been through some highs and lows in his life, as most people have. Times when he served God courageously. Times when he failed God miserably. In this verse, David has just seen the Ark of the Covenant coming home. It was a sign of God's presence with His people and it had been captured. Now it was coming back where it belonged. David was so filled with joy and happiness that he boogied down the road in front of it – wearing his fancy priest clothes!

Has joy and gratitude ever "exploded" from you? Have you ever been so blessed by God that you wanted to dance down the street? Can you celebrate regardless of who is watching? Or are you shouting "Hallelujah" on the inside but quietly reserved on the outside? That's OK. God made everyone different. Some could never do a dance of praise and some can't help themselves.

However God made you … celebrate! Dance and sing or smile and pray. Just be sure you celebrate!

How do you celebrate? Are you a lift your hands, shout Hallelujah kind of person? Or are you a quiet "in your heart" praise giver? Whatever your style, how often do you just purely praise God?

Your Body

Don't you realize that your body is the temple of the
Holy Spirit, who lives in you and was given to you by God?
You do not belong to yourself, for God bought you with a
high price. So you must honor God with your body.

1 CORINTHIANS 6:19-20

What does the command to honor your body have to do with grace? Well, a couple of things actually: First, God, through the sacrifice of Jesus paid for your life of freedom in Him. Second, God in His grace gave you the Holy Spirit to live in your heart. The Spirit is a gift because He lives in you to teach you and guide you in your walk with Christ. So, your body is the Holy Spirit's home – God's Spirit lives in you!

What does it mean to honor God with your body? The easy answer is to not do drugs, not take dangerous chances … take care of your body. An answer to that question that may be more applicable to you, is to take care of your body by getting enough rest, eating healthy, maintaining a healthy weight, getting exercise. Take care of the one body God gave you.

But, another answer is to consider how you honor God by what you do with your body – how you use your body to serve Him and others.

Use your strength and energy to serve Him. Your body is the tool God gave you.

How do you take care of your body? How do you use it to serve God? Do you feel that you honor God by how you treat yourself?

Your Prayers Matter

Confess your sins to each other and pray for each other so that
you may be healed. The earnest prayer of a righteous person
has great power and produces wonderful results.
JAMES 5:16

You have been given an incredible gift – the privilege of being able to talk to the Creator of the universe, knowing that He listens to you! This is a gift of God's grace. It's evidence that He cares about you and wants to hear what you're feeling and what's important to you.

When someone needs prayer to help them stay strong in their faith or for health struggles they're having, you can pray and God hears you. Your prayers make a difference. This is one of the blessings of living in relationship with other believers. You can hold each other accountable. You can pray for each other. No one needs to feel alone because they know others are praying for them.

Don't just say, "I will pray for you." Do it. Pray passionately and earnestly. Pray believing that God hears you and will answer. Don't neglect the caveat that God hears the prayers of a righteous person, so keep living obediently to Him. Allow others the privilege of praying for you, too. Build relationships of trust with others so you can each share things that are on your heart and share in prayer, knowing that God hears and cares.

When have you had the privilege of praying for
another person? When has someone prayed for you?

Measure Up

Lead a life worthy of your calling, for you have
been called by God. Always be humble and gentle. Be patient
with each other, making allowance for each other's faults
because of your love. Make every effort to keep yourselves
united in the Spirit, binding yourselves together with peace.
EPHESIANS 4:1-3

You've been called by God to a life that is filled with His love and blessings, a life framed by His forgiveness of your sins.

He asks you to live that life in a way that respects others and their lives well with them while honoring God with your actions. Unless you're going to live in the wilderness, you have to live and interact with others. Make it a good experience by following God's guidelines for getting along with them … humility, patience, forgiveness, love and unity. This isn't just "acting" these ways but showing others that you value them and that you are willing to make every effort to honor them and live in peace. Show people you love them instead of judging them. If people aren't exactly like you, love them anyway. If someone hurts you, forgive her. If someone is different from you, love her anyway. Pray for her. Be gentle and forgiving. Stay united by your love for God so that people who don't know Him can see Him in the way you treat others. Make every effort to be the person God knows you can be … that He called you to be.

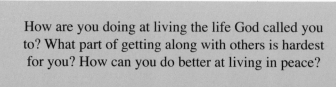

How are you doing at living the life God called you to? What part of getting along with others is hardest for you? How can you do better at living in peace?

God's Plans

"I know the plans I have for you," says the LORD.
"They are plans for good and not for disaster,
to give you a future and a hope."
JEREMIAH 29:11

When you were young did you have a plan for how your life would turn out? Did you plan for marriage, children, career, a home with white picket fences or a career that would take you around the world?

Did your life turn out the way you planned or did things take a left turn somewhere and you've ended up nowhere close to what you expected?

If you've submitted your life to God's will then it's quite possible that your plans were changed somewhere along the way. His plans for your life will, in the end, turn out a whole lot better than your plans would have.

When you gave your heart to Jesus, your new life came with the benefit of God's vision for your future … and it's a good one designed by His grace. He will direct your life by closing some opportunities and making others available. He will bring people into your life who challenge you to try new things. When you need courage to try something new, He will give it.

God's plans for your life will only be good and will lead to a future of serving Him and others.

Has God guided you to change directions
in your life? How has He guided you?
How can you see that God's plan is good?

The Benefit of Trust

I pray that God, the source of hope, will fill you completely with joy and peace because you trust in Him. Then you will overflow with confident hope through the power of the Holy Spirit.

ROMANS 15:13

"Fill you completely." What a beautiful prayer this is. When you give your heart and life to God completely holding nothing back, holding no control for yourself, He turns right around and fills you completely with joy and peace. What an act of grace!

Joy isn't the same as happiness. Happiness comes and goes based on what's happening around you. It's situational. It brings high highs and its absence brings low lows. But joy comes from deep inside your heart. You know that God has your back. He knows what's going on with you. Nothing surprises Him so your joy is in Him and because of Him. You trust Him.

Trust brings peace. You don't have to worry about what's happening or what might happen because you trust God's power and His Holy Spirit in your heart holds you steady. Peace doesn't mean you sail through life in a zombie-like trance. But when fear rises in your heart, you stop and say, "I know You have this God. I choose to trust You with my life and all those I love because Your power is greater than anything."

Trust God and He will fill you completely with joy and peace because of His magnificent power.

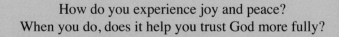

How do you experience joy and peace?
When you do, does it help you trust God more fully?

Life-Giving Water

Jesus replied, "Anyone who drinks this water
will soon become thirsty again. But those who drink the water
I give will never be thirsty again. It becomes a fresh,
bubbling spring within them, giving them eternal life."
JOHN 4:13-14

The image of a bubbling spring is pretty cool in a few different ways. A human being can't live without water. Our bodies are made up of 50% or more of water. When we drink water it gets absorbed into our body's organs and … we get thirsty again. So we must drink more.

Jesus compared the life He gives with water indicating that when you fill your life with anything other than Him, your satisfaction will not last. You'll thirst for something else … for more.

The life-giving water that Jesus gives is like a bubbling spring in your heart. That is an image of action … of life. The motion shows that the water Jesus gives is always moving, growing, changing. It is life. What He gives brings lasting satisfaction. When you accept Jesus you won't thirst for anything else.

This life-giving, life-forming, always changing, always satisfying water of life is a gift from God's heart of grace. It makes you feel alive. His Spirit in your heart moves and guides so your life is never stagnant. He keeps you moving and growing. It is life.

How do you feel Jesus' life-giving water bubbling in
your soul? How does He move and change your life?

The Important Commands

"You must love the Lord your God with all your heart, all your soul, and all your mind. This is the first and greatest commandment. A second is equally important: Love your neighbor as yourself."
MATTHEW 22:37-39

Jesus boiled down the process of obeying to pretty much as simple as you could ask for. Love God – completely, holding nothing back. Love Him from the submission of your heart, the depths of your soul and with every thought that skitters across your mind. Love Him. Make Him the ruler of your life and the guide for everything you feel, think, say and do.

Simple. Except it isn't always because so much fights against it. The world shouts, "This is better. There's more freedom here. You can handle life without God." But, it's ONLY by God's grace you were saved. A grace so sacrificial that He didn't even hold back His only Son from you. A grace you didn't deserve. The only thing you can give in return is your complete love.

Jesus said the second command – which is just as important as the first one is to love your neighbor as much as you love yourself. So … sacrificially, unselfishly? You take care of yourself and make sure you have all you need. You give yourself the benefit of the doubt when you mess up.

All the other commands are based on these two so … pay attention!

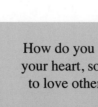

How do you struggle with loving God with all your heart, soul and mind? Why is it a struggle to love others as much as you love yourself?

Guilt-Free

Since we have a great High Priest who rules over God's
house, let us go right into the presence of God with sincere
hearts fully trusting Him. For our guilty consciences have
been sprinkled with Christ's blood to make us clean,
and our bodies have been washed with pure water.
HEBREWS 10:21-22

In biblical times, the high priest's job was to make a sacrifice to God to atone for sins of the people he oversaw. Only the high priest was allowed in the most holy part of the temple. He was a go-between for man to God.

Jesus is your High Priest. By His sacrificial death He became your bridge to God. Jesus changed everything. Because He intercedes for you, you can go directly into God's presence. You can talk to God. You can read His Word. You can know Him personally and you can trust His guidance and protection in your life.

Because of God's grace in providing your High Priest, you come before God cleansed. Your sins are washed away. Completely.

Stop for a moment and just think about that. Every act of selfishness. Every disobedience. Every anger or unkindness. Every time you deny God's power or love. EVERYTHING is wiped away by Jesus' sacrifice and God sees you as completely clean. Because of this gift of grace, you can be guilt-free. God forgives you so you can forgive your failures, too. Every day is new with Him – a new chance to love and obey.

Do you get lost in guilt at your own sin? How does
realizing that God sees you as completely sin free make
you feel? Does it help you forgive yourself?

Ask God Anything!

"What do you mean, 'If I can'?" Jesus asked.
"Anything is possible if a person believes." The father instantly
cried out, "I do believe, but help me overcome my unbelief!"
MARK 9:23-24

A heartbroken dad brought his son to have a demon cast out of the boy. Jesus' disciples had tried to release the boy but they couldn't do it. The father approached Jesus and said, "Help us, if You can." He obviously believed a little that Jesus could help, but he didn't believe completely, either because of the disciples' failure or just because he was afraid to believe completely.

Jesus' response is beautiful, "What do you mean IF I can?" He expected people to believe in Him and His power. He knew who He was and the power that He had from His Father.

The awesome part of this story is what the worried dad said next, "I do believe but help me overcome my unbelief." Do you see – you can ask God for anything. You don't have to get hung up on what you "should" be. You don't have to say words you think you're supposed to say or pretend faith that you don't really have (yet). God, in His grace-filled love will help you with what you need. If you need help believing, ask Him. If you're afraid to fully believe, ask His help. He will help you. That's what love does.

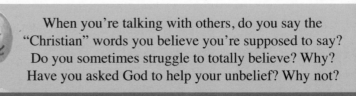

When you're talking with others, do you say the
"Christian" words you believe you're supposed to say?
Do you sometimes struggle to totally believe? Why?
Have you asked God to help your unbelief? Why not?

Choose Wisely

Do not love this world nor the things it offers you, for when
you love the world, you do not have the love of the Father in you.
For the world offers only a craving for physical pleasure,
a craving for everything we see, and pride in our achievements and
possessions. These are not from the Father, but are from this world.
And this world is fading away, along with everything that people
crave. But anyone who does what pleases God will live forever.

1 JOHN 2:15-17

There are many areas of life where you can split your devotion. You can support more than one ministry. You can split your vote between parties. You can be a fan of more than one genre of book, movie or music. However when it comes to God, there is no splitting God who is a jealous God (His Words in Exodus 20:5) and He will not share your devotion with anything or anyone else. He wants all of your heart.

It's hard because some of the things that the world offers are pretty attractive and are symbols of success that win you the praise of others. God warns you that you can't keep craving what the world wants and also enjoy the pleasures that a life devoted to Him gives, too. The things the world offers will fade because none if it goes into eternity with you. Make a choice. A wise choice. Don't try to hold on to both things. Give God your whole heart and receive the blessings He gives.

Be honest with yourself and God right now – are you trying to hold on to some things the world offers and still serve God? How's that going for you? What would happen if you let go of your affection for the world's things?

May

The Importance
of Thanks

Give thanks to the LORD, for He is good!
His faithful love endures forever.
PSALM 106:1

God knows that He's good. He knows that He gives you everything. He knows that without Him you are nothing, so why do you need to thank Him?

More than likely you spend quite a bit of prayer time asking Him for things. Thanking Him is just as important.

Thanking God for all He gives you is good for you to do because it causes you to stop and realize that all you have is from His hand. Your protection is from His heart. Your blessings are from His grace. His love is forever. There is nothing you can do that will make Him stop caring about you. He will never turn away from you.

A bond is built between you and God when you recognize how much He gives and you take the time to thank Him. You are nothing without Him. You have nothing without Him. Realizing that makes your gratitude deep and real and your dependence on Him more complete.

Thank Him for your salvation. Thank Him for His blessings. Thank Him for His forgiveness. Thank Him for His goodness. Thank Him for His love that goes on throughout eternity. He loves you now and will love you forever.

If you made a chart of your prayer time, how much time do you suppose would be spent on requests? How much time on thanks? For what are you most thankful for today?

Pruning Is Necessary

"I am the true grapevine, and My Father is the gardener. He cuts off every branch of Mine that doesn't produce fruit, and He prunes the branches that do bear fruit so they will produce even more."
JOHN 15:1-2

Pruning sounds scary, doesn't it? There's a reason for that … it is. When a gardener prunes a tree or bush, he cuts off unhealthy branches or branches that are crowding out new growth. It's necessary for the long-term health of the tree or bush.God has your future in mind. He sees how things in your life are either helping or hurting you move toward the goal of becoming more like Christ. Anything that isn't moving you in that direction needs to be cut out of your life – things, activities and even people. It doesn't mean that any of those things are bad. They just aren't useful in moving you to where God has planned. They have been good for a season, but you have grown past that season so changes must be made.

Do you trust God to move you forward? Are you willing to endure the pain of pruning in your life? Hold on tightly to Him. Trust His heart. Know that letting go of good things means there are different and better things ahead.

Remember that God only prunes the lives of those who are trusting Him and living for Him. He has good things ahead for you!

If you've been living for God very long, you've probably experienced pruning in your life. What has God cut from your life? What did He replace it with? Can you see how the pruning is benefitting your faith?

Brown Sugar Blessings

"Give, and you will receive. Your gift will return
to you in full – pressed down, shaken together to make
room for more, running over, and poured into your lap.
The amount you give will determine the amount you get back."
LUKE 6:38

The process of measuring out the amount of brown sugar you need for a recipe means pressing the sugar down into the measuring cup and adding more until the packed solid cup is full.

God's blessings are like that. He gives and gives. Just when you think maybe He's given all He's going to give, He packs more in. God is never finished giving to His children.

God encourages you to mimic His generosity as you give to others. Give generously of your time and energy. Care about people around you. Share in their pain and grief by understanding and comforting. Don't pull back from people who are hurting.

Share in others' joy and success, too. Celebrate and cheer with not a bit of jealousy. It's encouraging for your friends to have you celebrate with them.

Blessings will return to you, pressed down and shaken together – more than you could imagine. The friendship and support that you give will come back to you in the community you create. God will bless you with even more support and encouragement in your own life! He gives and gives in a multitude of creative ways!

How comfortable are you in sharing others' pain?
How do you comfort and help others? How well do you
celebrate with others? How do those blessings come back to you?

Grace-filled Unity

Is there any encouragement from belonging to Christ?
Any comfort from His love? Any fellowship together in the Spirit?
Are your hearts tender and compassionate? Then make me truly
happy by agreeing wholeheartedly with each other,
loving one another, and working together with one mind and purpose.

PHILIPPIANS 2:1-2

If people can't see kindness and unity among God's children, why would they be curious about His love? The characteristics of God's children are to show love for others, concern for others, understanding and kindness. Is it always going to be easy to get along with others? Probably not. But, think about it – every critical word you speak about a fellow believer, every public disagreement, is a negative advertisement about belonging to God's family. Is it *always* possible to agree wholeheartedly with your Christian brothers and sisters? No, but it is possible to keep your issues private and to handle them with respect and kindness.

You have the grace-filled benefit of God's Spirit encouraging you as you control your reactions and responses to others. He will help your heart to be tender and compassionate. He will strengthen you to react to situations with kindness. Keep your focus on serving God, loving others and the all-important purpose of honoring Him by the unity and love you show to others. Remember your purpose of drawing others into God's Kingdom. Don't let your behavior make this an unattractive option for them. Ask God to help you be kind and respectful as you represent Him.

Is there a particular person or situation you have difficulty with? Why is it so hard? Are you showing kindness and respect? Are you making Christianity appealing to others? How can you do that better?

Sin No More

They kept demanding an answer, so He stood up again and said,
"All right, but let the one who has never sinned throw the first stone!"
JOHN 8:7

Religious leaders brought Jesus a woman who was caught in adultery. They were trying to trick Him by asking if she should be stoned as Moses' law said. The woman must have been terrified. She was surrounded by her accusers. She knew what they wanted to do. As much as they wanted to punish her they wanted to use her case to have something to hold against Jesus. Would He join with them and say, "Yes, she must be stoned to death?" Would He free her and by doing that build His enemies case against Him?

The religious leaders couldn't have anticipated Jesus' response, "OK. Stone her and the one of you who has never sinned can start the process." That must have shocked them. One by one they quietly slipped away. Then Jesus told the woman, "Go and sin no more."

Grace. Jesus showed the guilty woman grace. Yes, she had sinned. She deserved punishment. What she got was forgiveness and a second chance to "sin no more." That's what God's grace does. He forgives and gives you another chance to obey. You're not convicted by the words of anyone else. His grace forgives and moves you forward.

How does this story make you feel? Have you been the victim
of someone trying to convict you? Have you participated
in the attempt to accuse someone else? How have you
experienced God's forgiveness and a second chance?

Moving Forward
in the Unknown

The LORD had said to Abram, "Leave your native country,
your relatives, and your father's family, and go to the land that
I will show you. I will make you into a great nation. I will bless
you and make you famous, and you will be a blessing to others."
GENESIS 12:1-2

Sometimes faith means stepping out in darkness. It means obeying what God says, going where He leads but without knowing the details of what's ahead. Abram did that. God said to go and leave behind everything familiar. He told him to pack up and leave, without telling him where he was going. Abram's obedience goes against all common sense, doesn't it? Would you set out on a move without knowing where you're going, where you'll live or how you'll support yourself?

Faith trusts God with everything about your life. When God says, "Go!" faith goes. Faith trusts that He has a plan for your life. It trusts that His grace will take you to something that's good and useful in serving Him and building His Kingdom.

No doubt, some of Abram's family questioned his decision. But he didn't let them cause his obedience to waver. Abram's faith in God was so complete that he obeyed, even when he didn't know what was next. He knew God's plan was best.

When was a time God told you do something
without giving you details of what was ahead? Did
you obey or wait? How did the situation turn out?

Grace-Honored Faith

When the woman realized that she could not stay hidden,
she began to tremble and fell to her knees in front of Him.
The whole crowd heard her explain why she had touched
Him and that she had been immediately healed. "Daughter,"
He said to her, "your faith has made you well. Go in peace."
LUKE 8:47-48

Crowds followed Jesus everywhere. It would be impossible to know every person who actually touched Him. Glance into the crowd. Notice one woman, trying not to attract attention as she pushed through the crowd to get close to Jesus. She had been sick twelve years, been to every doctor, spent all her money. No one could help her. She was down to her last hope but she knew it was her greatest hope. This sick woman's faith was so strong that she believed if she could just touch the hem of Jesus' robe she would be healed. She didn't need His word. She didn't need His attention.

The woman, perhaps in a last ditch effort as He moved forward, stretched through the crowd and touched Jesus' robe. Instantly she knew she was healed. Did you get that ... instantly!

Jesus knew power had gone out of Him. He asked who touched Him. Maybe the woman wanted to hide rather than call attention to herself. But she stepped forward and admitted what she had done.

Jesus' response was grace-filled love. "Your faith has made you well. Go in peace."

When have you taken a faith-filled risk? Are you
willing to take a risk that shows your trust in God?

Never Too Busy

But the other criminal protested, "Don't you fear God even when you have been sentenced to die? We deserve to die for our crimes, but this man hasn't done anything wrong." Then he said, "Jesus, remember me when You come into Your Kingdom." And Jesus replied, "I assure you, today you will be with Me in paradise."

LUKE 23:40-43

When Jesus was crucified, two criminals hanged on crosses on either side of Him. If anyone could be considered hopeless as far as Jesus' forgiveness is concerned, it could be the thieves who would soon be dead. The comments that one criminal launched at Jesus were cynical and critical. But the criminal on the other side of Him understood that Jesus had done nothing to deserve the punishment He was experiencing. He asked Jesus to remember Him when He got to heaven. It would be understandable to think that Jesus was a bit preoccupied in that moment. He had been tortured and now was dying a very painful death. But nothing stops God's grace. Jesus recognized the man's faith in Him and He promised him salvation.

Does God have time to pay attention to you? World situations are overwhelming. Crises are constant. He is bombarded with needs and requests. But God's love is bigger than any of that. His grace runs deeper. He cares about anything you care about. Tell Him what you're going through and how you long for His help. God is never too busy for you. You're His child.

The thief who asked Jesus to remember him was at death's doorstep. Jesus forgave Him anyway. What do you need to talk with God about today? Did you know God cares about you?

Grace Gets
Its Hands Dirty

Large crowds followed Jesus as He came down the mountainside. Suddenly, a man with leprosy approached Him and knelt before Him. "Lord," the man said, "if You are willing, You can heal me and make me clean." Jesus reached out and touched him. "I am willing," He said. "Be healed!" And instantly the leprosy disappeared.

MATTHEW 8:1-3

Leprosy is no fun. In Jesus' day there was no cure for this highly contagious disease. Touching the skin of someone who had it meant it was likely you would get it, too. Lepers were forced to live away from their families with others who suffered the disease. They couldn't be part of the mainstream of life.

So when a leper stepped close to Jesus and asked for healing the disciples must have collectively gasped. Did they hope Jesus would step away from the man? They knew He could speak a word and heal the leper if He wanted. That's all He had to do. They had seen Him do it before. But Jesus didn't do that. He touched the man. His touch could have made Him sick with the dreaded disease. Think about it – that man hadn't been touched since he got sick. He got no hugs from his wife. No snuggles from his children. No pat on the back from a buddy. No one wanted to touch him. Until Jesus.

Grace is willing to get its hands dirty to show love and care. It shows a person he matters ... that he is seen and heard.

How has God's grace touched you? Has He reached out in ways that others wouldn't? How have you "touched" those who are sick, lonely or scared in a way that shows God's grace and love?

Gentle Bandages

He heals the brokenhearted
and bandages their wounds.
PSALM 147:3

Remember when you were a child and you got hurt? Nothing felt better than the comfort you got from a much-loved adult. Whether it was your mom, dad or a grandparent ... when that special loved one pulled you close and told you everything was going to be OK, you believed. Your wound was gently cleaned and covered with a bandage. Once the wound was safely covered your comforter might have gently kissed it. You felt better and bounded back outside to play.

It's not so simple as an adult, is it? Some wounds can't be seen because they're deep in your heart. No one knows about them except you ... and God. There are no bandages or sweet kisses to make you feel better ... except from your heavenly Father. He loves you and He will comfort you. He will remind you that He's still with you and that one day things will be good again.

Maybe He doesn't take away the thing that's causing your pain but He holds you close. You're never alone. He bandages your wound with His presence and His grace that gently, lovingly says, "I know. I'm here."

God's comfort is so gentle and sweet.
How have you experienced His comfort when no
one around you even knew about your wound?

Thankful Prayer

Devote yourselves to prayer with an alert mind and a thankful heart.
COLOSSIANS 4:2

Why does this verse tell you to pray with a thankful heart? Are you supposed to be thankful for the situation that you're praying about, even if it's painful and frightening? Yes. Thankfulness is not meant to be situational. Should you be thankful for the good things God allows in your life but not the painful things? There are precious things to be learned through difficult times. Keep your mind alert to what you can learn. If the focus of your heart stays dependent on God, trusting Him regardless of what comes, then your faith in Him grows. That's something to be thankful for.

Your prayers should also be prefaced with the faith of thankfulness for the answer that is already on the way; even before your prayer is uttered. Thanking God for His response of care is important. It completes the circle of prayer: Need-prayer-response-thanks-need … because the needs go on and on.

God, in His grace responds to your prayers. Don't forget to thank Him. But also thank Him for the lessons learned in difficult times and give Him thanks, even before you see the answer. That's faith in action.

Do you remember to thank God for His answers to
your prayers or do you go right on to the next request?
What are some things you can thank Him for right now?

Iron-Strong Strength

I can do everything through Christ, who gives me strength.
PHILIPPIANS 4:13

How persistent are you when you're trying to accomplish something? For example when you start an exercise program are you persistent in pursuing it? Or do you work energetically for a few weeks then slowly fade away? When you're learning a new skill, such as, say playing piano, do you get discouraged when it doesn't go well right away? What about your efforts to live in obedience to God? Whether you're focusing on obeying the commands in His Word or the practical applications such as loving others who are not too loveable?

It's hard to stick with something that's hard. You get tired and weary. Here's the thing – you don't have to do it alone. You have the all-powerful strength of Christ available to help you. When you're obeying Him and living for Him, He will help you be successful. Ask Him. Tell Him what you're ready to give up on.

Tell Him when your strength is running out. Tell Him when something is harder than you imagined. Maybe He's just waiting for you to recognize that you need His help. Ask Him for the ironclad strength of Jesus. He wants to help you.

What do you need strength for today?
What are you about to give up on? Tell
God what you need. Ask for His help.

A Grateful Heart

The LORD is my strength and my song;
He has given me victory. This is my God, and I will
praise Him – my father's God, and I will exalt Him!
EXODUS 15:2

Thank God with a grateful heart. Thank Him for the strength He gives when you don't know how you're going to stand firm. Thank Him for the energy He gives when you're so tired you can't think. Thank Him for the perseverance He gives when you want to quit. Thank Him for the song in your heart on dark, dreary days. Thank Him for placing a song in a heart too grieved to recall one. Thank Him for songs of celebration and joy. Thank Him that others join in your song.

Praise God for victories over temptation. Praise God for answered prayer. Praise God for love and forgiveness. Praise Him for loved ones that make life sweeter. Praise Him for abundant blessings. Praise Him for peaceful rest. Praise Him for laughter. Praise Him for tears. Praise Him for health. Praise Him for illness. Praise Him for healing. Praise Him for loss. Praise Him for guidance. Praise Him in all things.

There's so much to thank God for every day. There's so much to praise Him for. Let your heart fill with gratitude and not regret. Filter your requests to Him through a heart that gratefully recognizes all He does for you.

Make your own Thanks and Praise List. What goes on it?

The Joy of Heaven

I heard a loud shout from the throne, saying, "Look,
God's home is now among His people! He will live with them,
and they will be His people. God Himself will be with them. He will
wipe every tear from their eyes, and there will be no more death
or sorrow or crying or pain. All these things are gone forever."
REVELATION 21:3-4

God's grace is evident in your life every day in the blessings He pours out on you. When you stop and think about it, you know there is no doubt that He loves you deeply. But, God's grace is not just about today. It is about forever.

When Jesus was on earth, teaching and training, He told His followers that He was going to go prepare a place for them. They couldn't go with Him right then, but one day they would join Him. He was preparing a place so magnificent they couldn't even comprehend it.

In the Revelation God gave John, He mentions that place again. In fact, He showed John a piece of His heaven. It's where God's children will live with Him for eternity. After the times of chaos, grief and pain on this earth, He showed John that in His heaven there will be no tears and no death. There will be no pain or sorrow at all. Heaven will be filled with wonderful joy and praise to God as His children live in His presence forever. What a wonderful experience that will be. No grief. Only joy, because of God's grace.

It's hard to comprehend the joy of heaven. What are you most looking forward to? Do all your loved ones know Jesus? Do you have any loved ones who don't have the assurance of heaven yet? Have you told them?

Who Are You Following?

"The one who enters through the gate is the
shepherd of the sheep. The gatekeeper opens the gate for him,
and the sheep recognize his voice and come to him.
He calls his own sheep by name and leads them out."
JOHN 10:2-3

Whose voice are you listening to? Jesus proclaimed Himself to be the Good Shepherd to His sheep. That's you. He said you would recognize His voice and when you heard Him speak you would come to Him and follow Him.

There are so many voices in the world shouting at you, trying to pull you away from God. Voices that insist their ways are best. Voices that cry out what their definition of success is. God's voice is in there but He may not shout. His may be the quiet voice that you can only hear when you sit in stillness before Him. Do you hear it?

How do you know that the voice you're following is the voice of the Good Shepherd? There's only one way – you have to spend time in His Word so that you can tell if the voice you hear is speaking God's truth. You must know your Shepherd in order to recognize His voice. If you don't invest in knowing Him, you may end up following a voice that leads you to disaster.

Listen for the voice of the One who truly loves you. Be sure it's Him you're following.

Honesty time – how much time do you spend
studying God's Word? How often do you sit quietly
waiting to hear His voice? Do you know His voice?

Methods and Motives

You want what you don't have, so you scheme and kill to get it.
You are jealous of what others have, but you can't get it,
so you fight and wage war to take it away from them. Yet you
don't have what you want because you don't ask God for it.
And even when you ask, you don't get it because your motives
are all wrong – you want only what will give you pleasure.

JAMES 4:2-3

Remember that Jesus said the second greatest commandment is to love others like you love yourself? Living that way pushes jealousy out of the realm of possibility. However, if you're not doing so well at loving others, jealousy easily creeps into your way of life. You want what someone else has – her house, her job, her status, her clothes. If you get really serious about it you might want her husband too. Gulp. Scheming, lying and cheating become a way of life just to get what you want. No element of that way of life speaks of love.

God says that better than jealous scheming is to ask Him for what you want. He loves giving you gifts. But, the condition is that you ask with the right motive. What would that be? It would not be to be better than someone else. Your motive should always be to have what would make you a better servant of Jesus. Of course it's OK to want "things" and to enjoy them. But not to want them more than you want to be an effective servant of the Lord or a good friend to those around you. Check your methods. Check your motives.

Is jealousy a struggle for you? What do
you most often yearn for? Why do you
want it? How are you dealing with this?

Being Near to God

Come close to God, and God will come close to you.
Wash your hands, you sinners; purify your hearts,
for your loyalty is divided between God and the world.
JAMES 4:8

When you see a celebrity out in public – someone really famous and popular, you'll probably notice quite a protection detail around the star. The guards' job is to keep people at arm's length from the famous person, make sure he isn't bothered by any nuisance fans, keep him safe and make sure he only has to talk to people he wants to speak with. You don't stand much chance of getting close to the star, regardless of how hard you try.

God isn't like that. He doesn't have a protection detail around Him. In fact, He hopes that you DO try to get close to Him. He promises that He will meet your efforts and come close to you.

Before you try to come near to God though you must prepare yourself. Just like you shower and put on clean clothes before going to a fancy event, clean yourself up to meet God.

Confess your sin and clean your heart by checking your motives. Make sure that your heart's desire is truly to meet the Almighty God and to know Him and serve Him. It is only by God's grace that you can come into His presence. Don't take this privilege lightly.

When you want to come close to God,
do you first spend time confessing your sin and checking
your motives? When was a time you felt very close to God?

The Generosity of Grace

At dawn Jesus was standing on the beach, but the
disciples couldn't see who He was. He called out,
"Fellows, have you caught any fish?" "No," they replied.
Then He said, "Throw out your net on the right-hand side of
the boat, and you'll get some!" So they did, and they couldn't
haul in the net because there were so many fish in it.
JOHN 21:4-6

The disciples had fished all night but didn't catch a thing. When they came to shore in the morning they were probably tired and discouraged. They saw a Man on the shore who told them to stop and toss their net out on the right side. They didn't know He was Jesus but they did what He told them to do. The net filled with so many fish they couldn't pull it in.

The grace of Jesus provided the needs of these tired fishermen without them even knowing it was Him. That miracle opened their eyes to the fact that it was Him!

Jesus provides your needs every day. Do you recognize His blessings? What does it take for your eyes to be opened to Him? Jesus wants you to have what you need. He wants you to know that He will take care of your needs – even before you know you have them.

Give Jesus credit for generously supplying your needs. It's a gift of His grace.

How does Jesus supply your needs?
Has His generosity ever surprised you? When?

Everything You Need

I am counting on the LORD; yes, I am counting on
Him. I have put my hope in His word.
PSALM 130:5

When life gets messy don't you want someone close by who you can count on? You want someone who will stick close so you're never alone. It's great if your friend is really wise and gives great advice. It's even better if your friend is super strong and can protect you.

You have that kind of friend in Jesus. He is always with you. He is wise and strong and He gives the best advice. God's wonderful grace has provided a source for you to gain His wisdom – the Bible.

Everything you need to know about obeying God and living for Him is written in God's Word. By reading it you will learn how to treat other people with the love that God wants you to show them.

So yes, God has given you all you need – a friend, protector and advisor. He has given you the guidebook for living for Him from which you can learn everything you need to know.

God's grace takes care of you in every way you need. That's what love does.

Is your confident hope in God's Word? What does that mean to you?
How does having God's Word at your fingertips make your life better?

It's All Good

We know that God causes everything to
work together for the good of those who love God
and are called according to His purpose for them.
ROMANS 8:28

Some things that happen in life are pretty hard. It's hard to believe that any of those hard things come from God. After all, He loves you, wouldn't He bring only good things into your life? Yes … but not in the way you think.

You see, this verse says that He makes everything that happens in your life work together for good. That means the wonderful things as well as the painful things. They're all pieces that when fit together to mold you into a more mature Christian.

Here's the thing – you have accepted Jesus as your Savior and you love God and want to serve Him. That's a prerequisite to the good life – love Him and be called for God's purpose.

So, you're God's child and He wants the very best for you. He has chosen you to do specific work for Him on earth. He will equip you to do that work and part of that equipping means going through hard times because those times will teach you things you need to know to do that work.

Have you seen difficult things and good things
work together to teach you good lessons for your
life? How? Does it make you trust God more?

Pay Attention to Others

We know what real love is because Jesus gave up His
life for us. So we also ought to give up our lives for our
brothers and sisters. If someone has enough money to
live well and sees a brother or sister in need but shows no
compassion – how can God's love be in that person?

1 JOHN 3:16-17

The homeless population in our world has grown quite large in recent years. When you walk down a street in any major city you see people living on the streets. Visit a shelter and you'll see mothers and children who have no home and no assurance of where their next meal will come from. Go beyond what you see in major cities and notice what's happening in poverty stricken nations around the world where drought has destroyed any food and water that used to be there. There are people everywhere who are hungry and thirsty. They want a clean bed to sleep in or a chair to sit in. These aren't luxuries. But they have no way to get these things. No way to pull themselves out of their poverty.

What does that have to do with you? Do you have compassion for people who are suffering? If you have more than enough to live on, do you share with those who don't have what they need? Do their needs touch your heart enough to help them? If it doesn't, there's little evidence of God's love in you. He blessed you and asks you to share His grace and love by helping others.

How do you share your blessings with
those who have needs? Could you do more?

Surrounded

You go before me and follow me. You place Your
hand of blessing on my head. Such knowledge is too
wonderful for me, too great for me to understand!

PSALM 139:5-6

You've seen the security that travels with government leaders. These
no-nonsense guards literally surround the leader on all sides, watching the crowd, guarding and protecting. That's their jobs. The safety
of that leader is their responsibility and they take it very seriously. He
or she can walk confidently, waving to the crowd because they know
they are being protected.

How cool would that be? If you were surrounded by security guards,
you could walk through life with no worries, waving at the crowd, going
to work, having coffee with friends, shopping, resting … whatever you
wanted to do because you'd know someone was watching out for you.
Someone is. Someone awesome! You are surrounded by God. He is
in front of you, beside you and behind you. His Spirit sees everything
around you – good and dangerous. He protects you in ways that you
don't even know: directing your steps, guiding your plans, calming
your heart.

It's hard to wrap your mind around His constant presence and protection but it's true. His grace shown in guidance, protection, love,
care and compassion is with you always!

How does the reminder that God's presence
is surrounding you change your view of
what's happening in your life? Does it make
you more willing to try new things?

Sin Surgery

When you came to Christ, you were "circumcised,"
but not by a physical procedure. Christ performed a spiritual
circumcision – the cutting away of your sinful nature.
COLOSSIANS 2:11

Look, the sin that kept you away from God is real. It was a barrier between you and Him because He cannot have sin in His presence. So, you were stuck. You were standing outside the family home and there was no way you could get in. No way. EXCEPT, Jesus opened the door for you. It wasn't easy; it took His death and resurrection but He did open the door. His work continued when you accepted Jesus as Savior because then Jesus did surgery on your heart. He cut out your sinful nature. So, shouldn't that be it – no more sin? If only.

You still struggle with sin, right? Yep, everyone does. You're still human and while that sin nature was cut out to make room for God … it isn't gone. God got rid of it but you bring it back in. You choose from day-to-day and decision-to-decision to allow sin to rule your heart or God to rule your heart.

God adopted you into the family when you accepted Jesus as Savior. It's your choice to behave like a member of the family but, you know that every time you fail, He will forgive you.

You have salvation because of God's grace. Sin could be
a thing of the past, but it isn't. Is there a particular sin you
struggle to keep out of your life? Why is it so hard?

Obedience Shows Love

"Those who accept My commandments and obey them are the ones who love Me. And because they love Me, My Father will love them. And I will love them and reveal Myself to each of them."
JOHN 14:21

Obeying God's commandments is not optional. It's hard but it's not optional. Jesus says that you can't claim to love God if you don't obey His commands. God, by His grace, had His commands written down in His Word so, you can't claim that you don't know what He wants. Read your Bible and you'll know. There are some commands that are easier to obey than others. For example, you'd never murder, right? But some are a challenge. It's hard to consistently keep them because doing those disobedient things comes so naturally.

With other things obeying God might make you unpopular with friends or family. Of course, you want to fit in with them and you might even argue that if you don't stay popular with them, then how can you tell them about God's love?

The thing about obeying God is that it won't always be easy. It won't make you popular. You can't justify your way out of it for any reason. God is God. His commands are His commands. You are to obey. That shows that your love for God is true.

He knows it isn't easy. He will give you strength and perseverance. Ask Him.

What commands do you struggle
to obey? Which acts of disobedience
seem to come so naturally to you?

Private Thoughts

"The words you speak come from the heart – that's what defiles you.
For from the heart come evil thoughts, murder, adultery,
all sexual immorality, theft, lying, and slander."
MATTHEW 15:18-19

Your thoughts are private, right? It's no big deal if you think things that a Christian shouldn't be thinking because who will know?

The problem is that your "private" thoughts are the things that are actually in your heart. They are the things you allow your heart to ponder. Those private heart thoughts reveal what you actually think about God, life, others and even yourself. Do you respect God, others and yourself? Do you want to obey God?

Oh, you can be careful to speak the Christian words that make you look good but if those words don't represent the ideas and opinions that are actually in your heart, then you're a liar. Do you think no one knows? You're wrong. God knows the things in your heart. He sees it all. You can say whatever you want but He's looking at your heart.

The hidden things in your heart will eventually come out in your words and actions. They won't stay hidden forever. Focus your heart on being honest before God. Confess the wickedness in your heart and thoughts. Ask God to fill your heart with thoughts that honor Him. He wants to help you. He will help you.

What are you not being honest about? Are you trying
to fool others and God? Are you trying to fool yourself?

Loving Those You Don't Love

"This is My commandment: Love each other in the same way I have loved you. There is no greater love than to lay down one's life for one's friends."
JOHN 15:12-13

"Aaaahhh … so and so makes me crazy!" Do you feel that way about someone? There are people who just rub you the wrong way, whether they mean to or not. There are others who seem to make it a hobby to be as annoying as they can. Then there are the people who just know how to push your buttons and they do it often. Does God really mean you have to love all these people?

He says to love others in the same way He loves you. How does God love you? Unconditionally. Completely. Sacrificially. That should be easy, right? No, some people can only be loved by God's Spirit loving through you. Thankfully He's willing to do that.

Making the effort to love someone you don't find loveable, is a sacrificial love. It means you're willing to overlook what annoys you. It's accepting that God loves someone through you – you're the conduit for His love to that person. That doesn't mean you have to be best friends. It means that God helps you see something positive in that person and shows you how you can coexist in love. Eventually, with His help, you may honestly love that person.

Is there someone you have difficulty loving? Have you experienced God loving someone through you? How did that change your opinion of that person?

Healthy Family

A peaceful heart leads to a healthy body;
jealousy is like cancer in the bones.
PROVERBS 14:30

Cancer eats away at the healthy cells of the body. It causes pain. It takes away strength and can, eventually, take life away.

Jealousy does all those terrible things too. It destroys healthy relationships, causes pain between friends and family, takes away the strength of community and eventually takes the life of the relationship.

Many times in Scripture God warns against jealousy because it only destroys. Being jealous of someone shouts dissatisfaction with what God has given you or how He has gifted you. Jealousy says, "God, what You've done for me is not good enough." Then the cancer of jealousy not only destroys your human relationship, it becomes a barrier between you and God.

Do you trust God? Do you believe He has your best interests in mind? Trusting that God's plan is best leads your heart to be at peace because you know His plan is best. Then you can enjoy your life and you can celebrate what's happening in others' lives. There's no room for jealousy because you're all on the same team working toward the growth of God's Kingdom. Unity in the family is preserved and relationships stay healthy.

Is your heart peaceful or filled with jealousy? God, in His grace has gifted you with certain things and has directed your life. What are you dissatisfied with? Have you talked with God about it?

Muscle Training

When your faith is tested, your endurance has a chance to grow. So let it grow, for when your endurance is fully developed, you will be perfect and complete, needing nothing.

JAMES 1:3-4

God knows what He's doing. He knows that difficult times make your faith stronger. Need proof? Think about a butterfly snuggled inside a chrysalis. He built his little home by himself, wrapping it around him. Then when his transformation to butterfly is complete he has to push his way out of the chrysalis. It's work. It takes a while to break the shell open and get free.

But, if you try to help the butterfly by peeling open the chrysalis and setting the butterfly free … it will, more than likely, die. The butterfly needs the struggle of breaking open the chrysalis in order to strengthen its beautiful wings and be strong enough to fly. Trying to assist so it can avoid the struggle doesn't help it, but actually hurts it.

That's how difficult times are for you, too. Each time you go through difficult things and see God help you and strengthen you, it grows your trust in Him. It strengthens your "trust muscle."

It's not easy on you and God knows that. But it's His grace that allows the struggles so that your faith can be strengthened and matured. It's a good thing.

What have you learned in the past when you've gone through a hard struggle? Has your faith grown stronger because of difficult times?

Lazy Obedience

Well then, since God's grace has set us free from the law,
does that mean we can go on sinning? Of course not!
Don't you realize that you become the slave of whatever you
choose to obey? You can be a slave to sin, which leads to death,
or you can choose to obey God, which leads to righteous living.
ROMANS 6:15-16

You don't have to be super careful about obeying God, right? After all, He promised that He'd forgive your sins. So, go ahead, have fun, do whatever you want – good or bad – then just ask God's forgiveness. It's no big deal.

Don't be foolish. If you don't take sin seriously, sin will seriously take over your life! Respecting the power of sin should make you focused on getting it out of your life. Respecting the grace of God that offers you salvation and forgiveness is even more important. Taking the sacrifice of Jesus so lightly that you willingly continue to sin because you know God will forgive you is an insult to what Jesus did for you.

Don't get lazy about obeying God. Keeping sin out of your life takes focus and perseverance. Every day you will be faced with multiple choices of whether to avoid sin and obey God or to just go on sinning. Choosing to go on sinning without making an effort to stop is disrespectful to God and shows that you don't value Him enough to obey Him. That's serious business.

Do you feel that it's a big deal to go on sinning when
you know better? Is there some particular sin that you have
found difficult to let go of? How are you working on it?

The Best News

"Go and make disciples of all the nations, baptizing them in the name of the Father and the Son and the Holy Spirit. Teach these new disciples to obey all the commands I have given you. And be sure of this: I am with you always, even to the end of the age."
MATTHEW 28:19-20

When you have good news, you want to shout it from the rooftop, right? Good news is made even better when it's shared. The more friends who celebrate with you, the more fun it is!

The best news you can share is the truth that God loves people. He loves mankind so much that He sent His Son to die for the sins that people can't help committing. His death makes possible a personal relationship with God and the promise of eternity with Him in heaven. This news is so good, so permanent, so unique … why wouldn't you share it with others?

Yes, it's hard sometimes – not everyone wants to hear this news. It's a challenge to know what to say. You have to be careful that your life matches what you say. But the news is so life-changing and the implications for those who don't hear it and have the opportunity to accept Jesus as Savior are very serious.

God, in His grace, promises that you don't have to do this on your own. Jesus promises to be with you every minute of every day until you join Him in heaven. He will help you share this wonderful news.

Who in your world still needs to hear about God's love? Have you tried to share with them? How did it go? How can God help you?

Deep Waters

"When you go through deep waters, I will be with you.
When you go through rivers of difficulty, you will not drown.
When you walk through the fire of oppression, you will
not be burned up; the flames will not consume you."
ISAIAH 43:2

Deep water, rivers of difficulty, fire and flames – those things show up in our lives in many different ways. For example, when the medical report is bad and you know the future holds a lot of serious procedures. Even with those procedures the future is scary … health is not guaranteed. That's deep water for sure.

You may feel very alone when you're facing something so serious and frightening. But, your God of grace reminds you that you're not alone in any of the difficulties you face. He promises that the problems you face will not destroy you. Does that mean you will physically survive anything that comes your way? No, He isn't talking about physical health or safety. What matters most to God is your spiritual life. If you hold tight to God when you're going through things that could shake your faith, then your faith won't be destroyed.

Believe it or not, staying closely connected to God is more important than your physical life. Your troubles may stretch your faith but they will not end it. God's presence will be known to you through His strength in getting you through tough times.

What deep water have you gone through,
or are you in right now? How is God
showing His presence? How does it help?

June

The Gift of Laughter

A cheerful heart is good medicine,
but a broken spirit saps a person's strength.
PROVERBS 17:22

It's awesome how practical God is – He knows that you need laughter in your life. He created laughter! It's His gift to you – another evidence of His loving grace. Laughter balances the sad times and helps you hang on until times get better. It makes the good times even better. What else does laughter do? It helps you not take yourself so seriously. It shoots endorphins into your system to give you energy and life – another grace-filled gift from God!

There are certainly times that are serious and demand a serious response. There are also times when a good laugh from deep in your gut releases some of the pressures and stress of daily life.

It's OK to laugh. God certainly has a sense of humor. Look around at some of the creative, funny things He made. Watch a video of monkeys or kittens playing. Think about some of the funny creatures He made – anteaters, hammerhead sharks.

If you are blessed to have a good friend with whom you can get silly once in a while and share hearty laughter, thank God for her. Enjoy the laughter and the break it gives you from the stresses of life. Laughter is a gift!

What makes you laugh? Do you have a friend with whom you often share laughter? How does a good, hearty laugh help relieve stress?

Never Alone

The LORD your God is indeed God. He is the faithful God
who keeps His covenant for a thousand generations
and lavishes His unfailing love on those who
love Him and obey His commands.
DEUTERONOMY 7:9

In the darkness of early morning when the stresses of life wake you and refuse to allow your heart to stop reeling in anxiety, you may feel alone. Of course, your mind knows that God is always present. He is aware of everything that's causing you stress and worry. But, even though you pray constantly about these situations, it doesn't seem as though He is doing anything. Nothing is changing. Then Satan slides in thoughts such as, "God doesn't care. He's busy with more important things. You don't matter to Him." If you allow your mind to accept those thoughts you will feel as though God has abandoned you and you're muddling through life alone.

Don't listen to those lies! God promised repeatedly in Scripture to be with you always. He keeps His promises because that's His character and He cannot go against who He is. When Satan starts whispering those lies to you, read verses like this one in Deuteronomy to be reminded that God, in His grace-filled love for you is present at every moment, in every circumstance, through every fear. He's present and He's working, even if you can't see His hand right now. Never doubt that.

What anxieties are waking you at night?
How long have you prayed about this?
How does God remind you of His presence?

God's Slow Anger

The LORD is compassionate and merciful,
slow to get angry and filled with unfailing love.
PSALM 103:8

The Christian life is compared to a journey because you didn't achieve perfection the moment you accepted Jesus. Yes, you have the Holy Spirit living in you. Yes, your sinful nature was pushed aside for a forgiven nature that longs to serve God. However, you're still human. You'll still fail Him sometimes. You'll learn from those failures and grow but you will fail. Do you fear that God will get tired of your failure? Do you worry that He will give up on you? News Flash – even if you feel like giving up on yourself, God will never, ever give up on you.

He has an amazingly deep capacity of being slow to anger – more than any human. It comes from His love for you which is so incredibly deep and because He believes in you so very much. So, even when you fail Him over and over, He doesn't give up on you. He doesn't get angry. He sees what you have the potential to become. He sees your heart that longs to serve Him and that you are disappointed in yourself when you fail.

He loves you and lifts you out of your own disappointment and keeps you trying again.

You know you fail to obey God sometimes?
What's your biggest struggle? How does God
encourage you to keep learning and growing?

God's Amazing Word

All Scripture is inspired by God and is useful to teach us what is true and to make us realize what is wrong in our lives. It corrects us when we are wrong and teaches us to do what is right.
2 TIMOTHY 3:16

A training book is helpful when you're learning something new. Explanations of how to do something or the rules to a game you're trying to learn are found in a rulebook or training book. It's difficult to learn new things without this help.

God knows that written down guidelines are helpful so He provided that for you to learn His commands. His inspired Word is another evidence of His loving grace. God's character is revealed in the Bible as you read how He interacted with His people in its stories. Reading of those interactions helps you know how He will interact with you – with honesty, love and high expectations.

Scripture clearly describes what it means to obey God. It gives you standards by which you can measure your own behavior so you know how you're doing in your efforts to obey Him.

Over and over Scripture tells you how very much God loves you. It tells you that His forgiveness is complete and constant. He never gives up on you and He is always, always with you. The Bible is not just a "rule book" it is a love letter to you from God, who loves you so very much.

How do you feel about God's Word? Do you love reading it? How often do you read it? Does it challenge you? Comfort you? Teach you?

Pursued by God

Surely Your goodness and unfailing love
will pursue me all the days of my life,
and I will live in the house of the LORD forever.
PSALM 23:6

If you've ever been pursued for something that you'd really love to have or do then you know how wonderful it feels. You could be pursued by a love interest and it tickles your heart to know he is interested enough to pursue you. Or perhaps you are pursued by a recruiter for a job that you'd actually love to have or a school you'd be honored to attend. How cool are those things? You feel valued as a person for who you are and what you bring to the table.

The most wonderful pursuer you have is God Himself. God loves you so much that He pursues you by His constant, unfailing love. When your faith is floundering some or your faith energy is fading away from Him, God pursues you by reminding you of His love and care. You will notice times when something so wonderful and so out of the ordinary happens that you know it has to be God. That's the only explanation for what you've experienced.

Yes, it's God reminding you that He's still with you. His love is deep and constant. His pursuing love pulls you back and holds you close.

When have you sensed God pursuing you? How did He do something out of the ordinary – something that could only be attributed to Him? Did that pull you back close to Him?

Shelter in Life's Storm

Those who live in the shelter of the Most High
will find rest in the shadow of the Almighty.
PSALM 91:1

Running through pouring rain, wind lashing the raindrops against your face. Thunder booming. Lightning flashing around you. It's terrifying. You just want to get out of the storm and be safe. Finding shelter in a storm protects you from the elements and from the dangers. The panic in your heart settles down as you take a deep breath, dry off and realize you're OK.

You have a shelter from the storms of life. And life does get stormy sometimes. Relationships fall apart and friendships collapse, sometimes with no warning and sometimes catching you completely by surprise. That storm hurts and the clouds hang low over your heart. Serious health issues pop up – something you had no idea was happening inside your body and your heart needs shelter from the fear of what might come.

God is your shelter. He may not stop the storms. He may not still the wind or stop the rain or quiet the thunder and lightning but He shelters your heart so that it doesn't question His love. He makes sure you know you're not alone in the storm. His comfort and presence allows you to rest, knowing that nothing surprises Him and He never leaves you alone.

When have you known that God
was sheltering you? How did you feel?
How did your faith grow from that experience?

Times of Silence

"If you look for Me wholeheartedly, you will find Me."
JEREMIAH 29:13

What about the times when it seems like God must be busy with other, more important people or requests? What about the times when you sit down to His Table of Grace and … it's bare? You feel that your needs must not be important to Him? Has He turned His back on you? It's a curious time when God seems to be silent. Of course He hasn't turned His back on you and He does care about you. But those silent times are not easy.

When you're feeling empty of God's presence and grace, reflect on the past. Remind yourself of the times He has blessed you generously. Recall the times you knew it was Him who rescued you and provided for you. Remember that He has shown Himself to you in the past. Dwell on those thoughts as you wait for His presence to be obvious to you again.

Sometimes all you have to hold on to is His promise to be with you always and to supply all your needs. Remember your needs are different from your wants. Focus your heart on His promises. Trust Him to do all He says He will do. Stay strong in His love.

Have you experienced times of
spiritual emptiness? How did you get
through it? How did God reveal Himself to you?

Not Thankful

Ever since the world was created, people have seen the earth and sky. Through everything God made, they can clearly see His invisible qualities – His eternal power and divine nature. So they have no excuse for not knowing God. Yes, they knew God, but they wouldn't worship Him as God or even give Him thanks. And they began to think up foolish ideas of what God was like. As a result, their minds became dark and confused.

ROMANS 1:20-21

Thanking God is no small thing. Refusing to acknowledge who He is and what He's done can apparently lead to some pretty bad things. Look at what Paul said happened to these people – they saw all the creation God made. They knew who God was but they wouldn't worship Him or thank Him for anything He did. That led to dark confusion in their minds. What does this say to you? Be thankful. Take time out of your busy days to realize all God has given you and the multitude of ways He blesses you every day. Be grateful – from the depths of your heart. Don't be satisfied with a surface "thanks" but let gratitude be so real that it explodes from your heart … so deep that you cannot find words that express how truly thankful you are. Realize that you would have nothing and be nothing were it not for God's loving grace showering down upon you. Then, tell Him how thankful you are. Tell everyone how thankful you are. Let your praise become a witness to all who know you of God's generous grace.

It's really easy to get bogged down in life and forget how grateful you should be to God. Take time to notice all He does for you. Don't expect His blessings. Thank Him from the depths of your heart.

Comfort Surprises

All praise to God, the Father of our Lord Jesus Christ.
God is our merciful Father and the source of all comfort.
2 CORINTHIANS 1:3

What does comfort look like to you? What does it feel like? When you pray for God's comfort do you expect something supernatural to happen like the sun to stand still so you can meet a deadline or a person who is bullying you to disappear for a while? Do you picture a grandfatherly guy in a pure white robe with a flowing white beard giving you a gentle hug?

All are interesting ideas. But, the reality is that God's comfort comes to you in many different ways. It may be in the form of an unexpected note you get in the mail from a friend. It might be a hug from a child. It could be a surprise visit from a loved one. The awesome thing about God is that He will send you comfort in the way that will mean the most to you at that moment.

The next time you need comfort it will come in a different way. You see, He's paying attention to you … so, be sure you pay attention to what He does for you. Notice how His comfort comes. Each time you see it, just know that it's God's grace in action!

You have undoubtedly received comfort
from God in surprising ways. Were you paying
attention? Did you notice? How has He surprised you?

A Web of Connection

Share each other's burdens, and in this way obey the law
of Christ. If you think you are too important to help someone,
you are only fooling yourself. You are not that important.
GALATIANS 6:2-3

Below the ground there is a web made up of fungus that grows around tree roots. It spreads from tree to tree to plant to plant. That web shares nutrition from trees that have plenty to some who have little. Even trees and plants that are dying can send nutrition. This web makes the trees all connected. They depend on one another for life itself.

This underground web presents an interesting image for how the family of God should work. God's children are all connected, so when one hurts, all hurt and when one celebrates all celebrate. When people around you are carrying a heavy burden, step up and help them with it. It's what God says to do.

Do you think you're too busy or too important to reach down and help someone who needs to be lifted up? If you think you're too important to help someone in need … get over yourself. You aren't that important. There will be times when you need help and you'll be quite thankful for your Christian brother or sister who stops his or her own life to help you. So, do the same for them. This act is God's grace flowing through you.

How has a Christian brother or sister helped you? How
have you helped someone? What kind of relationship
did the act of helping another build between you?

Tough Love

These trials will show that your faith is genuine. It is being tested as fire tests and purifies gold – though your faith is far more precious than mere gold. So when your faith remains strong through many trials, it will bring you much praise and glory and honor on the day when Jesus Christ is revealed to the whole world.

1 PETER 1:7

You've heard of tough love. It's when someone, usually a parent or family member, lets a loved one go through a difficult situation. That adult might have the wherewithal to end the situation but chooses not to because the person with the problem needs to learn a difficult lesson. It's tough for the parent to watch someone she cares about in pain. It's tough for the person going through the situation. But, sometimes going through difficult times is the only way to learn important lessons.

Imagine how hard it is for God, who loves you so completely, to allow you to go through painful things. He could change everything without even speaking a word. However, He knows that going through trials tests your faith. Staying strong through a trial shows you and Him that you're serious about obeying and serving God. Each time your faith is tested and it survives, your faith grows a bit stronger. So, as painful as it is, God's tough love teaches you and grows you to become more like Christ. In a strange way, God's tough love is God's grace to you.

What's your experience with tough love? Have you had to show it to someone? Have you experienced it from God? Did you learn important lessons through it?

Everyone Sins

"My wayward children," says the LORD, "come back to Me,
and I will heal your wayward hearts." "Yes, we're coming,"
the people reply, "for You are the LORD our God."
JEREMIAH 3:22

When you accepted Christ as Savior, you began your Christian life with great enthusiasm. You had great determination that you would live in obedience to His commands. You didn't enter your faith life expecting to fail. Even so, failure is inevitable because you're human and sin is a part of your DNA.

However, the temptation is to deny your sin because you don't want to appear "unchristian" to anyone around you. You feel shame by allowing your failures to be visible to others. So you try to hide your sin or perhaps even deny it to yourself and even to God. But there's no need to do that. Everyone … absolutely everyone sins. Whether they want to or not. They can't help it. You can't help it. God knows you sin. He knows that you sin when you don't want to. But more important than your sin is the intent of your heart. God looks at it to see if your desire is honestly to obey Him and honor Him. That matters to Him. He sees that you're longing, your desire is to serve Him and then His grace, over and over again, offers you forgiveness and restores your relationship with Him.

Have you tried to hide your failures from others?
From God? What is the honest desire of your heart?

Give Up Everything

Then Jesus said to His disciples, "If any of you wants to be
My follower, you must give up your own way, take up your cross,
and follow Me. If you try to hang on to your life, you will lose
it. But if you give up your life for My sake, you will save it."
MATTHEW 16:24-25

"You must give up your own way," which means give up control of your own life. Well, that's not easy, is it? But if you want to follow Jesus that's what you have to do. You can't keep one foot in the world of "I get to do what I want 'cause I'm #1" and one foot in "I want to follow You, Jesus." Keeping a foot in each of those worlds is actually keeping both feet in the first one because Jesus doesn't accept divided loyalties.

Look, Jesus wants to give you a full, blessed, amazing life but frankly, He can't if you don't let Him have control of your whole life. You can't let go of control if you don't trust Him. You can't trust Him if you don't respect Him. You won't respect Him if you don't believe His love for you. You won't believe His love if you don't believe His grace.

So, you see the process. Take step one. Know His grace. Accept His salvation. Believe His love. Respect His Holiness. Trust His Heart. Give Him control. Be blessed with a life more wonderful than you ever imagined.

Where are you stuck on the continuum of giving
up control? Why is it hard? Have you taken
step one of salvation? Do you trust His love?

Putting the Word into Practice

Jesus replied, "But even more blessed are all
who hear the word of God and put it into practice."
LUKE 11:28

When you're driving you see the signs telling you what the speed limit is for the road. You see it. You know it. But, do you obey it?

Do you always, every day, every single time, obey the speed limit? If you don't and you're stopped by a policeman, it won't do you any good to say, "Oh yes, I saw the sign. I know what the speed limit is." If you didn't put it into practice then it won't make much difference to the police officer.

That's what Jesus is saying here. God gave you His Word to be a help to you. It explains who He is. It shares His love. It shows you how He relates to His people. It explains what He expects from you in obeying Him and in how to live with other people. So, when you sin … disobey His commands … you can say, "Oh yeah, I read that one. I know it."

But, putting into practice the way God says you should live is what will change your heart and life to make you more like Christ. And … that's the goal.

How important is God's Word to you?
How would your life change if you didn't have it?

Overflowing Gratitude

Give thanks to the LORD, for He is good!
His faithful love endures forever.
PSALM 107:1

When you get a gift you believe you deserve, maybe because it's your birthday or maybe because you've given the giver a gift in the past and it's only fair that she give you one … your gratitude is minimal because you're getting something you deserve. But, a humble heart doesn't expect gifts. It's overjoyed when a gift is received.

Gratitude holds an important role in your worship. It's a response to all God does for you and all He gives you. Gratitude springs from the recognition that God doesn't have to do any of what He does and, more importantly, that you don't deserve one speck of His blessings. When you are truly grateful, it's because you realize that God's grace to you is displayed in generosity that extends from creating the world you live in all the way to the clothes you are wearing and the last bite of food you enjoyed.

Everything … absolutely everything you have is because of His gracious generosity. When you get your mind around that truth, even for a moment, gratitude flows from your heart faster than your words can express it to God.

For what are you thankful today?
Thank God for specifics.

What Is Truth?

"When the Spirit of truth comes, He will guide you into all truth. He will not speak on His own but will tell you what He has heard. He will tell you about the future."
JOHN 16:13

One thing you read says, "This is truth," then another thing that's diametrically opposed to the first thing also claims to be truth. Both may be reliable sources but different opinions. Or, one may be from a skewed viewpoint. How do you know? It's an important challenge. One that you must be careful about, especially when the truth relates to God's Word and following Him in obedience.

Thankfully you do not have to trek through the confusion alone. God, in His loving grace, gave you the Holy Spirit who will reveal real truth … God's truth to you. As you read and study the Bible the Holy Spirit will help you understand what God wants you to know. Pray about what you read. Ask God to give you clarity. Ask Him to help you see His truth.

Trust Scripture more than human writers, who, as knowledgeable as they are, and as good as they may be, are still human and can occasionally be off-center. The Holy Spirit is your best guide. He shares the truth from God.

Have you struggled to know what real truth is on a subject? How did you decide? How does the Holy Spirit direct your thoughts?

A Safe Place

The LORD is good, a strong refuge when trouble comes.
He is close to those who trust in Him.
NAHUM 1:7

You've probably seen pictures of a mother hen with her wings spread out as her chicks huddled beneath them. They know they are safe there. Mom is protecting them. She will keep them under her wings until the danger has passed. What's interesting is that her wings are always there but the chicks only run to her when danger is around. She only swoops them into protection when she knows they need it. The rest of the time the chicks run, play, eat … whatever chicks do.

God is your refuge … your hiding place. He tells you that often in Scripture. Because He loves you and wants to keep you safe, He encourages you to run to Him when you need protection. Now, you probably need protection a lot more often than you're aware of, a lot more often than you take advantage of. Sometimes He protects you when you don't even know it.

But, isn't it a blessing to know that when life does get tough, when you're afraid, or confused, when there's danger of any kind, you have a safe place to hide. Trust His heart of grace. Run to Him.

When was a time you ran to God for protection? How did He keep you safe? When you're afraid, is your first thought to run to God?

Use It or Lose It

"To those who use well what they are given, even more will be given, and they will have an abundance. But from those who do nothing, even what little they have will be taken away."
MATTHEW 25:29

You're good at some things. It's okay to admit that. You're good at some things because God gifted you to do them. You are to use those things to serve Him, to help His Kingdom grow. There are people you can reach by using your gifts who others couldn't reach by using theirs. Everyone is necessary. Every talent and gift is necessary.

God is the grace-filled Giver of abundance to those who deserve abundance. He will bless you even more if you use well what He's given you. So, if He has made you a counselor, counsel well. If He's made you a singer, sing well. If He's given you a heart for the hurting, comfort well.

Your purpose as a child of God is to bring glory and honor to His Name, to serve Him and do your part in sharing His love with the world. You can do those things by using the tools He gave you. When you do, He will give you more tools and greater opportunity. Use what you've been given.

It's not pride to acknowledge how God has gifted you. What are you good at? What do you enjoy doing? How do you use your gift to serve God?

Be Generous

"If you give even a cup of cold water to one of
the least of My followers, you will surely be rewarded."
MATTHEW 10:42

Generosity doesn't always mean money. It could simply mean taking a bottle of water to someone – maintenance worker, homeless person, coach of your child's team … anyone. Generosity pays attention. It notices when someone around you needs something. It might not be water, maybe a store clerk needs a smile or a waitress needs a kind word.

Be generous from your spirit. Give money when you see it's needed and you have it to give. Give out of your necessity not just your excess. Give kindness every day. In our fractured, grumpy, say-what-you-want social media driven world, people need kindness. You can always give a gentle word, a compliment, an encouragement, a smile. Connect with people instead of rushing past, eyes down, or on your phone. Give of yourself.

God in His generous grace gives so much to you. Pay it forward by giving to others. Show them how His love in your life causes you to pay attention and be generous with your time, energy, spirit and yes, your money. Don't reserve your generosity for those who "deserve" it. Just be generous and leave the "deserving" part between them and God.

Do you consider yourself a generous person? How does generosity flow from you? Do you give financially, of your time, of your spirit? What's your generosity personality?

David's Wisdom

Solomon, my son, learn to know the God of
your ancestors intimately. Worship and serve Him with
your whole heart and a willing mind. For the LORD sees
every heart and knows every plan and thought. If you seek Him,
you will find Him. But if you forsake Him, He will reject you forever.

1 CHRONICLES 28:9

David spoke these words to his son, Solomon. God called David "a man after God's own heart." That's quite a statement, isn't it? David certainly did some wonderful things in his life but he also had some pretty big failures. So David knew what he was talking about when he counseled Solomon to know God deeply and to serve Him whole-heartedly. The better Solomon knew God and the more he desired to serve Him, the better he would know God and the more he would serve Him. See how that works?

God knows you're going to mess up sometimes. He knows you're not perfect … yet. But, He doesn't give up on you. He searches your heart to see what your desires are. He wants to know if you truly long to serve Him and love Him more all the time. If that's your heart's desire, then He will meet you where you are – in whatever failure you are floundering. He will meet you, forgive you, pick you up and keep you going. That's what grace does. That's what love does. That's what God does.

What is the desire of your heart? Have you been only saying the Christian words expected of you without your heart being in them? Time for a heart check!

What Do You Hunger For?

I have told you often before, and I say it again with tears
in my eyes, that there are many whose conduct shows they
are really enemies of the cross of Christ. They are headed for
destruction. Their god is their appetite, they brag about shameful
things, and they think only about this life here on earth.

PHILIPPIANS 3:18-19

Paul knew that some Christians say all the right words … the Christian words that make them look good to other Christians. Then, they turn around and behave in ways that don't honor God or respect other people. Their appetite is hungering for something other than obeying and honoring Him. They can say the right words to make themselves look good to others but the way they behave actually makes them enemies of Christ. Whew. That's serious stuff. Your appetite controls so much of your life.

For what do you hunger? Whatever you're craving is where you'll put your energy. How do you spend your time? How do you treat others? Do you long for success more than humility? Or is your hunger to know God more deeply? Do you long to serve Him sacrificially? Are you devoted to helping others? Where your appetite is shows where your heart is. Do some self-examination to see if you're longing to serve God who has given you life. If your appetite is not there, time to make some changes.

This is a tough question: What do you hunger for? This is completely between you and God but you know where your thoughts and energy are focused. Do you need to do some heart cleaning to adjust your appetite?

Hidden Treasure

You died to this life, and your real
life is hidden with Christ in God.
COLOSSIANS 3:3

When you lose something special, you tear the house apart looking for it, right? You search and search until you find it. The more precious the lost item, the more intense your search.

The most precious thing you've been given is life and the truth is that your real life is hidden in Christ. Why would God hide something so important? He wants you to know Christ deeply and personally.

So, to find your true life in God you obviously must get to know Christ. How do you do that? By studying Scripture, especially the four gospels that tell you the stories of what Jesus taught, how He cared about people, healed the sick, raised the dead and helped the blind and lame. Jesus loved people. You read that He is the Messiah, the Son of God. You learn how He chose suffering and death to make a way for you to have a personal relationship with God and the promise of eternity.

That shows how much Jesus loves you and that He and His Father gave you the Holy Spirit to help you learn and grow. This is your future life – hidden with Christ in God.

Your goal is to become more like Jesus. What have you learned about Him? How are you like Him now?

New Life

My old self has been crucified with Christ. It is no longer I who live,
but Christ lives in me. So I live in this earthly body by trusting
in the Son of God, who loved me and gave Himself for me.
I do not treat the grace of God as meaningless. For
if keeping the law could make us right with God,
then there was no need for Christ to die.
GALATIANS 2:20-21

What does it mean that your old self is crucified? The old person …
the you before you accepted Jesus as Savior could only try to gain
favor with God by obeying laws, a set of rules. It was a lot of work and
completely impossible. Or maybe you didn't even think about obeying
God. Maybe God wasn't even on your radar.

But then you accepted Christ and God's grace gave you the Holy
Spirit to live in you and help you fall deeply in love with God. Now you
are a new person because of Him. Don't take that lightly. "Do not treat
the grace of God as meaningless." Grace changed everything for you.
You no longer have to obey laws. You are now a child of God and He
loves you, forgives you and guides you. He has given you a life filled
with more wonderful joy than anything you left behind. Why would you
even think about going back to that old way of life?

Thank God for His grace and love and the life He has given you
through the death and resurrection of Jesus.

Thanksgiving is a big part of your relationship
with Christ. As you look back at life before you knew
Him, what are you most thankful for in your new life?

Genuine Friendship

Love each other with genuine affection,
and take delight in honoring each other.
ROMANS 12:10

Do you know someone who is sugary sweet when you bump into her? She is chatty and over-the-top about everything she says. It's almost uncomfortable because you know you aren't really friends. Her chattiness is too much. Her concern is not real. The way she's treating you is not genuine.

A real friend honestly cares about you. She wants to know what's happening in your life – good and bad. She is available to you and willing to spend time with you. In fact it makes her happy to do that. She encourages you, lifts you up, cheers for you. A real friend loves you and celebrates you.

A friend like this is a gift from God and is to be treasured. He knows that real friends make life so much better. In His grace, He brings people into your life who have the potential to be genuine friends.

You have the opportunity to be the same to them. Cultivate friendship. Invest in those you meet. When you find a true friend, love genuinely and honor fully. Friends are God's gift to you because lives shared is a blessing to both of you.

Who are your genuine friends? How do
you share life together? Have you told them
how much you appreciate their friendship?

Serving God

Never be lazy, but work hard
and serve the Lord enthusiastically.
ROMANS 12:11

When you take on a task, do you give it your all and see it through to the end? Can your boss and co-workers count on you? Is there a sigh of relief when you say, "I will do it" or is there an apprehension that they may have to pick up the slack in the eleventh hour?

If you're getting paid to do a task, hopefully you are diligent in earning your salary. But what about when the job is a volunteer thing … maybe something at church? Does it go to the bottom of your priority list? Do you let preparations slide until the last minute then kind of slide through, doing something but not doing a great job? Or, do you just let it slide and not do anything?

Working for the Lord is the most important work you can do. However you contribute to His work is part of providing opportunities for others to meet the Lord or to grow stronger in their faith.

That's serious work and whatever your role is, it comes directly from God. He has, in grace, gifted you to do your job and provided the opportunity. Serve Him energetically and enthusiastically!

Take an honest look at yourself – how do you approach
doing God's work? Do you serve with energy and joy? Why?

Keep On Praying

Rejoice in our confident hope. Be patient
in trouble, and keep on praying.
ROMANS 12:12

You know how the story ends. You know God has promised eternal life with Him. You know His guidance and protection are constant. You know He promised never to leave you. You know that whatever messy stuff you go through in your life here, in the end God wins and all will be well because you belong to Him.

Knowing all that should help you get through the hard times. Your confident hope is in the promises God gives you in His Word. His grace-filled presence promises all those things. Yes, you will have trouble in this life. It's inevitable. But you have His presence, strength, comfort and love to get you through them. You are never alone in your trouble. He promised.

So, when trouble comes, and it will, pray. When trouble persists, and it will, pray some more. When things get worse, and they might, pray more and more. Never stop praying. It's your connection to God. He asks you to talk to Him. He commands you to talk to Him, not because He is a dictator, but because He cares.

Do you have the confident hope
Romans 12:12 talks about? Do you trust God
to be with you through your troubles? How
has He shown His presence to you in the past?

Caring for Others

When God's people are in need, be ready to
help them. Always be eager to practice hospitality.
ROMANS 12:13

You may have heard the saying, "Charity begins at home." There are certainly some problems with the narrowness of that idea but there is something important to consider too.

First, the problem – people everywhere experience need. Some of it is quite severe. People who are not yet part of God's family need help and you should be generous in any way and to whatever extent you can to help them.

Now, the important thing – family sticks together, right? So, when a Christian brother, sister, family, church or whatever, needs help; be ready to give it. Let the world see that family sticks together. Be an example of love and generosity. Open your home or church, make meals, share clothes. Do whatever you can to show and share God's love with your family members. Your kindness will be encouraging for them as they know they aren't alone in their troubles. It will be a witness to all who are watching. It may be reciprocated someday when you need help.

Remember that God, through His grace, has blessed you with all you have so that you can be a help to others – the family as well as those who haven't yet met your Father. Be kind. Be generous. Be hospitable.

How have you experienced the generous care of others?
How have you been able to help others? Do you share willingly
and unselfishly? With just the "family" or with others as well?

The Best Weapon

David replied to the Philistine, "You come to
me with sword, spear, and javelin, but I come to you
in the name of the LORD of Heaven's Armies – the God
of the armies of Israel, whom you have defied."
1 SAMUEL 17:45

Don't you just love the story of the little guy defeating the giant? Young David wasn't the least bit afraid of Goliath. None of King Saul's big, strong soldiers would fight the big guy … but a young boy with just a sling and five stones walked right up to him.

David knew who was on his side. He was defending the honor of his God. He knew that Goliath's size didn't matter. Goliath's weapons didn't matter. Goliath's shield didn't matter. David didn't even actually need his sling and stones because what he had inside, in his heart, was the weapon that would defeat Goliath.

What's your Goliath? What have you been cowering from? Why are you afraid? You have the same weapon David had. The same God who took down the giant is ready for you to say, "OK, let's do this, God." His power and strength are yours. He promises that His Spirit in you is all you need. You are strong in Him. You are powerful in Him. Call on Him for help and know that you will win because of Him!

What's your Goliath today? Have you
called on God's strength and wisdom to
fight it? How is He helping you?

Selflessly Interceding

Please forgive me if I have offended you in any way.
The LORD will surely reward you with a lasting dynasty,
for you are fighting the LORD's battles. And you have
not done wrong throughout your entire life.
1 SAMUEL 25:28

Abigail said these words. Her husband had behaved badly when David's men asked him for food. David was going to kill him for what he did. Abigail stopped David by reminding him of the good things he had done for God and that he had a bright future. She took food to him and his men. She asked forgiveness – even though she hadn't done anything wrong. Abigail stopped David from acting in anger that he would later regret. Abigail interceded for her husband. She saved David from sinning. There was no pride in Abigail's behavior, only concern for David.

God, in His wisdom and grace, has placed you in a community of people. Hopefully you all care about one another. Are there people that you care so much for that you would intercede for them? Would you even apologize for something they did in order to stop another friend from saying or doing something they could later regret? Jesus said that a true friend is willing to lay down his life for a friend and that's what this behavior is. Stepping up instead of stepping aside. Standing up for someone instead of turning away. It's brave and sacrificial behavior.

Have you interceded for someone? How did it go?
Has anyone interceded for you? How did it save you?

Would You Suffer?

God saved us and called us to live a holy life.
He did this, not because we deserved it, but because
that was His plan from before the beginning of time –
to show us His grace through Christ Jesus.
2 TIMOTHY 1:9

Are you willing to suffer for your faith in God? When someone makes fun of you for your beliefs or even worse, should you face persecution, do you stand strong or back down? Paul was in prison for his faith when he wrote to Timothy and it wasn't the first time he had been imprisoned for his beliefs. Still, he encouraged Timothy to be strong in his faith, regardless of what happened.

Paul shared with Timothy, and with you, that with your salvation God called you to live a holy life. "Holy" means set apart for a purpose. Your purpose is to worship and honor God. You didn't deserve it … no one does. But, it was God's plan for the beginning that because you choose to stand strong for God, His name is lifted up.

Ask God to give you the strength and courage to stand strong for Him, no matter what you face. Pray for His grace to be obvious in your life by how you respond to persecution and in your courage to never diminish who He is to you. Never be ashamed of your faith in Jesus. He gave everything for you.

Have you faced criticism, cynicism or out and out persecution for your faith? How did you respond?

Water into Wine

This miraculous sign at Cana in Galilee was the first time
Jesus revealed His glory. And His disciples believed in Him.
JOHN 2:11

Hopefully you know the story – Jesus was a guest at a wedding when they ran out of wine. At His mother's urging, Jesus performed His first miracle. He turned six giant jars of water into wine! He didn't touch the jars. He didn't touch the water. He didn't even really say a word to make the miracle happen. It just did.

Jesus' first public miracle was done to help His friends. It was done with simple ingredients … six jars of water. It was done privately. There was no big show. No one but the servants who brought the jars of water over even knew what had happened.

Jesus cares about you. He cares what difficulties you face. He cares what you need. You never need to feel that your needs are too ordinary for Him to bother with. You never need to feel that what you need is an impossibility.

Nothing is impossible for God. He can give you what you need with just a jar of water to work with. He can make something out of nothing. His heart of grace will take care of you in ways you don't even notice or see. Always.

Undoubtedly Jesus has cared for you in ways you
don't even know about. But, how have you seen His care
in your life? Have you witnessed a miracle on your behalf?

White As Snow

"Come now, let's settle this," says the LORD. "Though your sins are like scarlet, I will make them as white as snow. Though they are red like crimson, I will make them as white as wool."

ISAIAH 1:18

Think about red … red ink on white fabric is nearly impossible to get out. Even if you treat it with the best laundry product, there will likely be a faint pink stain you can't get rid of. And, what happens when you accidentally wash a new red piece of clothing with your whites? Yeah, you have a lot of pink clothing then.

God says that to Him your sins look like scarlet – red. Bright red. But, His grace to you makes them as white as snow. Newly fallen snow is about the whitest thing you can see. God turns your red sin into white snow with not even a hint of pink. God loves you so much that He takes away all evidence of your sin. You are a completely new person in His eyes. You did nothing to deserve this grace, in fact there's nothing you can do to deserve it.

Does that reality fill your heart with gratitude? Tell God. Let your gratitude fill your prayers. Let it show in your life.

Share the story of your salvation with others, to encourage and challenge them to know God's forgiveness, too.

How does God's forgiveness affect your outlook on life? How often do your prayers speak your gratitude?

The Golden Rule

"Do to others whatever you would like them to do to you.
This is the essence of all that is taught in the law and the prophets."
MATTHEW 7:12

The Bible, both Old and New Testaments teaches you how to live in obedience to God. In a nutshell you're told to love God with all your heart, mind and strength and to love your neighbor as yourself. This verse in Matthew takes that command a step further – treat others the way you'd like them to treat you. That's pretty simple, isn't it? This is often called the Golden Rule because it's a golden way to treat others.

You know how you'd like others to treat you – with respect, love, generosity, kindness and encouragement to name a few ways. That's the way everyone wants to be treated. Someone has to get the ball rolling. Be God's person in this. Take the initiative in treating those around you this way – even those who are unkind to you – even those who don't immediately respond with kindness or respect. Be careful not to show this behavior with the purpose of making others respond with this treatment for you. Show kindness from the depths of your heart because it is the right thing to do.

Living by the Golden Rule is obedience to God and shares God's loving grace with others.

Are there some people you have difficulty treating with kindness?
Why? How is your commitment to living the Golden Rule?

What's Your Heart's Desire?

"Don't store up treasures here on earth, where moths eat them and rust destroys them, and where thieves break in and steal. Store your treasures in heaven, where moths and rust cannot destroy, and thieves do not break in and steal. Wherever your treasure is, there the desires of your heart will also be."
MATTHEW 6:19-21

God warns you that putting your emphasis on the "stuff" that you can accumulate in life is a waste of time. Nothing you gather here on earth is going into eternity with you. Nothing you gather here will last. It's true that society shouts, "Get more! Buy more! Have more! The one with the most stuff wins in the end!" But … society is wrong. None of that "stuff" has eternal value. It's self-focused and selfish to make that your focus.

One day the world will see that the real "winners" are the ones who choose to know God and live in obedience to Him, those who show love, respect and compassion to others. Those are the treasures you store up in heaven. Worshipping, honoring, obeying and serving God are treasures. Treating others as God says to treat them is a treasure.

What's the desire of your heart? Do you focus on finishing life with the most stuff? Or to finish life with treasures waiting in heaven for you. Whatever your heart desires will be your focus.

You know what you're "supposed" to answer regarding what's important to you. In the quietness of your heart, answer these questions … what's the desire of your heart? Where is your focus? Where are you putting your time and energy?

Spiritual Training

Physical training is good, but training for godliness is much better, promising benefits in this life and in the life to come.
1 TIMOTHY 4:8

When you're training for a marathon, you run each day to strengthen and train your body. Muscle memory means your body remembers what it has to do to run because of what you've been doing each day. You put nutritious food into your body instead of junk food. Your body needs the fuel of those nutritious food supplies.

How does this physical training translate to training in godliness? And, why should you think about it in this way? Think about the second question first – training in godliness is important because by God's grace, you know Him. By His grace He provides ways for your faith to grow deeper and stronger. You don't immediately go to maturity in your faith walk. In fact, it's sometimes called a race.

Then what about spiritual training? What's your spiritual muscle memory? Does your heart remember how God has blessed you? Does it recall specifics of times He has protected you, guided you and taught you? What "nutrition" are you putting into your spirit? Feed on the truth of God's Word. Remember what you put into your mind and heart is what will come out. Take your spiritual training seriously so your faith will grow stronger and deeper.

How's your spiritual training going? What's your plan?
Are you noticing your spiritual muscle memory improving?

Self-Image Boost

You made all the delicate, inner parts of my body
and knit me together in my mother's womb.
Thank You for making me so wonderfully complex!
Your workmanship is marvelous – how well I know it.
PSALM 139:13-14

How are you feeling about yourself? Do you get stuck in the comparison cycle by looking at those around you as more successful, more pretty, more talented, and even more devoted, more spiritual and more useful to God? Comparing yourself to others is really dangerous because God made you unique and exactly as He wants you to be. In fact, it's not only dangerous to you; it's disrespectful to God. Are you saying that He didn't know what He was doing when He made you? Do you think He made some mistakes or that His workmanship was inferior? That's what your comparisons look like, right?

God's grace-filled heart saw you before you even came into this world. He made you to be who you are and to do what you do? Are you different from those around you? Yes. Are you less than those around you? No.

Don't question God's plan. Celebrate how He made you. Develop your strengths and talents. Be open to His plan and where it takes you in life. Be willing to take some risks and see how it grows you and gives you new opportunities to serve Him. Become the best YOU that you can!

What part of yourself are you critical of? What part of you do you like? How can you work on the parts you don't like? How can you develop the parts you do like?

The Riches of God

Yours, O LORD, is the greatness, the power, the glory,
the victory, and the majesty. Everything in the heavens
and on earth is Yours, O LORD, and this is Your kingdom.
We adore You as the one who is over all things.

1 CHRONICLES 29:11

God gives you everything you need to survive in this life and all you need to serve Him. It's all His. You are nothing without Him. You have nothing without Him. And, whatever you need, minute-by-minute and day-to-day is available to you from His storehouse of riches! Do you need strength? Ask Him. Do you need patience? It's yours. Do you need help loving? Tell Him. All of who God is becomes available to you when you accept Jesus as Savior. Think of the characteristics of God that you most admire: wisdom, joy, power, love … yours! Just ask Him and trust the timing of His response. He knows what you need. He wants to give you all you need. He wants to know that you know you need what He can give … and only He can give.

Does this mean you can ask Him for a million dollars? Sure, you can ask, but why do you want it? Examine your motives before you start asking for riches or for trouble to be poured out on your enemies. Be God focused and Christ-like in your requests – your Father has it all!

God wants to bless you because He loves you. What do
you need? Joy, patience, wisdom, love? Have you asked?

A Fresh Start

Create in me a clean heart, O God.
Renew a loyal spirit within me.
PSALM 51:10

When you accepted Christ you started out serving God with enthusiasm and joy. It was a new life! A wonderful life! You were forgiven by grace and made a new creature. But then … life started happening. Troubles came. Discouragement followed. Your enthusiasm dimmed. Your joy was replaced by "what ifs" and doubts. Sins you had kicked out of your life crept back in and you were on a downward spiral. Now what?

You've only one real choice. Come clean with God. Tell Him that you see how you've fallen away from Him. You know you've messed up big time. You've let sin back into your heart. What will He do? Forgive you. That's what God does. Because of His love and grace, He forgives and you have a fresh start to obey Him. He will give you a clean heart – ask for it. He will refresh your spirit's energy to know Him and serve Him – ask Him.

God wants your love and your worship. He won't force you but He will help you get back to it whenever you fall away. Just ask Him.

It takes discipline and strength to stay close to God
and keep sin at bay. How are you doing?
Do you need a fresh start on some point?
Tell Him about it and ask His help.

The Depths of Christ's Love

May you have the power to understand,
as all God's people should, how wide, how long,
how high, and how deep His love is. May you experience
the love of Christ, though it is too great to understand fully.
Then you will be made complete with all the fullness
of life and power that comes from God.
EPHESIANS 3:18-19

Paul wanted so much for the Ephesian Christians – but no more than what Jesus wants for you. Paul wanted the Christians in Ephesus to fully know the magnitude of Christ's love for them. It's so much bigger than what they apparently knew. Deeper than anything they could have imagined. Higher than anything they had seen. Long and wide – there are simply no words grand enough to describe His love. Paul knew that the more they could understand it, the more full their lives would be. But, even in saying that Paul knew that there is actually no way the Ephesians could have truly comprehended Christ's love. There's nothing to compare it to and no way to explain it.

Just as Paul wanted his friends to grasp it, so Christ wants you to grasp His love. The only way that can happen is if you spend your whole life learning about Him. Ask God to reveal His love, to lift the curtain, even for a moment so you can see the depth and riches of Christ's love for you. It's so amazing. You'll long for more knowledge and the fullness that His love brings to you.

Look up all the verses that speak of Christ's love.
What new understanding does that give you?
How does that knowledge affect your heart?

What Goes In ...

Fix your thoughts on what is true, and honorable,
and right, and pure, and lovely, and admirable.
Think about things that are excellent and worthy of praise.
PHILIPPIANS 4:8

What you put in is what comes out. You know that's true with your body. If you consume a diet of junk food, you'll gain weight. Your health will suffer. A junk food diet affects your skin, hair, sleep ... everything. So, what you put in is what you get out.

God reminds you to be careful to put good thoughts in your mind and heart because what you put in is what will come out. If you fill your mind with negative, critical, judgmental, mean and unkind thoughts that's what will come out in your words and behavior. That's no fun for people around you and it surely doesn't show that living for Jesus is the focus of your life. In fact, it shows just the opposite.

However, if your thoughts focus on Scripture, the reality of God's love, praise for Him, concern for others, gratitude for all God's blessings and a desire to honor God then that will show in your behavior and in what you say.

This kind of behavior blesses others and shows gratitude for God's grace of forgiveness and a desire to honor Him in your life. So, be careful what you think.

What kinds of thoughts fill your mind? If they are negative, do you fight them? How do your thoughts come out in words and actions?

Growing Up

I am certain that God, who began the good work
within you, will continue His work until it is finally
finished on the day when Christ Jesus returns.

PHILIPPIANS 1:6

When God saved you by His grace, His Holy Spirit came to live in your heart. Your old sinful nature was cut away and you were given a new desire to know God and serve Him.

However, that was just step one. You're not meant to stay a spiritual baby for all your life. God will continue to work in your heart, teaching you and growing your faith. But, only if you want Him to do so.

Your part of growing up is to study His Word so that you understand how He took care of His people in the Bible stories. You'll learn His character – how He is a jealous God, a loving God, a forgiving God and a protecting God. Scripture tells you how to obey Him – what He expects, what His commands are. You are to fill your thoughts with thoughts that honor God and others.

You also help your faith grow by talking to God. Tell Him what's on your mind, what you're worried about, what you want Him to do. Open your heart to His leading and guidance. Give Him complete control of your life. Your faith will grow as you see how much God loves you!

How has your faith grown since the day you
accepted Jesus? How has God changed you?

Help for Life

The LORD says, "I will guide you along the best pathway
for your life. I will advise you and watch over you.
Do not be like a senseless horse or mule that needs
a bit and bridle to keep it under control."

PSALM 32:8-9

Believe it or not, the older you get the more confusing life gets. It doesn't get easier. Every day there are a multitude of choices and even more changes that flow in and out of your life. Knowing which way to go and what to do can be overwhelming. You certainly don't want to make a big mistake that could have long-term effects and change the course of your life in a bad way. How do you know what to do?

Pray. God wants to guide your life. He wants to guide you down the best path. One that moves you forward to become more like Jesus in your knowledge of Him and in your behavior. Pray that He will protect you as you follow Him. There will be dangers. There will be those who fight your choices. You'll need His protection.

When you do ask God to guide you let Him have control of your life. Don't fight His every word and direction. Once you believe how much He loves you and how He wants the very best for you, your heart will submit to His leading. When you believe that you will completely trust His leading.

How have you experienced God's leading
in your life? How have you accepted His
leading? Or have you fought His leading?

The Most
Important Message

How beautiful on the mountains are the feet
of the messenger who brings good news, the good news
of peace and salvation, the news that the God of Israel reigns!
ISAIAH 52:7

God saved you by His grace. But, more than likely someone told you about God's love. Someone shared the story of how Jesus came to earth, died for your sins, rose again and how you can have a personal relationship with God through the forgiveness of your sins and then the promise of eternity in heaven. Someone told you. Now, as a member of God's family, you have the opportunity to do the same for others – share the good news.

The news of God's love is the best news you can share with anyone. If learning of God's love changed your life, wouldn't you want to share it with others and let them experience it, too? It's what God expects His family members to do – tell others. This is serious because Scripture tells you that one day Jesus will come back to take His followers to heaven. Anyone who hasn't accepted Him will have missed their chance and be doomed to eternity without Him. If you truly believe this, you'll eagerly share the Good News with your loved ones so they have the chance to accept Jesus. You will be a messenger of good news!

Who shared the story of God's love with you? Have you
taken the opportunity to share the Good News with anyone?

Teamwork

Two people are better off than one, for they can help
each other succeed. If one person falls, the other can reach
out and help. But someone who falls alone is in real trouble.
ECCLESIASTES 4:9-10

Look at the facts – God loves you. You know that to be true. God is all you need for your life. You know that to be true, too. God wants to give you the best things for your life. You know that, too. One of the best things He gives you is friendship because He knows there is comfort in the support you can give one another.

The grace of God wants you to have everything you need. A close friend or a spouse can pick you up when you fall. She can encourage you when you're sad … when you don't think you can keep going. She can cheer for your successes and cry with you for your sorrows. There is strength in numbers. Your friend can pray for you and you can pray for her. Sharing your burdens makes them lighter. Sharing your joys makes them happier.

Look around you. Who are the special friends God has put in your life? Have you opened your heart and embraced the friendship? Have you allowed yourself to build the trust for a vulnerable relation-ship?

Thank God for this friendship and for the strength you have because of it.

Do you have a special close friend or spouse with whom you can share your joys and sorrows? How has this friend made your life better? How have you worked together to encourage and help each other?

Knowing the
Right Thing to Do

Remember, it is sin to know what you ought to do and then not do it.
JAMES 4:17

If a police officer stops you for speeding, you will probably get a ticket. It's your responsibility to know the law and to obey it.

Think about that in relation to sin. Do you know the right thing to do? Then you need to do it. How do you know what God considers sin? He made sure you could know. It's outlined in the Bible, God's guidebook for you. In it you read quite clearly what it means to obey God. You learn that disobeying His commands is considered sin.

Of course, knowing what sin is doesn't make obeying easy, because you still must choose to obey. It does help, though, because you know what the parameters of obeying are.

Even knowing what the Bible teaches there will be times when you disobey God. Many times it will be not be by deliberate choice. It's still sin. Sometimes you make deliberate choices that you know are sin. That's kind of double sin, isn't it? The choice and the sin.

Of course, God forgives your sin because of His grace. But, if you know what that forgiveness cost Christ, why would you deliberately choose to sin when you know better?

Is there a time when you chose to do something
you knew was sin? How did you feel after doing that?
Did it make you think twice about doing so again?

Praise for God's Help

I cried out to Him for help, praising Him as I spoke.
PSALM 66:17

Instead of just, "Help me!" this psalmist prayed, "I praise You, O God, for Your help!" What amazing faith. Not only did the psalmist know he could ask God for help, but he so firmly believed that God would answer that he praised God even as he made his request.

What an amazing example! God promised that He would always be with you. He promised that He would always hear your prayers. He promised to take care of you.

Do you view those promises with such confidence that you can praise God for His help even as you first utter your cry for help?

The more times you call out to God and recognize His answers and His care, the stronger your faith will grow. Soon you will be so confident in His coming answer and His help that your heart will swell with praise as you cry out to Him.

Praise Him for His presence. Praise Him for listening. Praise Him for caring. Praise Him for helping. What a glorious example of His love, grace and care.

Praise God for how He has answered your cries for help in the past. Praise Him for His love and care.

God's Representative

The LORD demands accurate scales and
balances, He sets the standards for fairness.
PROVERBS 16:11

You go through a fast food drive-through, get your order and the change from the payment you gave the cashier. You drive out of the lot, stop at a park to eat your food and discover that the change you were given was wrong … very wrong. The cashier inadvertently gave you twice as much change as you had coming. What do you do? Stick it in your pocket and plan how you want to spend it? Drive right back to the restaurant to return it?

What does it mean to you that God says, "Be fair. Be honest?" He insists on your honesty in dealing with people because you are His child and a representative of who He is to those around you. If you don't deal honestly with people who know you are a Christian, what will they think of God? Will they trust His honesty if you aren't a good example of honesty?

You are to show honesty in all financial dealings. Honesty in filing taxes. Honesty in returning cash when the change you've been given is wrong. Honesty in how you pay people who work for you. Fairness and honesty are standards for how a Christian behaves.

Do you consider yourself an honest person?
Would God consider you to be honest? Is there any
area of honesty and fairness that you struggle with?

Good Fruit, Bad Fruit

"A tree is identified by its fruit. If a tree is good, its fruit
will be good. If a tree is bad, its fruit will be bad."
MATTHEW 12:33

What you are on the inside will eventually show on the outside. Two verses after this one Jesus explained that whatever kind of person you are on the inside will eventually show on the outside. It becomes a "what you see is what you get" kind of thing.

If you're a "good tree" your fruit will be good, tasty and healthy. If you're a "bad tree" your fruit will be withered and small. It won't be good to eat. That tree and its fruit will be useless.

What does this have to do with you? If you're healthy in your heart, then the "fruit" from your life will be good. Your life will be an honest reflection of God's love and kindness. Those godly qualities will come straight from your heart; an honest display of what your heart feels.

However, if your heart isn't healthy, anger, selfishness, judgment and other ugly things will show in your life. These are the result of the sin you allow to settle in your heart that keeps out the godly qualities which would make your fruit good.

It's your choice … what do you want in your heart?

What is the fruit from your heart? Are
you generally loving and kind (good fruit)
or selfish and critical (bad fruit)?

Your Conscience

Cling to your faith in Christ, and keep your conscience clear.
For some people have deliberately violated their consciences;
as a result, their faith has been shipwrecked.

1 TIMOTHY 1:19

A clear conscience helps you sleep well at night. There're no regrets waking you to think through because of bad behavior or bad choices. How do you keep your conscience clear? This verse tells you – cling to your faith in Jesus. Stick as close to Him as you can. God, in His wonderful grace, promised the Holy Spirit to live in your heart. If you hold on to Him as tightly as you can, He will teach you and guide your decisions and choices. He will convict you when your behavior is not good.

If you ignore when your conscience tells you that your behavior is not good, then you are deliberately choosing to disobey God. What happens then? This verse tells you – your faith is shipwrecked ... damaged. The longer you ignore your conscience, the less you care about what's happening and whether or not you are obeying God.

Cling to Jesus. Make knowing Him and understanding how to be more like Him your focus. Be intentional in reading your Bible. Be constant in prayer. Don't let Satan weasel his way into your thoughts so he can encourage you to ignore your conscience.

When has your conscience challenged your behavior? Did you pay attention? How do you feel when your conscience isn't clear?

Real Love

If I gave everything I have to the poor and even
sacrificed my body, I could boast about it; but if
I didn't love others, I would have gained nothing.
1 CORINTHIANS 13:3

What's your motivation? Why do you donate money to charities? Do
you feel that giving means you are obeying God's command to love
others? In your mind, does how much you give indicate how "good"
you are? Are you measuring yourself by what you give or even what
you do for others?

Giving money to people who need help and giving your time to help
others are good things. Those who receive help surely benefit from your
kindness. However, what you're doing does not mean that you actually
love others, which is what God says you should do. There could be
many reasons for your generosity without any of them being love.

Bragging about your generosity or kindness is a pretty obvious in-
dication of whether or not your giving or serving came from love or
pride. If you want others to know what a great person you are then
your motivation is wrong.

Real love motivates you to give and serve whether anyone else
knows or not. In fact, it's better if no one knows. Love flows
from your heart because God loves you deeply and sacrificially. Love begets love.

What's your motivation for giving to others? Have
you ever given a totally anonymous gift? How do
you feel when someone finds out about your gift?

Peace in Your Life

Those who love Your instructions have
great peace and do not stumble.
PSALM 119:165

Who doesn't want peace in her life? It doesn't come easily though and
it's difficult to maintain. Our world is chaotic and some parts of your
life may feel uncertain. Lack of peace can affect your sleep and your
health and your spiritual life.

How can you get peace in your life? Following God's instructions
as He gave them in the Bible is the only way. God's commands are
not meant to make you feel confined or burdened. His instructions are
a gift from His heart of grace because they guide you in how to live
in a way that keeps you at peace with other people and in obedience
to Him. Obeying His instructions gives you a better way of life. The
peace comes from the assurance that God is in control and His power
is stronger than anything else in the world.

Learning to love God's instructions requires your heart submitting
to Him and allowing Him to have control of your life. This won't happen
if you don't trust that His plan for your life is better than anything you
can imagine on your own. Believe that God's love is deeper, wider and
higher than anything you can comprehend.

Does following God's instructions come easy or is it a
struggle? Are there certain areas of His instructions that
are more difficult to obey than others for you?

No Arrogance

Because of the privilege and authority God has given me,
I give each of you this warning: Don't think you are better
than you really are. Be honest in your evaluation of yourselves,
measuring yourselves by the faith God has given us.
ROMANS 12:3

Do you feel like you're pretty hot stuff? Are you proud of yourself for your looks, intellect or talents? Guess what? You didn't have anything to do with those things. They are God's gift of grace to you.

The danger of pride is that you begin to think you're better than other people. You lift yourself up and in the process push others down. There's no love in that except for yourself. If you're honest with yourself you know that all you have and all you are is only because of God. He deserves all the credit.

Measure yourself by the faith that you have … do you love God? Do you trust Him with your life? Are you serious about obeying Him and honoring Him? This is what matters in life. Find your success in how serious you are about knowing and loving God. Don't worry about how you measure up to others with things that don't really matter. Be concerned only with loving God and letting His love flow through your words and actions to all those around you.

Is pride a struggle for you? How do you
push it aside when it raises its ugly head?

Peace in Trouble

Around midnight Paul and Silas were
praying and singing hymns to God,
and the other prisoners were listening.
ACTS 16:25

Paul and Silas were beaten, thrown in prison and their feet bound in stocks. Their crime was that they commanded a demon to come out of a young girl. Paul and Silas devoted their lives to teaching about God. Now they were in prison. What would your response be to that? Some people may have been resentful or angry. But Paul and Silas ... sang hymns of praise to God. They sat there in the prison with their feet bound in stocks and sang praise. Of course the other prisoners listened. Even the jailer listened. They were witnessing to their faith in God, even in a bad situation.

How do you respond to painful situations? Do you trust God's plan so that, regardless of what comes into your life, you can praise Him? Paul and Silas were convinced that God was in control and that His grace would give them the strength to get through their bad situation.

Do you have that same strength of conviction? Do you trust God's plan? Does that give you peace when you're in a time of trouble? God's grace will protect you no matter what. So you can be at peace.

When was a time you were in a frightening
or painful situation? What was your response?
Were you able to praise God as Paul and Silas did?

Looking Ahead

I have not achieved it, but I focus on this one thing:
Forgetting the past and looking forward to what lies ahead,
I press on to reach the end of the race and receive the heavenly
prize for which God, through Christ Jesus, is calling us.
PHILIPPIANS 3:13-14

God forgave your sins and gave you salvation by His grace. This is not because of anything you did. As a new Christian you were a baby in your faith. You had lived the life that you turned away from a lot longer than your new-found life of faith. So, it can be a challenge to forget your past or to forgive yourself for your past and look to the future. God in His grace forgives you and moves you forward toward the prize He promised you – your heavenly reward.

Paul understood that the Christian life is a journey. He knew he had a lot to learn about knowing God and living for Him. Do you understand that you don't just accept Christ then become immediately mature in your faith? You must keep your focus looking forward to the life you're growing into. Keep learning and growing in your faith. Satan will try to trip you up by reminding you of past failures and trying to make you believe that God could never forgive you. Don't look back. Look forward. Trust God's grace.

Is it hard for you to forgive yourself for past sins?
How do you keep your focus looking forward?

A Gentle Whisper

The LORD passed by, and a mighty windstorm hit the mountain.
It was such a terrible blast that the rocks were torn loose,
but the LORD was not in the wind. After the wind there
was an earthquake, but the LORD was not in the earthquake.
And after the earthquake there was a fire, but the LORD was not in
the fire. And after the fire there was the sound of a gentle whisper.

1 KINGS 19:11-12

How do you see God? Is He like an ultra-muscular, white-haired being whose powerful voice bounces off the mountains? Does He frighten you? Maybe that's what Elijah thought, too. He was a discouraged prophet who had been challenged and persecuted. He was tired. He felt very alone. God told him to stand on the mountain and listen for His voice. Elijah did and a mighty windstorm shook rocks loose from the mountain. That wasn't God's voice. Then there was a powerful earthquake. That wasn't God either. Then a fire, but God wasn't in the fire. Finally Elijah heard a gentle whisper. There. That was God's voice.

Because of His grace God speaks to you in the way that you will hear Him. Sometimes it may be in a mighty storm, earthquake or fire – powerful and booming. Sometimes He speaks in a gentle whisper that comforts your frightened, aching heart.

Your God is a mighty, powerful being who defends you and challenges you and insists on your obedience. He is also a gentle, loving Father who holds you close and comforts you through hard times. Thank God for both sides of His character.

How do you see God? Have you seen
both sides of His character? When?

Fully Equipped

"Now go, for I am sending you to Pharaoh.
You must lead My people Israel out of Egypt."
EXODUS 3:10

God gave Moses a job. God wanted His people freed from slavery in Egypt and Moses was the one to lead them to freedom. Moses had already had quite a life – from the time he was an infant God had protected and led him.

It was obvious Moses was someone special to God. But what was Moses' reaction to God's instructions? "I can't do it." He actually said that to Almighty God! "I can't do it. Send someone else."

What Moses didn't understand is that when God gives you a job to do He makes sure you're equipped to do it. Maybe Moses had never been a good speaker, but when he needed to be, God made sure the words flowed.

Has God given you a job to do? Do you question whether you have the skills or talent to accomplish it? Have you argued with God about it? Trust His heart of grace. He won't set you up to fail. If He asked you to do something, He will make sure you have what you need to do it. You may need to step out in faith – start moving before you know you have the skill. Trust Him. He won't fail you.

Have you ever questioned God's instructions? Did you obey Him and do what He wanted? How did it turn out?

By His Grace

They said, "Come, let's build a great city for ourselves with
a tower that reaches into the sky. This will make us famous
and keep us from being scattered all over the world."
GENESIS 11:4

Some crisis or problem comes up in your life and you know you should pray about it, but it's not all that big so you say, "No worries, God. I've got this I can handle it."

The men building this fantastically tall tower in Babel didn't think they needed God either. They wanted their accomplishment to show the world how intelligent and capable they were ... never mind God!

That didn't set well with God. He destroyed their tower. He made them all start speaking different languages so they couldn't even work together anymore.

God is very patient. He has a long fuse before He gets angry. But look, He made everything there is by His grace. He saved you by His grace. He gives you everything you need by His grace. You are nothing without His grace. You can do nothing apart from His grace. So, pushing Him aside thinking you can handle things without Him is not a good idea. Call to Him for help and guidance whatever you face in life. Give thanks to Him for all you can do and all you can be. It's all by His hand.

Are you sometimes guilty of thinking you can handle
some things on your own? How does that turn out for you?

One Hope

We were crushed and overwhelmed beyond our ability to endure,
and we thought we would never live through it. In fact,
we expected to die. But as a result, we stopped relying on
ourselves and learned to rely only on God, who raises the dead.
2 CORINTHIANS 1:8-9

Paul knew what persecution was. He had surely handed plenty of it out before he knew Jesus and now, as Christ's servant, he was the victim of it. In this current attack he and his friends thought they were actually going to die as a result of the persecution. Believing you're going to die must be a helpless feeling. There was no one who could help Paul, no one except God. So, in this terrible place Paul was in, thinking he would die, no help in sight, he found all he needed in God.

Hopefully you've never felt you were facing death because of your faith, but perhaps you have experienced being in a difficult place where there didn't seem to be any help on the horizon. Did you find that you could rely on God? Did He, in loving grace, meet you in your need? Did He give you the strength to get through your trial? Hopefully you learned that even when things seem hopeless; even when you can see no way through the trial, God's strength, power and wisdom will see you through. When you have nothing but God you'll realize He is all you need.

How has God's strength, power and
wisdom seen you through challenges?

So You Understand

Jesus called out to them, "Come, follow Me,
and I will show you how to fish for people!"
MATTHEW 4:19

If you don't know anything about sports and have no interest in sports, then using any example from the sports world to explain a point would be rather useless, right? For an object, lesson or example to make sense it must be relevant to your understanding. A good teacher makes sure you can understand what she is trying to teach you. Do you know who the master of relevant illustrations is? Jesus.

Jesus was careful to meet people where they were. So, when He started calling His disciples and He called some fishermen to follow Him, He gave the invitation in a way they would understand. He said, "Follow Me and I'll show you how to fish for people."

Because Jesus wants you to understand His love and His instructions, He will also communicate in ways that make sense to you. In His grace He will find a way to call you or tell you what He wants you to do. He will speak in a way that relates to your life so it helps you understand.

Jesus isn't about confusion, so just listen, pay attention, and you will hear His voice.

Have you found it to be true that Jesus speaks in ways that
make sense to you? How does He communicate with you?

Showing Grace to Others

"And since I, your Lord and Teacher, have washed your feet,
you ought to wash each other's feet. I have given you
an example to follow. Do as I have done to you."
JOHN 13:14-15

Jesus is an excellent example of how to show grace to others … serve them. Look at what He did; He washed His disciples' feet. Look, He knew who He was but that didn't stop Him. The Messiah, the Son of God knelt down and washed His followers' dirty feet. We don't have a record of any of them washing His feet. After all, foot washing was a demeaning job reserved for the lowest of the low.

Jesus wanted His guys to see that serving others isn't always attractive. It can mean doing things that aren't fun. Come on, feet? You have to get out of your own high opinion of yourself to show grace. If you get caught up in how important you think you are or feel that you are above certain kinds of service, then you miss opportunities to show grace to others.

Jesus didn't just tell His followers how to serve – He showed them. He gave an example to them and to you. Show others you value them by being willing to serve, even in ways that could make you feel lowly.

How has someone served you in a way that surprised you? Have you willingly served another in a way that you could have considered "below" your status?

Your God Is so Big

"I am the LORD, the God of all the peoples
of the world. Is anything too hard for Me?"
JEREMIAH 32:27

There's a little song with motions that children learn: "My God is so big, so strong and so mighty. There's NOTHING my God cannot do." What a great thing to teach children so they grow up knowing God is powerful and mighty. Children willingly believe God can do anything because nothing and no one can stop Him. Children have such a simple faith. As people grow up they can get cynical and while they believe in God's power, it may not be their first thought in a crisis. Adults sometimes believe they can handle some of life's issues without God's help. Or perhaps they feel it takes God too long to act so they don't turn immediately to Him.

Where are you on that spectrum? Do you right away go to God for help, regardless of how big or small your trouble is? Or do you try to handle some things yourself because they seem so urgent?

God controls everything. God is more powerful, strong and wise than all. The children's song is correct, "There's NOTHING my God cannot do." Trust Him in your trials. Wait for His response. Then thank Him for His care. Thank Him for being God!

Be honest with yourself – where is your faith on the
"There's NOTHING my God cannot do" spectrum? Is your trust deep
and constant? Do you daily thank God for His protection and care?

August

White Hair Service

That is why we never give up. Though our bodies are dying,
our spirits are being renewed every day.

2 CORINTHIANS 4:16

No one gets out of this life alive … until Jesus comes back. Everyone is growing older. Whether you're on the younger end, midway or closer to the end of earthly life expectancy, there are changes in your life. Your body changes. Your attitudes change as you mature. And your service to God changes. He brings different opportunities for you.

There's a danger you may face, too – the feeling that as your hair grows white, there's less you can do for God. It's simply not true. Even if you can't physically do what you did 20 years ago, it's not true. Even if your responses are slower than 10 years ago, it's not true. God, in His grace, adjusts the work He has for you. But, He always provides some way you can serve. He will make ways for you to share the wisdom you've gained from years of walking with Him. You always have the privilege of being a prayer warrior for His work – the most important job in His Kingdom.

Pay attention when God resets your service. Serve Him gladly! Thank Him that your service is renewed every day.

Where are you in the aging process?
How have you seen your service opportunities
change? Do you still feel useful to God?
Are you paying attention to His resets?

Keep Your Eye on the Savior

You have allowed me to suffer much hardship, but You will restore me to life again and lift me up from the depths of the earth. You will restore me to even greater honor and comfort me once again.

PSALM 71:20-21

God's loving grace is most apparent when you are going through difficult times. Of course you see His grace when life is peaceful and good because of His love for you. But when life is hard, when you're suffering, and you sense His presence surrounding you, holding you up and loving you, His grace becomes so very real.

What difficulties are you struggling with in your life? Have things happened that were unexpected? Did you feel blindsided by someone? Are you struggling with health problems? Are you struggling financially? Hardships come in many different forms. Some things that are a struggle for you may not be for someone else. Struggle is personal and unique as is God's rescue and restoration. Keep your focus on Him in your hard times so you can see how He's lifting you up.

God's grace meets you where you are in your struggles and lifts you from them. He knows how to comfort you in ways that will specifically encourage you and help you out of the pit of suffering you're in.

Thank God for His grace in restoring you from your hardships. Thank Him for His loving care.

Being in a place of hardship is painful.
Have you experienced it? How did God lift you
from it? How is He still working in your heart?

Talk with God

I am praying to You because I know You will answer,
O God. Bend down and listen as I pray.
PSALM 17:6

There is a big difference between talking *about* God and talking *with* God. As a child of God you have the incredible privilege of actually talking with your Father, God. This privilege is a gift of His grace to you.

Talking about God could actually be an act of pride. Talking about Him like you're best buddies sounds like bragging that you have the ear of God. Then, telling someone that you will pray for them is an affirmation that you do actually pray. Of course, it is meant to be a comfort to your friend but if you don't actually speak the prayer on your friend's behalf … what good is your promise to her?

Don't just talk about your relationship with God. Talk with Him about your life. Tell Him your hopes and dreams, ask His help for the things you struggle with, intercede on behalf of your loved ones and friends. Spend prayer time praising God, appreciating all He does for you and who He is.

Prayer is an unbelievable privilege and opportunity. Don't take it lightly. Trust God to hear and respond. He promises He will.

How important is prayer in your life?
Do you take advantage of this privilege?
Do you trust God to answer?

Time Out

The LORD ordered the fish to spit Jonah out onto the beach.
JONAH 2:10

You probably know Jonah's story by now. God gave him a job but Jonah didn't want to do it. He didn't want God to save the people of Nineveh. Of course, Jonah ended up in the belly of a big fish. That was God's "time out" for him. For three days Jonah thought about his disobedience and decided that he wasn't God but that God is God. Smart guy. Then, instead of being digested by the big fish, he was spit out onto the beach and God gave him a second chance to obey His command. That's grace.

Has God ever given you a time out? A chance to rethink something He wants you to do? Did you use that time to realize that God is God and you aren't? Did you experience God's grace of second chances? Obedience doesn't always come easily. You may think you have better ideas that the God who made you, but God, in His grace, doesn't make you fish food … He gives you time to think and realize His way is best.

Grace gives a second chance. Gratitude says, "Thanks" as it's on its way to obey.

Have you had the struggle of "your way or God's way?" Has God ever given you a time out to think things through? How did you respond?

A Little Bit of Judas

Judas came straight to Jesus. "Greetings, Rabbi!" he exclaimed and gave Him the kiss. Jesus said, "My friend, go ahead and do what you have come for." Then the others grabbed Jesus and arrested Him.
MATTHEW 26:49-50

How could Judas do it? He had spent the same 3 ½ years with Jesus that the other eleven disciples had. He saw Jesus do miracles. He heard Him teach. He knew that Jesus said He was the Messiah. How could Judas betray Him?

Heart issues. In Judas's heart, he didn't believe any of what he heard Jesus teach. He was a dishonest man who stole from the treasury. He didn't buy the truth that Jesus was going to die. He couldn't grasp that Jesus was God's Son, sent to save mankind through His own death. It's amazing that Judas walked side by side with Jesus and witnessed all that Jesus said and did but he still didn't believe.

It's easy to criticize Judas; but be careful. Look at your own heart. Do you slide over some of Jesus' teachings because you don't want to obey them? Are you ignoring things you know you should be doing because they aren't attractive or they look too hard? Is there a little bit of Judas in your heart?

If so, confess it. Admit it. Ask God's forgiveness. In His amazing grace, He will forgive you and strengthen your faith.

Is there something from God's Word that you don't want to obey? Is there something you're trying to hide from Him? Will you confess it and ask Him to strengthen your heart?

Restoration Grace

Suddenly, Jesus' words flashed through Peter's mind:
"Before the rooster crows twice, you will deny three times
that you even know Me." And he broke down and wept.
MARK 14:72

Oh Peter. So many people identify with this passionate, impetuous follower of Jesus. We know him as the disciple who leaped into the water, then sank. He's the one who said he would never deny Jesus. But did – three times in one night. Peter leaped into life and faith and sometimes his leap led to bumps in the road but Jesus saw something in Peter's heart that made grace smooth over the bumps.

In Jesus' darkest hour Peter denied that he knew Him. When Jesus looked at him, Peter must have wanted to cry. He must have been disappointed in himself because he felt like he failed Jesus big time. But, because of grace, God wasn't finished with Peter because Peter's heart believed that Jesus was the Messiah. He believed the purpose behind Jesus coming to earth.

So, grace restored Peter to active duty and he went on to do some amazing things for God. He preached about Jesus. He healed people. He was the first to take God's message outside the Jewish people.

God's grace will restore you from failure. God's grace will reappoint you to ministry. God's grace will always make you useful.

Have you ever felt that you failed Jesus? Why?
How did you feel about yourself? How did God restore you?

AUG

7

Recipient of Grace

Holding her hand, He said to her *"Talitha koum,"*
which means "Little girl, get up!" And the girl, who
was twelve years old, immediately stood up and walked
around! They were overwhelmed and totally amazed.

MARK 5:41-42

Don't you wonder how Jairus's daughter felt when she was told the story of how Jesus brought her back to life? Did she follow Jesus for the rest of her second-chance life? Did she feel that God must have some special plan for her because He gave her a second go around? She was a blessed young girl, wasn't she?

Wait … so are you. God has given you a second chance at life, too. He saved you from eternal death by His grace. You could ask yourself those same questions that you might ask Jairus's daughter. Are you following Jesus for the rest of your life? Do you feel that God must have some special plan for you? He does, you know.

God's grace saved you because He loves you. But He didn't save you then walk away. He wants your faith in Him to grow strong. You are part of His family now and that means He has jobs for you to do. You have an inheritance from your Father and everything you do for Him here is investing in that inheritance. So, don't take your "second chance at life" lightly. It's a gift and a blessing!

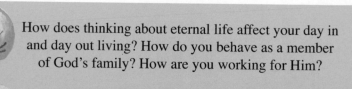

How does thinking about eternal life affect your day in and day out living? How do you behave as a member of God's family? How are you working for Him?

The Grace of Proof

"I won't believe it unless I see the nail wounds in His hands,
put my fingers into them, and place my hand into the wound
in His side." He said to Thomas, "Put your finger here,
and look at My hands. Put your hand into the wound
in My side. Don't be faithless any longer. Believe!"
JOHN 20:25, 27

Thomas wouldn't believe his friends' stories until he saw for himself that Jesus was alive. He wanted to see the wounds in Jesus' body … the body he had seen die. Then he would believe. Maybe he should have believed the other disciples. After all, they said the risen Lord had appeared to them. Just because Thomas wasn't there that day, did Jesus have to make another appearance?

He did. He cared enough about Thomas to come back and let Thomas actually see Him. He didn't have to – after all, Thomas was just one man. But He did because every person is important to Jesus.

You're warned against testing God by asking Him to prove Himself to you. But, there may be times when God, in His kind grace, gives you proof that He is paying attention to what you're dealing with. He shows you that He is present. He does that because He loves you. You matter to Him so, whether it's a sudden rainbow, a gentle breeze, words of a song … whatever He uses, He will make you aware that He's alive. He's with you. He's paying attention.

Perhaps there has been a time when God gave you a special awareness of His presence. How did He do it? How did it change your outlook?

The Hardest of Hearts

When Jesus came by, He looked up at Zacchaeus
and called him by name."Zacchaeus!" He said. "Quick,
come down! I must be a guest in your home today."
LUKE 19:5

If Jesus was going to give personal, unexpected attention to some-one, would you expect it to be a hated tax collector? Someone who didn't know Him? A man who cheated people out of their money?

That's exactly who Jesus singled out one day. Crowds of people lined the streets of Jericho because they heard Jesus was coming. Zac-chaeus, a hated tax collector who cheated people, was curious about Jesus. But he was a short man and couldn't see over the crowd who lined the streets. So, he climbed up in a tree and leaned out over a branch to see Jesus. As Jesus passed by that tree, He stopped. The people on the street must have filled with anticipation that He might do a miracle or speak to one of them. To their amazement He spoke to the tax collector! Not only did He speak to Zacchaeus, He wanted to go to the tax collector's house! As a result, Zacchaeus's heart was changed. He gave money back to people he had cheated. He gave back even more than he had taken.

What do you learn from this? God's grace reaches to the hard-est of hearts. No one is beyond His reach.

Have you ever thought someone was
beyond the reach of God's grace? Did you pray for
that person? What has happened in that person's life?

No Room for Pride

"I tell you, this sinner, not the Pharisee, returned home justified before God. For those who exalt themselves will be humbled, and those who humble themselves will be exalted."

LUKE 18:14

Jesus told the story of two men who prayed to God. One was a Pharisee, a religious leader. The Pharisee prayed, "Oh God, I'm so glad I'm not like other people! I'm not a sinner like all of them." He looked over at the tax collector and said, "I'm so glad I'm not like him!" The Pharisee seemed to actually be saying that God was lucky to have him as a follower and that he didn't really need God at all.

Meanwhile the tax collector prayed with his eyes cast down. He beat his chest in sorrow as he begged God, "I am a sinner. O God, please be merciful to me." His sorrow and repentance was real.

Why did Jesus tell this story? He was talking to a man who was arrogant and self-impressed. Jesus wanted the man to understand which man, the Pharisee or the tax collector found favor with God.

Which one do you think it was? Of course, it was the tax collector. Pride and arrogance have no place in God's family because a proud person believes she doesn't need God – she is more important than God and doesn't need His grace.

Pride is the enemy of a life of faith.
How does pride affect your faith walk?

Grace Instead of Revenge

But don't be upset, and don't be angry with yourselves
for selling me to this place. It was God who sent
me here ahead of you to preserve your lives.
GENESIS 45:5

If you could justify anyone wanting to get revenge on his brothers for their bad behavior, it would be Joseph. After all, they let their jealousy rule their hearts and they sold their own brother into slavery, lied to their dad and told him Joseph was killed by an animal. Goodness; they sold their brother and lied to their dad about his favorite son! Amazing. You probably know the story – Joseph went from being the favorite son (with the coat of many colors) to slavery to prison to being the second highest ruler in Egypt!

So when his brothers had to ask him to sell them food, Joseph could have just had them sent to prison or even killed. But, he didn't. Joseph understood that God was in charge of his life and that God's plan often involved hardship. He was willing to endure that for the greater good.

When someone hurts you and you have the chance to get even, do you take it or do you show grace and forgive as Joseph did? It's not easy. In fact, it takes submission to God's plan and an understanding that His plan is bigger than you could ever expect.

When have you had the chance to get
revenge but showed grace instead? Why did
you choose grace? How did you feel after that?

Unexpected Source

AUG
12

Soon Pharaoh's daughter came down to bathe in the river,
and her attendants walked along the riverbank. When the
princess saw the basket among the reeds, she sent her maid
to get it for her. When the princess opened it, she saw the
baby. The little boy was crying, and she felt sorry for him.
"This must be one of the Hebrew children," she said.
EXODUS 2:5-6

From the first days of his life, Moses knew God's grace. Infant Moses
should have been killed like all the other Hebrew baby boys. But, by
God's grace, he was saved through the courage of his mother. Then,
God used a princess who wasn't a believer to save Moses again.
God, in His grace, uses anyone He wants. The princess did not know
she was being directed by God and used by Him to save a baby who
would grow up to save God's people from slavery.

God's direction and protection in your life can come from anywhere.
Of course, He may speak through Scripture, through a sermon, through
a song or through a friend. He may even speak directly into your heart.
However, He may also guide or protect you through something or
someone totally unexpected. All of creation is under Him so God can
use whatever He wants and whatever will clearly connect with you.
Pay attention and when you sense Him speaking from an unexpected
place, ask Him to affirm that it's Him. Then thank Him for speaking.

Has God spoken, directed or protected you
from an unexpected direction? What was it?

Jesus Cares

The young man who had died was a widow's only son,
and a large crowd from the village was with her. When the
Lord saw her, His heart overflowed with compassion. "Don't cry!"
He said. Then He walked over to the coffin and touched it,
and the bearers stopped. "Young man," He said, "I tell you, get up."

LUKE 7:12-14

Jesus stopped a funeral procession. The young man who had died was the only son of a widow. Of course the woman was heartbroken at losing her son. No doubt she was weeping and her friends were trying to comfort her.

What was Jesus' response to her pain? His compassion and grace flowed freely. He stopped the procession and told the young man to, "Get up." He did! Jesus gave the grieving widow her son back. You see, Jesus' compassionate heart cared about that single woman. It mattered to Him that she was grieving her son. So, in His grace, He gave her back her boy. His grace-filled, compassionate act also proclaimed His power and love to everyone in that procession.

Jesus cares about your pain. It doesn't matter if your pain is because of a natural pattern of life such as death. He cares. Will He raise your loved one back to life? No. He doesn't do that anymore because you have the Holy Spirit living in your heart to comfort your grief. You aren't alone in your pain. You're never alone.

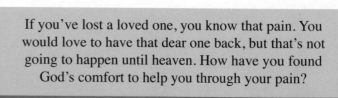

If you've lost a loved one, you know that pain. You would love to have that dear one back, but that's not going to happen until heaven. How have you found God's comfort to help you through your pain?

Humility

You must have the same attitude that Christ Jesus had.
Though He was God, He did not think of equality with God as
something to cling to. Instead, He gave up His divine privileges;
He took the humble position of a slave and was born as a human
being. When He appeared in human form, He humbled Himself
in obedience to God and died a criminal's death on a cross.
PHILIPPIANS 2:5-8

"You must have the same attitude that Jesus had." That's not a big order, is it? Love is certainly the foundation of His attitude. His love is clothed in humility. Jesus didn't cling to His "Godness" to keep from coming to live on earth as a man. He didn't pull a "God card" to keep from suffering and dying. He humbly, willingly gave up His heavenly position and agreed to obey God in suffering and dying for your sins. There was complete humility in His grace.

Humility doesn't come easily, does it? Your natural sin nature fights against it. It whispers in your ear that "you deserve recognition" … "you should get credit" … "you can do it better than someone else." Jesus is your example of humility and if anyone could say they deserve recognition or could do things better, it would be Him. He didn't do that though. He did the God-ordained work before Him and He did it gladly because of His great love for mankind.

Putting aside pride is not easy. Only with God's strength can you develop the Christ-like attitude of humility.

Complete humility is a struggle for everyone.
Where does pride attack your heart? How do you push it away?

The End Is Near

The end of the world is coming soon. Therefore,
be earnest and disciplined in your prayers.
1 PETER 4:7

This world, this life, won't last forever. God makes that clear. In His grace, He warns you to pay attention to that fact. Don't get lazy in your faith walk. Don't get slothful in your prayer life. You don't know when the end is coming – either your own life's end or the end of this world. So, be disciplined. What are you supposed to pray for in your discipline? The verses before verse 7 point out the friends you had before you accepted Christ may give you a hard time about your faith. Pray for them because this life will end and you don't want them to face eternity without Jesus.

Pray for yourself too, that the taunts you face for your faith in God will not weaken your resolve and pull you away from Him. Pray for opportunities to share your faith with your friends and family. Pray for compassion and kindness in your behavior so that your life with God will be appealing to those who are watching.

God has warned you – this life doesn't go on forever so make each day count!

How disciplined are you? Is your prayer life
healthy and strong? What needs to improve?

The Gift of Life

The wages of sin is death, but the free gift of God
is eternal life through Christ Jesus our Lord.
ROMANS 6:23

When you're applying for a job one important consideration is how much the job pays. You need to earn enough to pay for your life: rent, food and whatever you need.

Your way of life earns a wage too. The life you had before accepting Christ earned a simple wage: death forever, a separation from God. It's forever, it cannot be changed. Now maybe that doesn't seem fair since that life is what you were born with and you think you can't help it. However, you can change it – by accepting Jesus as your Savior. You can choose to turn away from your natural, sinful life. You have the option and freedom to do that. When you do, your wage increases to life: forever life with God. This change is free. It's God's gift to you for the choice you made.

What is your response to this free gift? It should be a heart overflowing with gratitude for the love and generosity God shows you through His salvation and the promise of eternal life with Him. Don't take this wage change lightly. It changes everything for you. Everything.

How often do you even think about what it cost God to
give you the free gift of salvation? How often do you sincerely
thank Him for it? Does gratitude overflow from your heart?

Just Love

Most important of all, continue to show deep love for each other,
for love covers a multitude of sins.

1 PETER 4:8

Love one another. It shouldn't be that hard but it sure is sometimes. Love and grace are woven together. You can't do the one without the other. Love overpowers pride and selfishness. Love has open eyes and an open heart.

Just look at the benefit of loving – little annoyances from treatment that might not even be intentional are forgiven without a word. Love covers it. Friends and family are given the benefit of the doubt. Love makes it all better. People who are different from you in culture, beliefs, religion and behavior become a little less scary because love leads the way. Those who have hurt you, wounded so deeply it will take a long time to heal are forgiven, whether they ask for it or not. Love makes the way. Love cheers for the winners even if you wanted so badly to win yourself. Love accepts defeat. Love slips into the background so someone else can shine. Love binds together instead of breaking apart. Love unites. Love celebrates. Love is filled with grace. It is humble. Love is deep, strong, generous, powerful, life-changing and obedient. Love changes everything. Love one another. Just love.

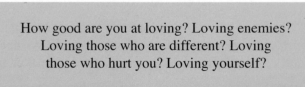

How good are you at loving? Loving enemies?
Loving those who are different? Loving
those who hurt you? Loving yourself?

Transformation

Don't copy the behavior and customs of this world,
but let God transform you into a new person by changing
the way you think. Then you will learn to know God's will
for you, which is good and pleasing and perfect.
ROMANS 12:2

Do you need a reason for your heart to burst with gratitude? Here it is; if you let Him, God will change you. He will change the way you think. The self-centered it's-all-about-me thoughts will go away. You will be able to look at life in a different way, concerned for others and how things you do and say or situations you are involved in affect them, not just you.

If you submit to Him, God will change your behavior so it doesn't copy or reflect any of the actions of those who do not know Him. You won't look like or be like those who do not have the Holy Spirit living in them.

Here's a reason for even deeper gratitude – God does the transforming. All you have to do is let Him. Submit to Him. Trust His plan for your life. Trust His work in your life. Trust the changes He makes in your heart as He transforms you to be more like Christ. Trust His will even when you don't understand exactly where it's taking you. Thank God for all His grace does for you.

How have you seen God transform your thoughts
and ideas? How has He revealed His will for you?

Double Blessings

*Cheerfully share your home with those
who need a meal or a place to stay.*
1 PETER 4:9

It's easy to speak words of grace, generosity and kindness. But speaking them without putting these behaviors into action is a waste of time. Just speaking words of obedience does not make obedience.

Showing grace, generosity and kindness to others should become a natural outgrowth of the grace you receive from the Lord. This verse in 1 Peter 4 follows one that warns that the end of the world is coming soon. Time is running out to tell others of Christ's love. It also follows one that instructs God's children to love others deeply, then, this verse tells you how to do that. Pay attention to those around you. Notice if someone needs a place to rest, short term or long term. Do you see someone who is hungry? Share your food. Do you notice someone who simply needs the comfort of sharing a meal with another person – a time of fellowship and conversation for someone who is lonely? Share what you have been given.

Remember that God has blessed you so that you can bless others. Receive the blessings of His grace and pass them on to others. You will be doubly blessed by sharing what you have.

Have you been blessed by someone's generosity?
When have you shared what you have with
others? Did you find joy in doing so?

Innocent Choices

All of us, like sheep, have strayed away.
We have left God's paths to follow our own.
Yet the LORD laid on Him the sins of us all.
ISAIAH 53:6

Sometimes sinning starts with wandering. Think of a sheep that's munching on grass and takes one or two steps away from the protection of the shepherd, then a few more steps and a few more until finally it is away from the flock unprotected and alone. It didn't intentionally leave the place where it was safe. However, its own appetite led it away from the path it should have stayed on.

Does that happen with you? One small choice leads to another and another until you find yourself in a place of disobedience to God's commands. It's not where you intended to go, yet in the depths of your heart, you knew you were wandering onto your own path and away from God's path.

Even though your wandering started innocently, it continued to take you farther away from God. Still, your loving God, in His grace and compassion, placed your sin on Jesus. He paid the price for even what began as unintentional disobedience. There is no accidental sin in God's eyes. Jesus paid for all of it. So, pay attention to your innocent choices and where they may lead you.

When have you made what appeared to be an innocent choice
that became the first step of wandering away from God?

The Gift of Wisdom

I love all who love me. Those who search will surely find me.
PROVERBS 8:17

Do you know who is speaking in this verse? What will you find if you search? Wisdom, which you know is God because God is wisdom. The thing is that God wants you to be wise.

With wisdom you will make good choices, you will see the big picture of how your individual decisions and actions play into all of life. In fact, you will see how they affect not just your life but those around you, too.

All of Proverbs 8 talks about the characteristics of wisdom – wholesome, good judgment, truth, understanding and something more valuable than gold or silver. Since it's so important, God promises that you can find wisdom if you honestly search for it. A prerequisite for finding it is loving God. His wisdom is a gift for those who love Him.

Submit your heart to God in love and ask Him to give you His wisdom. Incorporate His wisdom into your heart and life. Live by its guidelines and it will make your life with those around you kinder and more compassionate. God's wisdom is a gift of grace.

What wisdom has God given you since you accepted Jesus? How has wisdom made your life better?

A Heart to Honor God

Noah found favor with the LORD.
GENESIS 6:8

The people of the world had turned their backs on God. They no longer cared what He thought or how He wanted them to live. Every person was only concerned about self. Life had gotten ugly because of their self-centeredness and unkindness. Dishonesty ruled, cheating was normal. Immorality filled their hearts. People's hearts were totally and consistently evil, except for one man: Noah.

When God decided to wipe out all humanity and civilization and start over again, He saved Noah – the one man who sought to honor and obey Him. Was Noah perfect? Was he totally sinless? No, of course not, but God saw that Noah's heart wanted to obey Him and because of that, He used Noah and his family to restart the population of earth.

You see God looks past your immediate behavior. He looks at your heart to see if you actually desire to obey Him and honor Him. Then, even though you have sin and failure, His grace forgives and renews. He gives you new life, as He did Noah. He uses you to do His work as He did Noah. Make sure your heart is honestly seeking to obey and honor God.

The lesson from Noah is to be honest about where your heart is. Are you seriously seeking to honor and obey God? Do you need to confess your failures and ask God to cleanse your heart?

Loyalty and Honor

I have heard how you left your father and mother
and your own land to live here among complete strangers.
May the LORD, the God of Israel, under whose wings you have
come to take refuge, reward you fully for what you have done.

RUTH 2:11-12

Ruth left everything familiar to move to Judah with her mother-in-law after both of their husbands died. Ruth left her own family, culture, religion and friends to make sure Naomi got safely back to her own country. Then, once they were there, Ruth did manual labor in the fields of Boaz in order for her and Naomi to have food to survive.

Boaz, the owner of the field, saw Ruth's loyalty and honored her for it. In fact, he grew to love her so he married her and took care of her and Naomi.

Ruth began this journey as a woman who was loyal to her mother-in-law. She respected Naomi's faith in God but Ruth didn't know Him herself. Her desire to honor her mother-in-law and learn more about Naomi's faith changed the outcome of her life. God, in His grace, honored her and even though she had to go through some difficult times, in the end she was rewarded for seeking Him and honoring Naomi.

Your heart is so important. It's the seat of how you really feel and what you really believe. Guard your heart. Keep it focused on God.

Are you hiding secrets in your heart? God sees
to the depths of your heart, you know. What's
there that you might not want Him to see?

Grace Passed On

"Lord, when did we ever see You hungry and feed You?
Or thirsty and give You something to drink?
Or a stranger and show You hospitality?
Or naked and give You clothing? When did we
ever see You sick or in prison and visit You?"
And the King will say, "I tell you the truth,
when you did it to one of the least of these My
brothers and sisters, you were doing it to Me!"
MATTHEW 25:37-40

You're busy. There are dozens of things on your "to do" list and some of them involve a looming deadline that you truly do not want to miss.

Then a friend calls. She's in desperate straits, "Can you help?" It will take all day, maybe a couple of days. You look at your full calendar. You hear your friend's desperation and, you go. Praying as you do that God will honor your sacrificial service to your friend and help you fulfill those deadlines.

Will He? Maybe. Maybe not. But what He will do is fill your friend's heart with gratitude, building the bond between you even stronger. He will show your friend that your help comes from a heart of love and grace that He has given you.

Your sacrificial help is an example of His grace and love. And, more than likely, God will help you with that deadline, or soften the heart of those who are waiting for you to make it. Grace for grace.

Have you ever put aside your own agenda to help a friend and by that missed deadlines yourself? How did your friend respond to your help? How did it feel to help her? How did the deadline situation work out?

Grace and Peace

May God the Father and our Lord
Jesus Christ give you grace and peace.
GALATIANS 1:3

The Apostle Paul began most of his letters with "grace and peace." Interesting words. In this letter to the Galatians, he expands his greeting to call on God and Jesus to give the Galatians grace and peace. Paul knew that all grace and all peace begin with God and therefore as the Galatians received that grace, they could pass it on to others.

God's grace to you goes all the way back to creation. He made this beautiful world for you and filled it with nature and animals and people who He knew would bring you happiness. Then His grace had Jesus leave heaven and be born as a man, die for your sins and be raised back to life. His grace sent the Holy Spirit to live in your heart, guiding, blessing, challenging and comforting. God's grace is why you have life and all that you enjoy in this life. His grace provides peace.

Because you've received all these blessings from God's grace you can pass grace along to others. You do that by kindness, forgiveness, serving, loving and sharing. Extend grace and peace to those around you and by your example they will learn of God's grace and peace.

How do you extend grace and peace to others? Does that action come easily to you? Does God sometimes need to work in your heart and extend grace through you?

Walking in Darkness

Do not be afraid or discouraged,
for the LORD will personally go ahead of you.
He will be with you;
He will neither fail you nor abandon you.
DEUTERONOMY 31:8

The Israelites were ready to enter the Promised Land. They had wandered in the wilderness for 40 years because they didn't listen to God. Moses led them all those years but now, because of his own disobedience, he wasn't allowed to enter the land. He was handing the leadership over to Joshua and Moses had to stay behind.

This must have been a scary time for the people. They had been wandering for 40 years! They had seen God do amazing miracles to take care of them but they were unsure what the future held. Moses was the only leader they had known. Did they question the choice of Joshua to take over? Joshua must have been a bit anxious, too, about this big responsibility. But Moses encouraged Joshua and the people by reminding them that God would be with them every step of the way.

Do you feel you're stepping out into darkness sometimes? Are you afraid because you can't see the whole pathway of where you're going? That's what walking by faith means. Step by step, trusting God's grace to protect you and place your feet on solid ground. He will never abandon you. Never.

Have you ever felt a little abandoned by God because you couldn't see what the future held? Did God reassure you? How did you get through it? Are you certain of God's presence with you right now? Even if you can't see what tomorrow holds?

Grace and Kindness

The LORD said to Moses, "This is the land I promised
on oath to Abraham, Isaac, and Jacob when I said,
'I will give it to your descendants.' I have now allowed you
to see it with your own eyes, but you will not enter the land."
DEUTERONOMY 34:4

Moses was one of a kind. He led God's people out of slavery. God gave the Law to Moses. You read later in Deuteronomy 34 that God Himself buried Moses and that, "since then, no prophet has risen in Israel like Moses, whom the Lord knew face to face." Yet Moses, for all of his blessings, was not allowed to enter the Promised Land because he sinned.

Does God's punishment seem harsh after 40 years of the people complaining to Moses and all the problems they had? To his credit, Moses never complained about his punishment and he continued leading the people right up to the border of the Promised Land. Even in His punishment, God showed grace to Moses. He told Moses to climb up Mt. Nebo and He allowed Moses to see the land God was giving the people.

God's heart of grace is compassionate and kind. Even when He must punish your disobedience, He cares about your pain. He wants you to learn from your mistakes but remember, He sees your heart and if there is true repentance and humility in it, He just may "let you see the land" that your punishment is keeping you from entering.

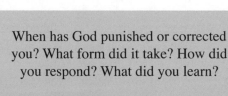

When has God punished or corrected you? What form did it take? How did you respond? What did you learn?

Not On Your Own

"I am the vine; you are the branches.
Those who remain in Me, and I in them,
will produce much fruit.
For apart from Me you can do nothing."
JOHN 15:5

There is a fine line between confidence and humility. The key to the difference between the two is at the end of this verse: Apart from God you can do nothing. It is only by God's grace that you can accomplish anything. He made you who you are. He gave you what you have. He guides and directs your steps.

You can be confident of the abilities God has given you and acknowledge that who you are is because of Him. But when pride takes control of your heart, your understanding of who God is and what He does for you are pushed aside. You no longer have any sense of gratitude. Why should you when you feel that all you have and all you are is by your own hand?

But when you realize that without God you are nothing you know that you wouldn't even have life if you didn't stay connected to Him for nurturing and feeding. Pride is pushed aside and humility at His greatness makes gratitude pour from your heart. There are no words gracious enough and loving enough to express your feelings.

What abilities and talents are you confident of?
Do you give God credit for these? Do you struggle
with pride at what you think you accomplish on your own?

Guided Steps

The LORD went ahead of them.
He guided them during the day with a pillar of cloud,
and He provided light at night with a pillar of fire.
This allowed them to travel by day or by night.
And the LORD did not remove the pillar of cloud
or pillar of fire from its place in front of the people.
EXODUS 13:21-22

The Israelites had been slaves in Egypt for years and years when Moses told them to pack up because they were leaving. God did amazing miracles to convince the Pharaoh to let them go. The last one cost every Egyptian family the life of their firstborn. Tough stuff.

So when Pharaoh told them to go and thousands of Israelites started marching, were they afraid? Were they nervous that he would change his mind and send his army after them? God knew their anxiety. He planned a way for them to know that He was with them every step of the way. The pillar of cloud in the day and pillar of fire at night proved to them in a tangible way that God's presence was with them.

Have you ever wished for a tangible presence or word from God? A cloud pillar or handwriting on the wall? You actually have something better. God, in His grace-filled love gave you the Holy Spirit. He lives in you as a constant reminder of God's presence. He directs your path as the pillar of cloud and fire did in the Exodus. Your God who loves you never leaves you.

How does God guide you? What assures
you of His presence with you?

Check Your Heart

The LORD said to Samuel, "Don't judge by his appearance
or height, for I have rejected him. The LORD doesn't see
things the way you see them. People judge by outward
appearance, but the LORD looks at the heart."
1 SAMUEL 16:7

Attractive people tend to get more respect than folks who are not as impressive. Is it right? No, but it happens. How do you judge people? Does a person who is fit, attractive and dressed nicely command your attention? Do you seek out a person like that but tend to feel that one who doesn't command attention is less worthy of your time?

God doesn't make judgments based on physical appearance. He said that to Samuel when the prophet was figuring out which of Jesse's sons God had chosen to be the next king. It wasn't the oldest or tallest or handsomest. It was the youngest – who had a heart submitted to God. None of the external stuff mattered to God, He only cared about the internal. David wasn't perfect. He made some big mistakes in his life but in his heart he cared about serving God, honoring Him and celebrating Him. God, in His grace, forgave David's failures because He saw his submitted heart.

How's your heart? Is it submitted to God? Do you care more about that than anything external … success, appearance, career? Your heart condition is the foundation of your submission to God. Check your heart.

No one really knows your heart condition except you and God.
Do a heart check right now. Is yours submitted to God? Do you trust
Him completely? Are you willing to obey whatever He directs?

Follow Your Leader

Thank God! He has made us His captives and continues to lead us along in Christ's triumphal procession. Now He uses us to spread the knowledge of Christ everywhere, like a sweet perfume.

2 CORINTHIANS 2:14

Some days are good and some not so good in the journey to live for God. Do you get discouraged? Do some days seem like you take one step forward and three steps back? Some days are like that. But the good news is that God, in His grace, doesn't leave you alone for this journey. See in this verse that He leads you along?

Follow your Leader. If you pay attention to God's commands and seek to obey them, pay attention to His Spirit guiding and convicting your heart, you will find that He helps you stay on the right path.

Thank God that you don't have to reach a certain point of accomplishment or growth for God to use you to bless others and share His love with them. He uses you in your journey. At whatever point you are in your spiritual growth, He gives you opportunities to share what you're learning about Him.

As you mature your understanding grows and He gives you more opportunities. Praise God that from the first day you know Him and every step of the way He has a purpose for you. You're part of the family!

How are you doing at following your Leader?
Who has been a sweet perfume of God's love
to you? What opportunities has God given
you to be a sweet perfume to others?

September

Take the Pressure Off

"There is only one thing worth being concerned about.
Mary has discovered it, and it will not be taken away from her."
LUKE 10:42

If you are a "Martha" who diligently works to make wonderful dinners and lovely tables and have everything perfect, maybe you have thought Martha's frustration with her sister was well-founded. After all, Jesus and His friends were going to enjoy Martha's meal. If Mary helped her then they could both sit and talk to Jesus. But, Jesus said that Mary had discovered the most important thing to be concerned about and that was time with Him.

It's quite possible that Jesus' comments to Martha were based on what He saw in each of their hearts. While Martha may very well have wanted to talk with Him, her first priority was her chores. Jesus came second. Perhaps Martha needed to cut back on the preparation and focus on time with Jesus – serve sandwiches instead of a five-course meal.

It's hard to change your expectations of yourself and do things in a different way but if doing so puts your focus more on Jesus, maybe you should. Jesus, in His grace would have been fine with a smaller dinner. He came to Mary and Martha's house for time with them, not the meal. Take the pressure off yourself, just be with Jesus.

Do you have to do things a certain way? What kind of pressure do you put on yourself? How does that impact your time with Jesus?

Free Indeed

"But for you who fear My name, the Sun of Righteousness will rise with healing in His wings. And you will go free, leaping with joy like calves let out to pasture."
MALACHI 4:2

Are you tired? Are you suffering? Has illness beaten you down so that movement is difficult and painful or perhaps even impossible? Has your freedom been impacted by the changes in your body? It's hard when you feel your body betrays you either because of aging or illness. You are forced to become dependent on other people to do things for you that you used to be able to do yourself. It's especially hard to give up activities you enjoy.

Your limitations are not forever, though! Healing is coming. Someday your time on this earth will come to an end and you will be carried to heaven, free of limitations and free of pain. You will be able to run, leap or dance – all in praise to God! Maybe you'll be of the ones who gets to experience Jesus coming back while you're still on this earth. How awesome that will be to be pulled heavenward even as you sense your physical limitations being left behind!

God's grace promises eternity. He promises healing. He promises a forever of healthy running, leaping, dancing, celebrating! Praise God!

Do you have physical limitations from illness or the normal things of aging? How are you handling that? Do you know someone who struggles with these things? How can you offer encouragement?

Getting to Know God

But they delight in the law of
the LORD, meditating on it day and night.
PSALM 1:2

When you're physically far away from a dearly loved one you miss him very much. Your heart aches for a reunion. You think about him each day, wondering what he's doing each moment. You wonder if he's thinking about you (and hope he is). You have a deep longing to be together again.

When you are reunited, you talk nonstop. You touch. You laugh and cry and your heart sings thankfulness at being together again.

Do you have that same kind of longing for closeness to God? Do you long for deep intimacy with Him? Do you think about Him day and night? Do you hunger for His Word?

If you want that intimacy, you have to make time to be with Him. The more time you spend with God the better you will get to know Him. Just as in your human relationships, quality time with God leads to intimacy with Him. A deep trust is built so conversation grows and vulnerability becomes possible. The more you know Him the more His thoughts become your thoughts. Your will becomes aligned with His. A part of God's grace is that He will come near to you when you seek Him. He loves you. He wants to be close.

Be honest with yourself … how much time
do you spend with God? Reading His Word? Praying?
Meditating? Do you hunger for a closer relationship with
Him? Are you willing to invest the time to have that?

Christ's Ambassadors

So we are Christ's ambassadors; God is
making His appeal through us. We speak for
Christ when we plead, "Come back to God!"
2 CORINTHIANS 5:20

What are your responsibilities as Christ's ambassador? It sounds like a pretty important job, right? That's because it is. An ambassador is sort of like a marketing representative who presents her client to potential customers. As Christ's ambassador you represent Him to others. You share what you want people to know about Him, making sure they know His wonderful qualities, His love for them and all He does for them. Of course you do this by telling about Jesus' death and resurrection and how His sacrifice paid the penalty for their sin. But, you also are an ambassador with your life. As important as your words are, your behavior and actions are what show that you mean those words and that your belief in them has changed your heart and life.

Being Christ's ambassador is a responsibility He has given you. He loves and trusts you because you have given Him your life. It's an honor and a privilege to share Christ, who means so much to you, with those around you. He changed your life. He will change the lives of those you care so much about.

How are you doing as an ambassador?
Do you share Christ with others?
Does your life show His presence? Do you
seek out people who don't yet know Him?

The Joy of Gate Keeping

A single day in Your courts is better than a thousand anywhere else!
I would rather be a gatekeeper in the house of my God
than live the good life in the homes of the wicked.
PSALM 84:10

If you really truly believe that what God offers you is the best there is, then this verse should speak volumes to you. The peace and fulfillment that life with God offers, even if you are only the guard at the door of heaven is better than living in the nicest home, eating the best food, surrounded by wealth but ensconced in evil.

Is that true for you? Does God mean that much to you? Do you crave Him or money?

If you feel that you're missing something by belonging to God, then you haven't let His grace grab your heart. You're holding back from Him.

Open your heart to the blessing of God's grace and peace controlling your thoughts, actions and attitudes. Ask Him to help you understand the joy of eternity with Him. These things begin with knowing the blessing of His salvation through Christ's sacrificial death for your sins. Once you grasp the magnitude of His love and grace and notice the daily blessings He pours out on you, gate keeping in heaven will be just fine for you. In fact, it will be your joy and your privilege!

Where are your priorities? What matters most to you? Do you crave time with God and growth in your spiritual life? Or do you crave money and success by the world's standards?

Let the Whole World Know

Give thanks to the LORD and proclaim His greatness.
Let the whole world know what He has done.
PSALM 105:1

When you receive a gift, you say "Thank you" or you send a note to express your gratitude. When someone does something nice you hopefully also express your pleasure. It's nice to verbally express your thanks with more than a smile or a high five – really speak your gratitude.

If you are willing to openly express gratitude to people who are kind to you, shouldn't you be even more openly grateful to God for His multitude of blessings? Speak your thanks to Him, but, not only to Him. Your gratitude to God can be a testimony to the world to His kindness, love and grace. Share your thanks with others. Give God credit for His blessings to you.

His grace is why you have what you do and why you are who you are. It's so easy to get "used to" God's blessings and take them for granted. Don't let that happen – let gratitude spill from your heart and lips! Make sure others hear that you believe God's blessings have given you what you have. Let your gratitude to God be your testimony to others. What an amazing way to share who God is and how He loves.

What are you grateful for? Does thanksgiving
explode from your heart so all know that
you credit God for all He does?

All In or All Out

"You cannot become My disciple
without giving up everything you own."
LUKE 14:33

Do you know the term, "Riding the fence?" It refers to someone who simply can't make up her mind on an issue. Perhaps she doesn't know how she feels about a situation because she is so influenced by the opinions of others that she can't make up her mind.

Or perhaps she is unwilling to disagree with others because she doesn't like conflict. Either way, she tries to stay right in the middle of two opinions and never takes a stand for her own beliefs.

Jesus says you can't do that when it comes to faith. You're either in or you're out. Trying to hold on to the life you have before you accept Jesus as Savior and still claim you've given your heart to Him just doesn't work. His grace paid for ALL your sin. He wants more than only a part of your heart. God's love is so deep and unconditional, why would you try to embrace it but hold back a part of your own heart and life?

Of course, it's a journey to get to the point of complete submission to God but He will see if your heart's desire is moving in that direction.

Are you holding some part of your life back from God?
Is there something you don't want to give up?
Why? How can you move toward letting it go?

The Gift of the Spirit

8

On the day of Pentecost there was a sound from heaven like the roaring of a mighty windstorm. Then, what looked like flames or tongues of fire appeared and settled on each of them. And everyone present was filled with the Holy Spirit and began speaking in other languages.

ACTS 2:1-4

Imagine being in that room. What emotions do you think were flowing? It had been seven weeks since Jesus had gone back to heaven. Were His followers still grieving that He had died? Were they still somewhat confused about what He came to do? Were they frightened for the future? They must have found comfort in being together. They probably gained strength from each other.

Imagine sitting in that room, doing the business of being Jesus' followers, filling the position left by Judas, figuring out how to move forward when suddenly the sound of a mighty wind fills the inside of the room! Then floating flames hover over each person's head. God's grace was fulfilling Jesus' promise – the Holy Spirit had arrived!

God did not leave His people alone when Jesus went back to heaven. His Spirit came and is still here, living in your heart. He is the physical evidence of God's love and care for you. He guides and directs you. He twinges your conscience when you are disobeying. He prays for you when you can't find the words to speak. He is God's loving grace living in you.

In what ways are you aware of the Holy Spirit's presence in your life? How does He guide or direct you? Have you thanked God for His gift of grace: the Holy Spirit?

Helping Others

They sold their property and possessions and shared the money with those in need. They worshiped together at the Temple each day, met in homes for the Lord's Supper, and shared their meals with great joy and generosity – all the while praising God and enjoying the goodwill of all the people. And each day the Lord added to their fellowship those who were being saved.

ACTS 2:45-47

There are people around the world who have so very little to live on. Perhaps you even wonder sometimes how a loving God could so richly bless some parts of this world and leave others with so little. These verses might be a part of the answer to that concern.

God gave His followers the Holy Spirit after Jesus returned to heaven. The Spirit gave them the power and authority to do miracles. They continued God's work that Jesus started. But what's most amazing (and convicting) is how the believers took care of each other. Remember Jesus told them over and over to love one another as He loved them. Love one another as you love yourselves. Love one another sacrificially. Love. Love. Love. They sold their stuff to have money to help one another. They shared meals so no one went hungry. They looked out for one another. And, they did it with joy. They gave generously, holding nothing back, simply loving one another.

Perhaps that's what God wants believers to do today to care for those around the world who have so little. Love. Just love.

How does the plight of people around the world affect you?
How do you help people around the world who need so much?

God's Temple

*Don't you realize that all of you together are the temple of God
and that the Spirit of God lives in you?*
1 CORINTHIANS 3:16

Your body is your body. You can treat it any way you choose. You can take care of it, feed it nutritiously, exercise it and make sure it gets the rest it needs.

Or, you can abuse it, feed it junk food, lie on the couch all day and watch TV then stay up all night and never rest. Which one of those scenarios is going to give you the best health? Of course you know that the first one will. Why should you care? You've got one body to use on this earth and how you take care of it determines how it will serve you.

But an even more important reason to take care of yourself is that your body is God's temple. He lives in you. God, in His grace, uses you to do His work on earth – to share His love and to spread the message of Jesus' death and resurrection with those who don't know about it.

If you aren't here then one part of His work is missing. So, take care of yourself, remembering that your diligence is not just for you but also for the Kingdom.

Are you diligent about taking care of yourself?
Do you struggle with any part of self-care?
Why? Do you tend to put everything and
everyone else before caring for yourself?

Pay Attention

Stay alert! Watch out for your great enemy, the devil.
He prowls around like a roaring lion, looking for someone
to devour. Stand firm against him, and be strong in your faith.
Remember that your family of believers all over the world
is going through the same kind of suffering you are.

1 PETER 5:8-9

Satan is no joke. He'd like you to think he is so that you don't take him seriously but you can be sure he isn't. The devil is never off-duty. He doesn't take weekends or holidays. His moment-by-moment goal is to pull you away from God. The quicker he can trip you up and the farther he can make you fall, the happier he is. Be careful not to take him lightly.

God warns you that Satan is sneaky. He prowls back and forth like a caged animal watching for opportunities to trick you. God wants you to pay attention. Be alert so that Satan's efforts don't catch you unaware. By paying attention you will be ready to stand firm. You'll be ready to call on God for help to push Satan away and resist the temptation of whatever he is throwing at you. God, in His loving, powerful grace will step up and help you.

Stay prepared to fight off Satan's attacks with the weapons God has given you – His Word, His Spirit and the power of talking with Him. In His grace He has given you everything you need!

Do you think about the reality of Satan very often? How do you stay prepared to fight him? What is your weakness that he attacks to try to pull you away from God?

Your Inheritance

Long ago God spoke many times and in many ways to our ancestors
through the prophets. And now in these final days, He has spoken
to us through His Son. God promised everything to the Son as
an inheritance, and through the Son He created the universe.
HEBREWS 1:1-2

The foundation of God's grace to you is built on His Son. Before
Jesus came to earth God used the prophets to get His message to the
people. Then Jesus came and He taught the people about God. He
told the people how to live for Him, how to obey Him and how to serve
Him. Jesus had firsthand experience because He is God.

When you accepted Jesus as your Savior, you became a child of
God. You were adopted into the family by God's loving grace. That
means that you share in the inheritance God has promised to His
children. That's no small thing. God promised everything to His Son,
Jesus. Everything that He made or will make, it all goes to Jesus. Because you are His child too, you share in that incredible inheritance.

Does that mean you are going to enjoy great wealth on this earth?
Possibly, but probably not. The wealth that God gladly shares with you
is eternal. It's the wealth of eternity in heaven with Him.

Riches here on earth cannot compare with that inheritance. It's
glorious. It's forever.

Understanding that your communication from God
comes through Jesus and that your inheritance from
God is built on the foundation of your relationship
with Jesus – how can you get to know Him better?

My Soul Thirsts for God

O God, You are my God I earnestly search for You.
My soul thirsts for You; my whole body longs for You
in this parched and weary land where there is no water.
PSALM 63:1

Have you ever gone for a long walk on a very hot day and forgotten your water bottle? By the time you figure that out you're pretty far into your walk. Then by the time you get home, your thirst is pretty intense. You can't wait for that first gulp of cool, clear water. It refreshes you. It cools you down. As you take drink after drink, your body is revived. Your muscles get the liquid they need to keep from cramping and to begin to revive. Quenching your thirst is important.

What do you thirst for in your life? Do you thirst for a deeper relationship with God? Do you long to know Him in a more intimate way? Do you long for Him to guide your life and direct your steps? Or is your thirst for something that's opposed to God? What do you long for? Money? Fame? Power? Are these things more important to you than knowing God?

By God's grace you have the opportunity to know Him as deeply as you wish? The only thing holding you back from an intimate relationship with Him is you. What do you thirst for?

You're the only one who can ask the question of what you thirst for. What occupies your thoughts? What do you spend your time on? Where do you put your energy? Is your thirst for God?

All Praise to God

Now all glory to God, who is able to keep you from falling away
and will bring you with great joy into His glorious presence
without a single fault. All glory to Him who alone is God,
our Savior through Jesus Christ our Lord. All glory,
majesty, power, and authority are His before all time,
and in the present, and beyond all time! Amen.

JUDE 1:24-25

All praise to God because you are not alone! God knows that life is going to be a challenge sometimes. You're going to face temptations that really challenge your faith. There may be days when you honestly don't know how you're going to make it. The path seems uncertain and with each step you take it feels like you're going to fall flat on your face. You may stumble sometimes but you won't fall because God is holding you. Praise Him for His strength to keep you from face planting. Praise Him for His guidance that directs your steps – even in the darkness. Praise Him for His wisdom that guides your decisions. Praise Him for His love that is the reason He provides all these things for you.

Let praise and gratitude spill from your heart for His daily provisions for you: His moment by moment care and protection and His constant guidance. He loves you so very much. You are His child and He alone can protect you from the temptations Satan throws at you and from your own weakness. God's power, strength and wisdom are yours. Always yours.

Praise God! Praise Him for all He does
for you. Speak your praise to Him.
Let Him know how you feel.

Showered with Kindness

He has showered His kindness on us,
along with all wisdom and understanding.
EPHESIANS 1:8

God showers His kindness down on you. When you get caught in a rainstorm, the water showers down on you. If it's a powerful storm, you quickly get soaked. You can't avoid the raindrops. That's how God's kindness is – it's powerful. It's constant. You are quickly covered in His kindness every day of your life. God loves you so much that He can't get enough of showering kindness on you. He wants to give you more and more blessings and kindness. He will find new ways to shower them down on you all the time!

God thinks of everything, in fact He wants you to understand what He's doing in this world. So He lets you in on His plans and His work by giving you wisdom and understanding. As you learn, you begin to see His love in action and how pieces of His work fit together.

You may not immediately understand everything He does or asks you to do but as you gain that wisdom, you learn a bit more about how you can trust Him. All He does is done with love and grace.

What kindness and blessing does God shower down on you?
How is your wisdom and understanding growing?

Grace-Fueled Compassion

Jesus saw the huge crowd as He stepped from the boat,
and He had compassion on them because they were like sheep
without a shepherd. So He began teaching them many things.
MARK 6:34

Is your compassion level affected by how tired you are? On a day when you've been very busy and you just want to rest but a friend stops in and she has a real problem. You could help but you're so tired! Does compassion for your friend's problem override your weariness?

If anyone had reason to be tired, it would be Jesus, right? He was constantly surrounded by people who wanted something from Him. So when Jesus got off the boat and saw a crowd of people waiting, was He so tired that He was annoyed to see them waiting? No. He had compassion for them. He knew the people were free-floating. They didn't have a leader to follow. What He could teach them would give them a new way of life – with God. It would change everything for them. So, in His grace-fueled compassion, Jesus taught.

Do you have grace-fueled compassion for any who need to know about God's love? Can you rise above your weariness to help people around you who need something? Does your heart fill with compassion for any who have needs? It's what Jesus would do.

Grace-fueled compassion serves with humility and sacrifice. How are you at that kind of service to others? Does it come easily to you?

Speaking Love

If you want to enjoy life and see
many happy days, keep your tongue from
speaking evil and your lips from telling lies.
1 PETER 3:10

Remember that Jesus said to love one another? He taught that often. What does it look like to love others? One way your love for others shows is by how you speak to them. If you say bad things about another person, how can you turn around and say you love her?

If you gossip or tell lies about another person then how can you say you love her? So often what comes out of your mouth reflects what's in your heart. Scripture tells you to guard your heart which means to be careful what you let stay in it.

You will have negative or critical thoughts about other people. That's part of being human. But if you immediately confess that thought and cast it from your heart, it won't take root and eventually go from a thought to an attitude to words that spew from your mouth.

To reflect Jesus' love to others and to treat others with grace and kindness, as Jesus treats you, guard your heart and your lips. Let your heart be filled with love and kindness so that the words you speak will reflect that.

Are you allowing critical and judgmental thoughts to
take root in your heart? How often do those attitudes
come out in how you speak to or about others?

Perfect Love

As we live in God, our love grows more perfect. So we will
not be afraid on the day of judgment, but we can face Him
with confidence because we live like Jesus here in this world.
Such love has no fear, because perfect love expels all fear.
If we are afraid, it is for fear of punishment, and this shows
that we have not fully experienced His perfect love.

1 JOHN 4:17-18

When you love someone you want to take care of them, right? You'll
do pretty much anything to protect a loved one. You will go out of your
way to help a loved one. You take risks yourself in order to protect
your loved one. You serve your loved one. It's a wonderful thing to
love someone. Only good things come from your love.

Now, if you can love that well, how well do you think God loves?
Right, even better. His love is perfect and powerful and complete. So,
you can trust that when you have given your heart to Him, He will protect it. He will help you as you grow to be more like Jesus. You have
nothing to fear, especially from God, if your heart's desire is to live for
Him and learn from Him.

If you are afraid, then perhaps it is because you have not fully trusted God. Are you still trying to live life on your own? Are you holding
back from Him? Are you afraid simply because you haven't accepted
His perfect love? His grace is the source of your love.

Are you afraid? Why? Could you be holding
some part of your life back from God? Why?

More Than a Memory

This is a day to remember. Each year, from generation
to generation, you must celebrate it as a special
festival to the LORD. This is a law for all time.
EXODUS 12:14

Celebrations are important because they recall some special experience or event. Celebrations are happy times that are usually shared with others and make for a fun party.

Celebrations are important to God too. He told His people to remember things He did for them and celebrate them. It's important to remember what God does for you. Every time God blesses you or protects you or guides you, mark that experience in your heart.

Remember what He's done because that memory feeds your faith and helps it grow stronger. Your memories will build one upon the other as your experiences with God grow. You'll learn to trust Him more with each experience. Celebrate your memories – the times God saves you, helps you, teaches you. Share it with others to God's glory.

But try to gain more experiences, don't simply be satisfied with the memories you currently have. God is alive and active so build on the new experiences you have with God. Then you will know your relationship with Him is alive and growing and you will have new memories to celebrate and share.

What experiences with God do you celebrate? How has God
worked in your life? Has His work made your faith stronger?

Promises Kept

Let us hold tightly without wavering to the hope we affirm, for God can be trusted to keep His promise.
HEBREWS 10:23

God will always keep His promises. It would be against His character to not do so. God is honest. He is trustworthy. He is perfect. Every promise that is given to you in the Bible can be trusted. So when He promises to save you by His grace, He does.

When He promises to forgive your sin, no matter how terrible it is or how often you sin, He will forgive. When He promises to help you be brave or courageous, He will. God promises you eternity in heaven with Him and you can trust that promise.

Nothing else on earth is as trustworthy as God. When a person disappoints you by breaking a promise, it's hard to trust her again. It's very hard to rebuild a broken trust. It may even be that a friend's broken promise makes you wonder if you can trust God.

Don't let human failure make you question God. Look at your relationship with Him. Has He ever failed you? Has He ever disappointed you? Hold on tight to God and all He says. Remember how much He loves you. His love is the reason His promises can be trusted.

God's word is filled with promises.
Which promise is special to you?
Do you trust Him to keep every promise?

An Important Job

If you keep quiet at a time like this, deliverance and
relief for the Jews will arise from some other place,
but you and your relatives will die. Who knows if perhaps
you were made queen for just such a time as this?

ESTHER 4:14

Esther won a beauty contest of sorts, which put her in a position to become queen. She was very beautiful but it was amazing that a Jewish girl became queen of Persia. God knew what He was doing though. He had a plan and Esther was an important part of it. An evil man who had the ear of the king was going to wipe out the entire Jewish population.

Because she was queen, Esther was in a position to save them but it was dangerous. Either the Jews would all be killed, or by approaching the king to ask for their salvation, she could have been killed herself. Esther's cousin, Mordecai said, "Maybe you became queen for this very moment." Maybe she only had one important thing to do in her life. It was dangerous but if God put her there, would He pave the way for her? Of course He would.

Maybe you have a "for such a time as this" task in your life. It's possible that God has an important job for you – it might not be dangerous but it's definitely important. Pay attention for what God, in His grace, has for you to do.

Do you have a clear idea of what God wants you to do? Has there been a one-time, specific job? Do you have an ongoing task for Him? What is it?

Building Bridges

A gentle answer deflects anger, but harsh words make tempers flare.
PROVERBS 15:1

When your spouse, child or friend snaps at you, what's your response? If you snap right back then a battle develops with sharp words being shot back and forth. If you can control yourself and respond gently, then a battle may be avoided. Which of these responses reflects God's grace? God showers His forgiving grace on you; forgiving your sins and you can pass grace on to those around you by how you respond in certain situations.

You have the power to diffuse an argument before it gets going and keep a relationship or friendship from being damaged. It takes self-control to not get angry. It takes humility to not shout that you're right. It takes patience to allow your friend enough time to hear your side of things.

Is it easy? Not always. Does it always pay off with a mended relationship? Not always. Does it always please God for you to be gentle, gracious and kind? Yes. Always.

Ask God to help you see things from both sides – yours and your friend's viewpoint. Ask Him to help you respond slowly, kindly and gently instead of impetuously, selfishly and loudly. Ask Him to give you grace to share with others so that you can build bridges rather than destroy relationships.

Do you need God's help in responding gently instead of angrily? When have you been successful in doing this? How did the situation turn out? Are you most often gentle or harsh?

Carefully Chosen Words

Even fools are thought wise when they keep silent;
with their mouths shut, they seem intelligent.
PROVERBS 17:28

Some people seem to have an opinion about absolutely everything and they loudly and frequently spout their opinion for all to hear. It's annoying and after a while it's hard to take them seriously. In fact, perhaps you've thought something like, "Oh that's just so-and-so's opinion. Don't take it seriously."

That's where the wisdom of this Proverb comes in. A person may be a complete fool – no wisdom at all, very little common sense, but if she keeps her mouth shut, no one will know she's a fool. In fact, people may think she's quite wise.

On the other hand if a person constantly spouts her opinions and thoughts without ever being asked and especially if she tries to force her opinions on others, people will think she is a fool.

By the strength of God's grace, keep your opinion to yourself unless you are specifically asked for it. Protect your reputation by keeping quiet. Remember that everything you do and everything you say is as a representative of God. Be diligent in sharing His love and grace, so be slow to speak so that His love and grace flows through your words.

Do words fly out of your mouth quickly and often? Do you
share your opinion whether you're asked or not? Do you need
to ask God to help you be silent a little more often?

Grace-Focused Living

Don't be selfish; don't try to impress others.
Be humble, thinking of others as better than yourselves.
PHILIPPIANS 2:3

What would your life of grace look like if Jesus had been selfish? He wouldn't have given up heaven to come to earth. He wouldn't have suffered and died for your sins. He wouldn't forgive you every time you mess up. Without Jesus' humility, sacrifice and unselfishness, you wouldn't have a life of grace. You wouldn't have anything.

So, as you learn to be more like Christ, what does His grace look like in you? There isn't any way to "be Jesus" to someone else if you are all about yourself. Wanting things to be all about you or always go your way certainly is not focusing on others and what's good for them. Being so full of yourself that you're constantly trying to impress others with how smart, successful and yes, even spiritual, you are is not a way of thinking about others.

How should you live? Unselfishly. Serving others as kindly, sacrificially and gently as possible. Don't try to impress with how great you are, but instead lift others up. Make it your goal to encourage others to be all they can be. Help them in any way you can. Be grace-focused to them, don't focus on yourself.

Is it hard for you to be unselfishly focused on others? Is it harder with some people than others? Why? How can you work on that?

Playing with Fire

The LORD said, "I will wipe this human race I have created
from the face of the earth. Yes, and I will destroy every
living thing – all the people, the large animals, the small
animals that scurry along the ground, and even
the birds of the sky. I am sorry I ever made them."

GENESIS 6:7

The people in Noah's day had become evil. They were focused on self. They didn't care at all about God's commands, serving Him or obeying Him. People cared only about fulfilling their own desires, no matter how that affected others. They had turned completely away from God. He saw what was happening and He was sad, hurt, disappointed. He had enough of them. So, He decided to wipe out creation and start over with Noah and his family.

What do you learn from this story? Sin is no joke. God does not take it lightly. His grace extended to you and all mankind through Jesus' suffering and death has limits. Look at the world today – does it look similar to Noah's day? Are you living for God as Noah did or are you fitting in more with the rest of the world? If you're justifying your sins because what you're doing is what society says is good, realize that you're playing with fire. God takes sin seriously. He desires your obedience. He desires your worship. His grace is why you have life with Him. Where is your priority? Obeying and serving God or living by society's standards?

Honesty time: What's in your heart? What sins are you justifying away? How are you fitting in with society even when those choices go against God's teachings? What matters most to you?

Your Choices

When people escape from the wickedness of the world by knowing our Lord and Savior Jesus Christ and then get tangled up and enslaved by sin again, they are worse off than before. It would be better if they had never known the way to righteousness than to know it and then reject the command they were given to live a holy life.

2 PETER 2:20-21

God takes sin seriously – it would be better if you had NEVER KNOWN the way to righteousness if you're going to reject it anyway! Wow.

God's grace to forgive your sins and give you salvation was not free. It cost Him something precious – His Son's suffering and death and the taking on His own shoulders the sin of all mankind, your sin. God's grace to you was not without cost.

If you live by the mantra of "Oh well, if I sin God will forgive me. No biggie" you are disrespecting the magnitude of what your forgiveness cost Him.

You've seen the "other side" of life. You've experienced grace and forgiveness. You've been given a new start, time after time. But when you consciously choose to go back to living the way you did before – making informed choices to not follow God's way, you are consciously rejecting God's grace. Of course you'll sin, even without consciously choosing to do so, because that old nature is always pushing to be back in control. But, do not choose sin over obeying God. The next verse in 2 Peter says that it's like a washed pig returning to the mud.

Are you making conscious choices to sin rather than obey? Why? Is it too hard to obey God? Have you thought about how you are disrespecting the cost of God's grace to you? What are you going to do about it?

Fight for Joy

Always be full of joy in the Lord. I say it again – rejoice!
PHILIPPIANS 4:4

There are some people who are always "down." They see pretty much everything in life as a "glass is half-empty" scenario. They have a difficult time finding positive things to say about most of life. People like that are tiring to be around. It's hard for those around them to keep a positive attitude about life when the negativity is pulling at them all the time.

Happiness and joy are not the same thing. There are solid reasons to be joyful regardless of what's going on around you. Joy comes from God. It swells up in your heart and spills out in your face, your words and your actions.

Can you be joyful even when faced with difficulties? Yes. But that doesn't mean you aren't sad about your troubles or what's happening in the world. It means that in your heart you know God is in control. You believe that He knows what's going on and He will either change the circumstance or strengthen you to get through it. He won't leave you alone.

Your joy is a testimony to His grace in your life. Fight to have joy instead of letting negativity pull you down.

Do you consider yourself to be a person of joy or negativity? What would your friends and family say? How can you let God's joy show in your life even more?

God's Timing

The LORD kept His word and did for Sarah exactly
what He had promised. She became pregnant, and she
gave birth to a son for Abraham in his old age. This
happened at just the time God had said it would.
GENESIS 21:1-2

Through God's grace He cares about the things you care about.
Abraham and Sarah had prayed and prayed for the privilege of
becoming parents. God had blessed them in so very many ways.
He had directed their lives in countless ways but still they had no
children. Now they were old. Sarah was 90 – too old to become
pregnant and give birth. Abraham was 100! The baby boy born to
them was most definitely a gift of God's grace!

If you ever think that God doesn't care about your concerns,
go back and read this story. God honored Abraham's and Sarah's
prayers in His own time. By giving them a son in their old age, it was
apparent that Isaac was a gift from God!

God hears your prayers. He sees the desires of your heart.
If you're honoring and obeying Him, as Abraham and Sarah did,
He will answer your prayers. Remember that living for Him and
knowing Him intimately will make your will and His will more aligned.
Then, trust God's heart and grace and pray your desires.
Then enjoy the blessings His heart of grace gives in His
own time – the right time.

It's hard to wait on God's timing but do you ever question
whether He hears your prayers? Have you had an
experience of God giving what you asked in prayer, in
His timing? How did you see that His timing was best?

Loved Forever

The love of the LORD remains forever with those who fear Him.
PSALM 103:17

God's love and grace are interchangeable. One of the characteristics of His grace is that it is everlasting. It never stops. It doesn't turn away because of your sin. In fact His grace grows stronger and more necessary to you because of your sin. If there wasn't sin in this world there would be no need for God's grace or forgiveness.

God loves you. God, the Creator, loves you. Yes, Scripture says God loves all mankind, that's true. It tells you that Jesus died for all of humanity's sin, but that doesn't diminish that Jesus' sacrifice and God's love is personally yours. Have you grasped the personal aspect of this? Good.

Now, grasp this – God's love sticks with you forever. He doesn't throw His metaphorical hands up in disgust and walk away when you sin. He doesn't say that you only get one more chance. His love and grace are yours for all eternity.

Look around and see the evidences of God's grace beginning with your salvation and forgiveness and then exhibited in the blessings of Scripture, the beauty of nature, the love of family, the joy of friends. He never stops gracing and blessing you. He never will.

Meditate on the personal aspect of God's love and grace to you. Does that give you any new revelations about His love?

God's Grace Is His

*"Friend, I haven't been unfair! Didn't you agree to work
all day for the usual wage? Take your money and go.
I wanted to pay this last worker the same as you. Is it
against the law for me to do what I want with my money?
Should you be jealous because I am kind to others?"*
MATTHEW 20:13-15

Jesus told a story about a man who hired some workers. They agreed to a certain wage for the day and went to work. Much later in the day the man hired more workers who worked a much shorter time but he paid them the same amount of money. The first workers weren't happy! They didn't think the latecomers should earn as much as they did when they had a much shorter workday. The boss's response was, "It's my money. I get to do with it what I choose. You're earning what you agreed to so what if I'm kind to someone else?"

Do you look at others and wonder why God blesses them more than He seems to bless you? Or do you question why He uses some people in such magnificent ways? Do you allow your attitude to make you feel that you're on God's "B" team?

God's grace is His and He can dispense it any way He wants. Do you believe He has a plan for your life and that He gives you what you need to accomplish it? Don't worry about what others are doing. Just do your job and thank Him for the privilege of serving.

Do you struggle with jealousy at how God
blesses others? Do you let yourself feel that
you are not as important to God as others?
How can you get over that feeling?

Forgiven!

"He returned home to his father. And while he was still a long way off, his father saw him coming. Filled with love and compassion, he ran to his son, embraced him, and kissed him."
LUKE 15:20

The story of the prodigal son tells of a self-centered boy who asked for his share of his dad's inheritance while his dad was still alive! Then he wasted all the money. He ended up alone with nothing to eat except the stuff he fed the pigs that he took care of. He realized he would be better off becoming one of his dad's servants. He felt he no longer deserved to be treated as his father's son. So he headed home to beg his dad for a job.

What happened? His dad saw him coming and he ran to meet him. He forgave his son. He restored his place in the family and celebrated his boy!

Did you see that? The dad *ran* to meet his son. He didn't even wait for the boy to make it to the house. That's a beautiful picture of your Father, God. He loves you so much that He runs to meet you when you return from sinful behavior. He runs to meet you and forgive you and restore you to your place as His child. His forgiving grace sends Him running to meet you!

You know how it feels to ask God's forgiveness for your sins. It's humbling. Have you ever pictured God running to meet you and to forgive you even before your request is fully uttered? How does that make you feel?

Law vs. Grace

God's law was given so that all people could see how
sinful they were. But as people sinned more and more,
God's wonderful grace became more abundant.
So just as sin ruled over all people and brought them to death,
now God's wonderful grace rules instead, giving us right standing
with God and resulting in eternal life through Jesus Christ our Lord.
ROMANS 5:20-21

God gave the law so that Moses could teach the people how to live. He even wrote some of the commands out on stone tablets Himself. His law gave structure to life. It showed people how to live in the way that pleased, honored and obeyed God. It also gave structure for how to treat other people with fairness and respect. The law is good but just keeping the rules does not give you a personal relationship with God. If it did, then Jesus didn't need to die for your sins.

God's grace wanted more for you than just keeping a list of rules and commands. He wanted you to have the privilege of a personal relationship with Him – a friendship – no, more than that – to know that you are His child! That was accomplished through Jesus taking your sins on Himself and dying for them. The price of your forgiveness was the sacrifice of His shed blood through His death.

So you see, the law has its purpose. But your relationship with God is through the grace of His gift of Jesus. Do not take that gift lightly. It gives you life.

It's easy to get caught up in keeping rules and forget about the grace of God's gift of Jesus. What's the difference between the two things in your mind?

God's Masterpiece

We are God's masterpiece. He has created us anew in
Christ Jesus, so we can do the good things He planned for us long ago.
EPHESIANS 2:10

How's your self-image? Do you compare yourself to others and come up short? Do you feel you aren't smart enough? Does it haunt you that you were mostly a "B" student in school? Do you feel that the boss or CEO has a way more important job than you do? Is your talent mundane compared with musicians or actors or writers around you? Have you pushed yourself down to a point of feeling that what you bring to the table doesn't matter much in God's Kingdom?

Well, stop that. This verse says that we, and this includes you, are God's masterpiece. What's the definition of masterpiece? It's the masterwork, a work of genius, a stunning success. That's you. Not because of anything you've done but because of God's grace. He made you exactly the way He wants.

He gave you abilities and talents, which of course, you can develop and grow. But you can only do that because He is preparing you for the specific, unique, "can be done only by you" work He has for you. He has a plan. It includes you doing exactly what He planned for you to do. You matter!

Do you struggle with self-image issues? Why? Have you considered that you are God's masterpiece? What are you good at? How does He use that in His plan?

Strength in Numbers

All of this is for your benefit.
And as God's grace reaches more and more people,
there will be great thanksgiving,
and God will receive more and more glory.
2 CORINTHIANS 4:15

Paul wrote to the Corinthians that he had endured terrible suffering because of his faith in Jesus. He was persecuted because he kept preaching. He refused to stop, even through the difficulties, because he knew that what he was doing would encourage the Corinthians in their faith.

There's strength in numbers. When you go to a sporting event or political rally or anything where there's a crowd of people all cheering for the same team or person, the bigger the crowd, the louder the cheers, and the more enthusiastic the crowd grows.

Paul is saying that as more people are saved by God's grace, the louder the thanksgiving will be and more people will hear and be saved so God will be glorified, and there will be louder thanksgiving so more people will be saved and God will be glorified and ... well, you see the pattern. There's strength and power in numbers.

Your praise and thanksgiving will be heard by others which could draw them into the Kingdom, adding their praise to God which will be heard by others and draw them into the Kingdom ... you get it, right? Praise God so all can hear.

Are you open about praising God? Trouble
didn't stop Paul from praising, how is
your praise during difficult times?

The Power of Jesus' Name

Let me clearly state to all of you and to all the people of Israel that he was healed by the powerful name of Jesus Christ the Nazarene, the man you crucified but whom God raised from the dead. There is salvation in no one else! God has given no other name under heaven by which we must be saved.

ACTS 4:10, 12

Jesus had gone back to heaven and the Holy Spirit was sent to indwell believers. God, in His grace, gave Jesus' disciples the power to do miracles and Peter healed a crippled man. Because of that many people believed in Jesus. The religious leaders arrested Peter and asked him where he got the power to do the miracle. These two verses are part of Peter's response – the healing was done by the powerful name of Jesus!

The religious leaders were responsible for Jesus' death. They didn't want to give Him any glory. They wanted Him to go away but His death didn't do that. Instead, His followers spread the news of His death and resurrection by teaching and doing miracles in His name!

There are two wonderful points here – first, salvation comes only through Jesus. There is no other pathway to heaven, only through Jesus. Second, God, in His grace, uses His followers to tell people about His love. His followers, that's you. You can't heal people but you can certainly pray for those around you and share His love.

God uses you to spread the message of His love and grow His Kingdom. How do you work in that responsibility? How do you share?

Blended by Grace

We will speak the truth in love, growing in every way more
and more like Christ, who is the head of His body, the church.
He makes the whole body fit together perfectly. As each part
does its own special work, it helps the other parts grow, so that
the whole body is healthy and growing and full of love.
EPHESIANS 4:15-16

Paul called for unity among believers. Get along with each other. Stop the petty arguments and power struggles. Be kind to each other. Be honest, yes, but in your honesty, speak with love. Don't call each other names or belittle others' opinions or ideas. You wouldn't see Jesus doing that with other believers so how can you feel it's OK? You're supposed to be growing in your faith so that you're more like Christ, not less like Him. If you're letting Jesus work in your heart to make you more like Him, He will give you patience with those around you. He will help you see their viewpoints and understand their ideas and dreams.

The gifts God gave you equip you to do the work He has for you. Others have different gifts and different work. God blends you all together to accomplish great things for His Kingdom. What you bring to the work is just as important as what someone else brings. All the parts are necessary. The super cool thing is that as you each do your work, you encourage each other's faith so that you all grow stronger by working together.

So, do you "play well with others?" Do you
cooperate with and encourage others in their work?
Do others consider you easy to work with? How has
working together with others grown your faith?

The New You

Throw off your old sinful nature and your former way of life,
which is corrupted by lust and deception. Instead,
let the Spirit renew your thoughts and attitudes.
Put on your new nature, created to be like
God – truly righteous and holy.
EPHESIANS 4:22-24

Throwing off your old way of life gives the image of taking off a heavy jacket on a very hot, humid day. Taking it off quickly and then throwing it far away from you because you don't want any part of it still close by. Just as a heavy jacket would make you hotter on a warm day, your old, sinful nature will keep tempting you to do sinful things.

The tricky thing is that you have to take off that heavy sinful nature every single day; even many times a day because it's your natural way of thinking and feeling. Sounds like a lot of work, doesn't it? But, the good thing is that when you take it off and put on your new nature – a gift of God's grace – you get some help. God's Holy Spirit – another gift from His grace – helps you grow a new way of thinking and shapes your attitudes to be more like Jesus.

You don't have to do it all by yourself. God's Spirit helps you and His strength and persistence are amazing. His goal is for your heart to be loving, gracious and kind like Jesus' heart.

Growing to be more like Jesus takes time. It's not immediate or automatic. How are you doing in the process? Is one part of learning to be Christ-like more difficult than other parts for you?

Praise God!

Honor and majesty surround Him; strength and joy fill His dwelling.
1 CHRONICLES 16:27

This one short verse is in the center of a song of praise that David sang. It pours out praise for God for everything from the miracles He did for the Israelites to every segment of creation praising Him through its beautiful existence.

God has always saved a remnant of His people to keep His message alive. He has always preserved His Word from the first written copies of it until today so that you can know Him.

God's first act of grace for mankind began with, "In the beginning …," when He spoke the first words of creation. With His intelligence and imagination He made every animal, insect, flower, tree, mountain, ocean, waterfall and everything else there is come from His mind. The masterpiece of His creation is you. He made people in His own image and loves all of humanity with an eternal, uncompromising and pure love.

His ultimate act of love was in sending Jesus to die for mankind's sin then come back to life and return to heaven making a personal relationship with God possible for all people.

All these things and millions more are reasons to praise Him.

Spend some time in prayer but don't ask God for anything. Just praise Him. Praise Him for all He does for you, how He's blessed you, your favorite things He does for you and your favorite part of His creation. Just praise.

Training Ground

For He knows how weak we are; He remembers we are only dust.
Our days on earth are like grass; like wildflowers,
we bloom and die. The wind blows, and we are gone –
as though we had never been here. But the love
of the LORD remains forever with those who fear Him.

PSALM 103:14-17

Life on this planet is just a blip in the scheme of all eternity. It's like a second of time in a century of years. Of course for now this life is important. It's your life and each day is a gift. You fill your days with productive activities, you love your family and friends, you serve your God. You have good times and hard times. But before you know it, this life is over and your physical body returns to the dust that the first man was created from. Within a generation few people will remember who you were or what you were like.

Do those thoughts depress you? Well then, focus on the bigger picture – what matters much more than this earthly life is what's beyond. God's grace has been poured out on you so that you can spend eternity with Him. That's the thing to celebrate. You will have forever with God to celebrate His love and enjoy His presence in His beautiful heaven. This earthly life is but a training ground, providing an opportunity to learn to know God deeply and prepare you for spending forever with Him!

Are you certain of your position in heaven? Do you anticipate it? Are you laying up treasures for your life in heaven by how you live your life here?

God's Thoughts

"My thoughts are nothing like your thoughts," says the LORD.
"And My ways are far beyond anything you could imagine.
For just as the heavens are higher than the earth, so My ways are
higher than your ways and My thoughts higher than your thoughts."
ISAIAH 55:8-9

Do you think you're so smart? Do you have answers for the world's problems? Social media these days makes it seem like everyone has an answer for everything and a criticism for anyone else's viewpoint, even fellow Christians who believe they are following God's teachings, too. It gets ugly and complicated and not much love is shared between opinions.

Even the best human ideas though are only microcosms of God's ideas. God simply doesn't think the way people think. Because He can see a larger slice of reality (like ALL of it) than you do, His thoughts prepare and grow you toward what's next in your life. His plans are for more than what this world offers you. His plans may take you through some pretty deep waters in order to grow your faith stronger and stronger. What's important to Him may not be what's important to you.

Trust God's heart in preparing you for what's ahead and how you can most effectively serve Him. His grace is in that preparation and it includes all you need to do His work. Even when you don't understand His thoughts, you can trust God's heart.

When have you not understood God's thoughts or ways? When did you begin to see how His plan was coming together?

Grace Teaches Grace

God can point to us in all future ages as examples
of the incredible wealth of His grace and kindness toward us,
as shown in all He has done for us who are united with Christ Jesus.
EPHESIANS 2:7

When you read the Bible you see how God interacted with His people in those days. It's encouraging to see His care, direction and guidance for them. You see His compassion and love for His people. It grows your faith and trust in Him as you see His character in those stories.

You may also read books and hear stories of how God has blessed generations just before yours. You may hear how your grandparents were showered with His guidance and grace in their lives. You can read of missionaries, evangelists and just regular people who He blessed and protected. His grace covered them.

These stories are an example of why God pours out His grace on you today. The stories of how He takes care of you and guides your life will be a blessing down the road someday for others who are learning to trust Him. In His grace, He builds one generation on the stories and examples of past generations. This is why you should share your stories of how God shows kindness and grace to you. It will bless and teach future generations of believers. Grace to grace.

Which Bible stories of God's work in people's lives
especially bless you? Which of His work in more modern
day people encourage you to stay close to Him?

Why Jesus Came

> He gave His life to free us from every kind of sin,
> to cleanse us, and to make us His very own people,
> totally committed to doing good deeds.
>
> TITUS 2:14

Jesus' suffering and death was not just to gain heaven for you. That's certainly a blessing of what His sacrifice gave you, no doubt about that. But God's grace gives you so much more through Jesus' time on earth. His teachings, recorded in Scripture by those who walked beside Him help you learn to obey and honor God by how you live your life. He taught how to relate to people and treat them with respect and kindness. Jesus' work while He was on earth is also a big part of why He came.

Jesus' interactions with the people He came in contact with show His love and compassion for all people – from a child who had died to a widow who lost her son or a man concerned about his sick servant. He helped the lame, the blind, the sick and the dead. His compassion was deep and sincere.

From Jesus' teachings and examples you learn to turn away from sin and focus your heart on purity – pleasing God and serving Him as Jesus did in the way He lived. The bonus of Jesus' work is heaven – eternity with Him!

What have you specifically learned from
what Jesus taught on earth? How does His
example of how to live influence you?

Thanks Be to God

LORD, be merciful to us, for we have waited for You.
Be our strong arm each day and our salvation in times of trouble.

ISAIAH 33:2

God's kindness is poured out on you every day. You experience His grace, compassion and mercy many times daily. It happens so regularly that you may not even recognize His work. He protects you before you even know you need protecting. He guides you so subtly that you may not even know He is doing anything until you look back on it later. He guides and protects you because He loves you and wants good things for you. He showers you with His grace. When problems arise in your life, you call on Him for help and you wait for His actions. You know that God is your hope for salvation and strength in your difficult times.

You know these things but do you take advantage of them? Is conversation with God the first thought when you wake in the morning? Is His strength the first thing you call for in times of trouble? Is His grace and compassion what keeps you going each day?

Do you thank Him for His care and protection? Do you acknowledge His guidance? Start each day with thanks for God's mercy and care. Thank Him for His guidance and love. Thank Him for being your everything.

What do you thank God for? How does He show His love
and care to you? How has He seen you through problems?

Hang In There

Sing to the LORD, all you godly ones! Praise His holy name.
For His anger lasts only a moment, but His favor lasts a lifetime!
Weeping may last through the night, but joy comes with the morning.
PSALM 30:4-5

Your life will be very unusual if you get through it without some tough times or problems. Trouble is simply a part of being alive. Even as a Christian you will have difficulties. As nice as it would be, accepting Christ as your Savior doesn't mean a problem-free life.

How do you handle the problems that come into your life? Do you praise God for your trouble? Do you depend on Him to get you through the difficult times? Is all your trouble a punishment from God? Of course not, some difficulties are just the natural outcomes of life. Some problems are for learning a lesson.

Regardless of why you're experiencing problems, remember that your troubles don't last forever. However, God's love and care does last forever. So even if you're going through very painful times, don't give up. Things will get better one day and God's grace will get you through. He will be with you step by step. One day you will know joy again and you can praise God for getting you through a difficult experience.

What problems have you faced thus far in your life? How has God's presence been apparent as you've gone through them?

Before You Were Born

You know what I was like when I followed the Jewish religion – how I violently persecuted God's church. I did my best to destroy it. But even before I was born, God chose me and called me by His marvelous grace. Then it pleased Him to reveal His Son to me so that I would proclaim the Good News about Jesus to the Gentiles.

GALATIANS 1:13, 15-16

God's plan for your life began before you were even born. If you've taken a few wrong turns in your life, don't give up. Paul is an example of this. In the beginning of his life he was against Jesus and anyone who followed Him. He made it his goal to lock Christians in jail, or worse. He tried his best to wipe out all Christianity.

But then, Paul met Jesus. He believed, turned away from his previous life and spent the rest of his life telling others about Jesus. It's a hopeful lesson that God used Paul in such wonderful ways – He used Paul to write much of the New Testament. Did Paul's change of heart surprise God? No, God had a plan for Paul. He knew what he was going to do before becoming a Christian and He knew what Paul would do after accepting Christ.

God knows the same about you. Whatever your pre-Christ life was like will not prevent you from serving God after you become a Christian. His grace forgives all you were before. His grace covers all your sin. He knew His plans for you before you were even born.

What was your life like before accepting Christ? What is your life like now? Can you see God's plan in your life?

Memorizing Scripture

I have hidden Your word in my heart that I might not sin against You.
PSALM 119:11

God gave you the Bible – His Word – so that you have a constant guidebook to teach you how to live for Him and serve Him. Everything you need to know about how God will help you in life is described in the stories you read there.

Scripture challenges you to obey God and explains how that looks in your life. If you follow what Scripture teaches you, you will be obedient to Him and you will treat other people with kindness, compassion and respect.

God also blessed you with a mind that allows you to commit things to memory. So, if you commit Scripture verses to memory, then whenever you need the strength and wisdom they provide they are available to you.

At times when you are frightened and confused a verse will float into your mind. It will be God speaking to you through His Word that's in your memory. He will use those memorized verses to comfort and encourage you at just the right moment. God's grace, given through His Word, is multiplied with every verse you memorize.

How often do you memorize Scripture? Do verses
come to mind that apply to situations you're facing?

God Is Good

O Lord, You are so good, so ready to forgive,
so full of unfailing love for all who ask for Your help.
PSALM 86:5

You never have to beg God to pay attention to you. You don't have to make an appointment to get time with Him. You don't have to stand in line for Him to hear your prayers. God loves you and He is always available to you 24/7. You can talk to Him anytime you want to or need to. He is with you, waiting for you to pay attention to Him.

God always shows goodness to you in His love and compassion. He cares about what's happening in your life. He cares about your struggles and temptations and He will help you through them all.

When you sin, God understands your embarrassment and sorrow at needing to ask forgiveness, but because of His unending grace, He quickly forgives. He doesn't make you beg for His forgiveness because His love for you is deep and unconditional.

God gladly comes to your aid when you ask for help. In fact, He's constantly waiting for you to ask for Him to help you. That's what love does. It forgives and helps in order to make life better for the loved one … that's you.

When was a time you called on God for help? How did
He help you? Is His love apparent to you each day?

What You Chase
Is What You Catch

Whoever pursues righteousness and unfailing
love will find life, righteousness, and honor.
PROVERBS 21:21

What you pursue in life is what you get out of life. If, in seriousness you pursue a life of righteousness and love then that's what you'll get. What does that mean? A life of righteousness means you make every effort to obey God's commands. You seek to honor Him by your thoughts, words and actions. A righteous person treats others with fairness and honesty. She respects others by how she speaks about them and to them. A righteous person is one who strives to learn to be more and more like Christ each day of her life.

What does it mean to pursue unfailing love? Pursue God. His love for you is uncompromising and unconditional. He loves you even when you sin. He loves you even when you fail to love Him back. He patiently waits for your love for Him to grow as your understanding of His love for you grows. As you grasp how deep and strong His unfailing love for you is, your response will be to love Him more.

So, when you pursue righteousness and unfailing love, that's exactly what you find – a life filled with righteousness, love and honor.

What are you pursuing in your life?
Are you learning to obey God more fully?
How have you recognized God's love in your life?
Has it changed your love for Him?

Your God

For Your kingdom is an everlasting kingdom.
You rule throughout all generations. The LORD always
keeps His promises; He is gracious in all He does.
PSALM 145:13

This is your God – He has always been present. He will always be present. His Kingdom is forever. There may be times when it seems to you that His Kingdom is shrinking – that evil is winning. But it never will. Because God's Kingdom is forever God will rule all generations of mankind that will ever exist. He is the most powerful. He is the wisest. He is love. This is your God.

He has promised to guide you and protect you from whatever happens in your life. He always keeps His promises so don't be afraid that you are alone in your struggles. You are not. Even when you lose a job. Even when you fight with your spouse. Even if your spouse dies. Even if your child rebels. Even if the medical report is bad news. You are not alone.

God promised to be with you in everything life brings – good and bad. He promises to graciously be present with you to give you strength and persistence to face whatever comes and to have victory in it because of His presence with you.

How does God's presence help you through the trials of life? Are you aware of His constant presence? How does He make Himself known to you?

The Wisdom of Solomon

I will give you what you asked for! I will give you a wise
and understanding heart such as no one else has had
or ever will have! And I will also give you what you did
not ask for – riches and fame! No other king in all the
world will be compared to you for the rest of your life!
1 KINGS 3:12-13

Like his father, David, Solomon obeyed God. When God appeared to
him in a dream and told him to ask for what he would like God to give
him, Solomon prayed for the wisdom of an understanding heart to rule
God's people. God was pleased with Solomon's prayer so He gave
Solomon what he asked for. Because of the king's unselfish prayer,
God, in His grace, also gave him wealth and fame.

Solomon did become the most famous king, not just because of his
wealth but because of how he used the wisdom God gave him. When
two women each claimed to be the mother of an infant, Solomon ordered that the baby be cut in two and a half given to each woman. He
knew that the real mother would stop the murder and allow the other
woman to have her child, just to keep it alive!

God's grace gives you what you need to do the job He has for you.
Solomon probably didn't have this level of wisdom before he asked
God for it, but God gave it when he needed it. He will also give you
what you need. Ask wisely!

What would you like to ask God
to give you? What do you feel you
need in order to better serve Him?

Humility and Submission

"Don't be afraid, Mary," the angel told her, "for you
have found favor with God! You will conceive and give birth
to a son, and you will name Him Jesus. He will be very great
and will be called the Son of the Most High. The Lord God
will give Him the throne of His ancestor David. And He will
reign over Israel forever; His Kingdom will never end!"

LUKE 1:30-33

Have you ever wondered what Mary did that allowed her to find favor
with God? Most experts agree that Mary was just a young teenager
when the angel appeared to her. What had she done that drew God's
attention to her?

We know from God's previous statements that His primary concern
is with a person's heart. So apparently, He looked at Mary's heart and
saw that she was humbly submitted to Him. That was obviously true
since she was willing to be made pregnant without being married and
bear the shame that came with that situation.

Is your heart submitted to God? If He asks you to do something difficult, are you prepared to say, "Yes?" Do you trust Him enough to step
out in faith, even if He asks you to do something difficult or dangerous?
Do you believe He will protect you and stand with you in the situation?
Do you trust His grace to shower down blessings on you as you obey?
Are you prepared to obey even if the blessings don't come until far
down the road?

How deep is your trust? Has God ever asked you
to do something completely based on your faith in
Him as He did with Mary? Were you willing?

Grace Always

Now swear to me by the LORD that you will be kind to me and my family since I have helped you. Give me some guarantee that when Jericho is conquered, you will let me live, along with my father and mother, my brothers and sisters, and all their families.
JOSHUA 2:12-13

Rahab was a prostitute – not someone you would typically expect to hear about in the Bible. However she played an important role in God's army being able to capture the strong city of Jericho. Joshua sent spies in to check out the city and they stayed at Rahab's house. The king heard the spies were in the city and he sent soldiers to capture them. Rahab lied to protect the spies and after the soldiers left, she asked the spies to save her and her family when the army came to capture the city. She recognized the power of God was with Joshua's army and they would defeat the army of Jericho.

The spies showed grace to Rahab by agreeing to save her. They kept that promise when Jericho fell. Rahab and her family were saved.

An evil person can do a good thing, for the right reason and through that find salvation and grace. Do not turn away from someone who believes differently than you, God may have chosen that person to help you with a part of His work and by the grace you show her, she may come to faith in God. Show grace whenever you can.

Have you had the opportunity to show grace to someone who was different from you and refused? Or if you did, did you show grace? What was the result?

Your Burning Bush

There the angel of the LORD appeared to him
in a blazing fire from the middle of a bush.
Moses stared in amazement. Though the bush
was engulfed in flames, it didn't burn up.
EXODUS 3:2

God got Moses' attention. Moses was watching out for his sheep, walking around the fields when he saw a bush on fire. As a shepherd, his first thought may have been to get his sheep away from the fire. But then he saw the bush was burning but not burning up. Weird. Then, he heard someone call his name! As he approached the burning bush God said, "This is holy ground. Take off your shoes." Yes, God got his attention in a dramatic way because He had an important message for Moses.

God will do whatever He must to get your attention. Maybe your "burning bush" has been an illness that kept you in bed for a while. Maybe it's been a voice in your heart as you looked out over the ocean. It would be nice if He would set a bush on fire and say, "Here I am. Listen to Me." He doesn't usually do that kind of dramatic thing anymore, but when you sense Him speaking to you through your stillness or through nature – pay attention. By His grace, He has found a way to get His message to you.

What's your "burning bush?" How has God spoken to you? Does He have to get you silent and still in order to get your attention?

Truly Loving God

"I want you to show love, not offer sacrifices.
I want you to know Me more than I want burnt offerings."
HOSEA 6:6

Don't get caught up in rules. If you demand that everyone live by the set of rules that you've decided are the correct way to honor and obey God (even if you're right) people will turn away from God rather than to Him because of your pharisaical rule keeping.

There's one way to be sure that doesn't happen; couch everything you say and do in love. More important than offering sacrifices or religiously keeping a set of rules is to live in love. Love God with all your heart, soul, mind and strength – that means with all of your being. Love Him more than anything else. Love Him more than you love yourself.

Love others as much (or more) than you love yourself. Give of yourself sacrificially to serve others. Be available to help, encourage, minister. Even when you're tired. Even when it's hard. Even when people are very different from you. Even if it takes a lot of grace. If it was easy it wouldn't be a sacrifice.

Love God. No matter where you are, who you are
or what you have you should always love God.

Living for God

This is what the LORD of Heaven's Armies says:
"Judge fairly, and show mercy and kindness to one another.
Do not oppress widows, orphans, foreigners, and the poor.
And do not scheme against each other."
ZECHARIAH 7:9-10

God's instruction from early times has been to show grace to one another. After all, you receive grace from Him in so many ways, be willing to pass grace along to others as you represent God to the world.

God mentions a few times to be especially gracious toward the weak and vulnerable in your world – widows, orphans, foreigners and the poor. Those groups are often the ones who have little or no voice in our society today. Show them grace. Help them when you can. Serve them when you can. Be their voice when you can. In our world today, more than ever, these groups need allies who are loving, steady, constant and unafraid to speak out. Your help for them should be aligned with what God would do.

God also warns against scheming against others. Be humble, don't scheme to get ahead. Work together to help those who need help and to grow God's Kingdom through how you live His love and show His grace to others.

What impact do you have on any of the vulnerable people groups mentioned in these verses? How do you show love and grace outside your own family or circle of friends?

Ask God to Listen

Answer me when I call to You,
O God who declares me innocent.
Free me from my troubles.
Have mercy on me and hear my prayer.
PSALM 4:1

Because of God's grace, you can actually ask God to listen to your prayer. Do you realize what a privilege that is? You can talk to God and you can start by saying, "God, listen to me please!" It's OK. He won't get angry with you for asking. You can even ask Him to answer you. God has forgiven your sin through His generous grace and He invites you to talk with Him. He wants to hear what you have to say!

Because of His grace to you, God cares about what's troubling you. He wants to know how you feel about it. He even wants to hear how you think He might solve the problem. That's what you do in a conversation. It doesn't mean He will take your suggestion because He probably has a better idea, but He wants to hear what you have to say.

The privilege you have to actually talk to your Creator is not one to overlook. It can be easy to get out of the habit of praying if you don't feel you're being heard. So ask God to listen and to answer.

Thank Him when He does!

How do you feel about prayer? Is it a priority
for you? Have you ever asked God to listen
or does that seem inappropriate to you?

Heart Filter

Never let loyalty and kindness leave you!
Tie them around your neck as a reminder.
Write them deep within your heart.
PROVERBS 3:3

What's the best way to remember something important? Write it down, right? If something is very important – like a command from God – write it on your heart. How do you do that? Repeat it to yourself over and over each day until it becomes the filter by which every other thought is measured. In this case, God says that to live as a person of grace, you should write loyalty and kindness on your heart so that everything you do is through these two attitudes.

Loyalty – to God. Do not let anything trip up this loyalty and you can bet that Satan is going to try very hard to break your loyalty to God. Don't let him. Start your day with committing your thoughts, words and actions to God and refresh that commitment often through the day. Keep your loyalty to God at the forefront of your mind.

Kindness – to others. Watch how you speak to and about others. Let the filter of kindness guide each word you speak and each attitude you show. Remember that God, in His grace, is always kind to you. Reflect that kindness back to others.

What filter does your heart work through? Loyalty
and kindness or complete selfishness? What do you
need to talk with God about related to your heart filter?

Put on Christ-like Clothes

Since God chose you to be the holy people He loves,
you must clothe yourselves with tenderhearted mercy,
kindness, humility, gentleness, and patience.
COLOSSIANS 3:12

When you have a special event coming up, do you start thinking about what you will wear for it? When the day arrives, you do your hair, put on makeup and get dressed in the special outfit that you possibly purchased just for this event. What you put on is important. If you feel good in what you wear then you're more confident for the event and you often end up enjoying it more. You know the saying, "Clothes make the man (or woman.)"

Have you thought about your "clothes" in relation to your Christian life? You should, because God tells you in this verse what "pieces of clothing" you should put on so that you reflect Him to others. The five qualities shared in this verse impact how you relate to other people. Since the verse says to put these on, it must be intentional to think about these characteristics and pray for them to be evident in your life. Wear the attitudes that show care, compassion, kindness, patience and humility to others. Treat others the way you'd like them to treat you. Show Christ-like love to others so that they will be drawn to know Him.

Which of these five characteristics is your
strongest? Which do you struggle with?
How do you show these in your life?

Supportive Friends

No discipline is enjoyable while it is happening – it's painful!
But afterward there will be a peaceful harvest of right living
for those who are trained in this way. So take a new grip
with your tired hands and strengthen your weak knees.
HEBREWS 12:11-12

God, in His grace, and because He is your Father, disciplines you. It's not fun – in fact, sometimes it's downright painful. It's for a good reason, of course, so that you learn and grow in your faith. If God didn't love you, He wouldn't discipline you. He wants your faith to grow stronger and your trust to grow deeper.

Is it OK to let others know when you're hurting because of discipline? Yes it is because as they see your honesty in your struggle, then they can be free to share their own struggles. They can pray for you and you can pray for them. Encouragement comes from sharing your pain with those who care.

Remember that when you "take a new grip with your tired hands" you have to let go of the bar to grab on again. Your prayer partner friends can hold you up with their prayers and encouragement until you get a new grip. Getting through the struggle of discipline doesn't have to be done alone. God disciplines because He loves. He gives you friends and supporters because He loves. Appreciate both.

How have your friends or family helped you through difficult times? How have you been able to help someone else?

Doing Your Part

Light shines in the darkness for the godly.
They are generous, compassionate, and righteous.
PSALM 112:4

Alright Christian, have you sometimes wanted to ask God, "Why?" Why are some people so blessed while others struggle to even have enough food to eat, water to drink and a bed to sleep in? Why doesn't He dispense the blessings more evenly? Why is His grace more generously bestowed on some parts of the world and some people groups? Does your heart break for those who have so little?

These are difficult questions with no easy answers. But, just maybe God expects you, and all Christians He has so richly blessed, to step up and help those who have so little. Maybe Christians aren't doing all they could. Remember that the early church believers pooled their resources so that no one went hungry. Granted, this is harder to do today with all the suffering in the world, but, God says right in this verse that godly people are generous.

They share from how He has blessed them. They are compassionate. They see people suffering and it hurts their own hearts. They are righteous. They see the disparagement in how the world's resources have been distributed and they want to do something about it.

How do you feel when you hear of people suffering in dire straits? Have you willingly shared your own resources, whether in the form of cash or time and energy given? In whatever way you can help?

Loving When You Don't Want To

"Love your enemies! Do good to them.
Lend to them without expecting to be repaid.
Then your reward from heaven will be very great,
and you will truly be acting as children of the Most High,
for He is kind to those who are unthankful and wicked."

LUKE 6:35

What? God, do you mean this? Love my enemies? Not only love them but be good to them and lend them money, even though I know I'll never see that money again? This is asking a lot. In fact why would You even ask me to do this stuff?

OK. Stop and think. God showered down His grace on you while you were still His enemy. He forgave your sin and made you His child. He loves you more than you can ever know. He blesses you generously. If God does all that for you, can't you love your enemies?

You don't have to do it alone. You can ask God to love through you. He will send His grace and love through your heart, your words, your smile, your handshake right to those you consider to be enemies; even if they never say thank you and never change their behavior. He will help you learn to love them as they are. Through your love for them, He will bless you! You will reap the reward of behaving like Christ, loving as God loves, doing good as God does. You will be rewarded.

Who do you have difficulty loving? Why? Have you asked God to love that person through you? Are you willing to let that happen?

November

Salvation Story

As he was approaching Damascus on this mission,
a light from heaven suddenly shone down around him.
He fell to the ground and heard a voice saying to him, "Saul! Saul!
Why are you persecuting Me?" "Who are You, Lord?" Saul asked.
And the voice replied, "I am Jesus, the one you are persecuting!"
ACTS 9:3-5

God's grace saves the most unlikely people. Saul had spent his adult life persecuting Christians. He made it his life goal to get rid of anyone who followed Christ – anyone who claimed that He was the Son of God: the Messiah. In fact, Saul was on this way to Damascus to persecute the Christians there when Jesus spoke to Him.

Saul got an actual verbal interaction from Jesus to prove Jesus' reality. It worked. Saul fell to the ground, blinded, but he did believe. His was a very dramatic conversion and his life completely turned around. Some people have dramatic conversion stories, either because of the messed-up life they lived before or because God knows it will take something very unique for them to believe. Maybe your conversion story seems mundane compared to others. That's OK. God works in the way He must for each person. He knows how to get an individual's attention and that's what He does.

God's grace is not just for those who have lived a pretty good life. It's not just for those who have done terrible things. It's for everyone. God's grace and forgiveness is freely given to all.

What's your conversion story? Have you shared it
with others? Did God speak uniquely into your heart?

Grace and Trust

The Lord said, "Go over to Straight Street, to the house of Judas.
When you get there, ask for a man from Tarsus named Saul.
He is praying to Me right now. I have shown him a vision
of a man named Ananias coming in and laying hands on
him so he can see again." "But Lord," exclaimed Ananias,
"I've heard many people talk about the terrible things
this man has done to the believers in Jerusalem!"
ACTS 9:11-13

If God asks you to do something difficult or dangerous, would you do it? Would you question Him and remind Him of the danger He's putting you in? He asked Ananias to go talk to Saul. Ananias didn't know that Saul had met Jesus. He didn't know that Saul's heart had changed. He only knew that God was asking him to go right to the house where this guy was staying – this guy whose goal was to get rid of all believers. Ananias had to wonder what God was doing to him.

But, he obeyed. God told him there was a plan to grow the church and that Saul was a part of that plan. So, Ananias went. He helped Saul and look at the amazing things Saul went on to do for God.

When God showers His grace down on you, a trust is built between you and Him. You know His love. You believe He wouldn't put you in danger without walking along beside you. Grace shows love and love builds trust and trust builds obedience.

Has God asked you to do something you didn't understand? Has He ever put you into what seemed to be a dangerous situation? How did it turn out?

Grace in Times of Trouble

The LORD was with Joseph in the prison and showed
him His faithful love. And the LORD made Joseph a favorite
with the prison warden. Before long, the warden put Joseph
in charge of all the other prisoners and over everything that
happened in the prison. The warden had no more worries,
because Joseph took care of everything. The LORD was
with him and caused everything he did to succeed.
GENESIS 39:21-23

Joseph got a raw deal. Sure, he had bragged to his brothers and his dad favored him over all of them. But, their dramatic action was to sell their own brother into slavery! Then Joseph was unjustly accused of something and ended up in prison! But this was all part of God's plan. He allowed Joseph to go through some very dark days in order to get him where He wanted him to be. Joseph became the prison boss and eventually, through some pretty cool acts of God, he ended up second in command of Egypt.

Joseph never seemed to doubt God during those dark days. He never seemed to question His plan. He trusted God and because of that, he succeeded in all he did because of God's grace.

Do you trust God in the hard times? Do you believe He is leading you to His ultimate plan for your life? Are you learning through the struggles? He has a plan for you. His grace will honor your trust in Him and He will help you succeed.

What difficult things have you gone through? Did you
sense God's presence in those times? Did your heart stay
obedient to Him? How did you see God's plan unfold?

Your Purpose

We keep on praying for you, asking our God to enable you
to live a life worthy of His call. May He give you the power
to accomplish all the good things your faith prompts you to do.
Then the name of our Lord Jesus will be honored because of the
way you live, and you will be honored along with Him. This is all
made possible because of the grace of our God and Lord, Jesus Christ.
2 THESSALONIANS 1:11-12

Why are you here? What's the goal of your life? Is it to be worthy of
God's call on you? Are you striving to make His name known? What
does your faith prompt you to do?

God has given you a work to do for His Kingdom. You may feel a
nudge in your heart to do this or that – it will be His work and He will
give you the power you need to do it. Nothing else you do really matters except to lift up Jesus' name and make Him known to all around
you. The daily living you do: eating, working, visiting with friends, playing with your children is all a part of your life.

But, the purpose, the reason you're here is to lift up the name of
Jesus using the talents and abilities He has given you. That's what
He saved you for. That's your work in the Family. There is no greater
calling, and you get to be a part of it because of God's grace.

What's your role in making the name of
Jesus known? How does He use your
talents to share His love and grace?

What's Inside

> "A good person produces good things from the
> treasury of a good heart, and an evil person produces
> evil things from the treasury of an evil heart.
> What you say flows from what is in your heart."
> LUKE 6:45

What's in your heart makes such a big difference. You see, you can fool people into thinking you are a serious Christ-follower. You can even sort of fool yourself. But you can't fool God at all. And, eventually, what's hiding in your heart comes spilling out through your lips.

God saved you by His grace. He gave you His Holy Spirit. He gave you His Word. But the learning and growing to develop your new nature of trust and dependence on God … well, that takes some effort from you. What you put into your heart is what will eventually come out. If you're harboring envy, a critical spirit, judgment, unkindness and even hate, those attitudes will eventually spill out of your mouth. It won't be pretty.

Allow God to make your heart healthy. Ask Him to clean up all the negative, evil things in it and replace those with His grace, love and compassion for all people. Ask Him to fill your heart with good things. Then, what spills out will be loyalty to God, compassion for people, love, kindness, honesty and all things that show your heart belongs to Him. Make your heart healthy.

You know what's in your heart, what do you hear spilling out
of your mouth? If you're honest with yourself, do you need
God to do some housecleaning in your heart? Ask Him to do so.

God Is a Devouring Fire

Since we are receiving a Kingdom that is unshakable,
let us be thankful and please God by worshiping Him
with holy fear and awe. For our God is a devouring fire.
HEBREWS 12:28-29

God is not your buddy. Oh yes, He loves you. He cares about you. But, He's a greater being than your best friend. God saved you because He loves you. His love is real. It's deep. It's unshakeable. It's forever. He gave you membership in His family and His Kingdom where He will reign forever and ever. It has no end. Nothing can shake it. God rules supreme.

Your response to His actions is not to treat Him with the comfort of a good friend, but to worship Him with holy fear and awe. So, you're supposed to be afraid of God? No, you're supposed to respect Him for His power, His position, His judgment, His greatness and His holiness. He deserves to be treated with respect and awe.

God insists that your worship be of Him only. He will not share your heart with any idol. He is a devouring fire – consuming whoever refuses Him and absorbing whoever worships Him into His unshakeable, never-ending Kingdom.

So, thank Him for His power, His love, His Kingdom and for receiving you into it. Respect Him. Worship Him and love Him.

How do you treat God? Are you casual
about Him? Do you respect Him and worship
Him with awe? Are you trying to share your
heart between God and something else?

Where Is the Grace?

"I am leaving you with a gift – peace of mind
and heart. And the peace I give is a gift the world
cannot give. So don't be troubled or afraid."

JOHN 14:27

Jesus promised peace of mind and heart. So why is life so hard some-times? Why do people suffer? Why are there wars and bombings that leave innocent children parentless and homeless? Why are there nat-ural disasters killing thousands of people at once? Why do marriages break up? Why do children rebel? Why is there illness? Why? Why? Why? Where is God's grace in all this?

Maybe, just maybe those things are God's grace. They are hard, yes. They hurt, yes. But, in them, through them, because of them, we see God's love and care. We experience His strength to get us up and moving each day. We have the opportunity to help our fellow humans get through the messes of life. Is it possible that these terrible things are the gift because they turn your heart to cry out to God and that's where the peace is to be found? There is grace in saying, "OK God, this is what we've got today. Let's see how You're going to get us through it."

What's happening in your heart is where your faith growth is. Your faith growth is what matters to God. See His love. See His care. Em-brace His peace.

How do these thoughts make you feel –
that the struggles of life might be His grace?
Have you seen your faith grow stronger through trials?

Who Did Jesus Come For?

When Jesus heard this, He said, "Healthy people
don't need a doctor – sick people do."
MATTHEW 9:12

Why did Jesus come to earth? Because people needed the message of love that He came to share. He came to teach about God so the people knew how to obey God and live for Him and how to treat one another. When He was calling men to follow Him as His disciples, He chose some who were known sinners – tax collectors.

The Pharisees thought they knew more than Jesus did. They questioned why He would work with such creepy people as tax collectors. Jesus called their bluff. Since the Pharisees considered themselves spiritually healthy and so far above everyone else, He just said He came for the sick people of the world, which is actually everyone.

The Pharisees' arrogance kept them from grasping the message of God's love for all. His grace didn't even make sense to them.

Understanding your own sinfulness and need of God's grace means that it can change your life. You know you need Him. You know you don't deserve His salvation so when you receive it, you embrace it and everything changes.

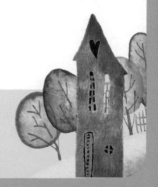

Does arrogance creep into your heart when you
think about your sinfulness? Do you feel as though
you're doing pretty good compared to others?

Who Deserves God's Grace?

For the person who keeps all of the laws except one is as
guilty as a person who has broken all of God's laws.
JAMES 2:10

Don't get arrogant about your goodness. You may be proud that you haven't committed adultery; you haven't murdered; you haven't stolen money. Yeah, you're a pretty good person. But look at all of God's laws. Have you gossiped? Have your judged another person? Have you said hurtful things, even in jest?

Scripture tells you that if you've broken any one of God's commands – any one – you're just as guilty as someone who has broken all of them. That's sobering, isn't it? No one is perfect. No one can keep all of His laws. What this means is that you need God's grace as much as anyone else does. You need His forgiveness as much as anyone else. It puts you even with people who have done the worst things you can imagine and those who are the best. You all need God's grace.

So, don't let yourself feel you are better than others or that you actually deserve God's goodness. His grace is a free gift to you and it comes from the heart of God.

Honesty time – do you sometimes feel a bit
proud of what a good person you are? Does that
impact how grateful you are for God's grace?

Jesus Is God's Grace

The Word became human and made His home among us.
He was full of unfailing love and faithfulness. And we
have seen His glory, the glory of the Father's one and only Son.
JOHN 1:14

If you've been a Christian for a while there is the danger that you get used to hearing that Jesus became human, lived among us and died to pay for your sins. You might get so used to hearing this you begin to forget that Jesus is God. He was living in His holy heaven where He is the Ruler. Life is perfect there. He gave that up to come to earth and live as a human being. He made His home among people. He was Emanuel – God with us. That, in itself, is a sacrifice.

But, Jesus' sacrifice was even greater. He was criticized, then persecuted, arrested, tortured and murdered. He had done nothing wrong. He never even sinned. He was loving to all people. He simply wanted people to know His Father. So He taught about God's love for all people. He taught people how to live for God. He encouraged people to love one another. He taught people to be fair and kind and to respect each other. Jesus did miracles to show His power and love. He showed what God is like by how He lived.

The grace of God's love is seen in every one of Jesus' actions, in every word He spoke, all He did. Jesus is the visible image of God's grace.

Do you find yourself getting lulled a bit by the stories of Jesus' humanity and death? When you stop and think about the magnitude of His sacrifice, how do you feel?

Most Important

"Don't lay a hand on the boy!" the angel said. "Do not hurt him in any way, for now I know that you truly fear God. You have not withheld from Me even your son, your only son."
GENESIS 22:12

Abraham and Sarah had waited a long, long time for the blessing of becoming parents. Their son, Isaac, was born to them in their old age and they loved him very much. So, when God asked Abraham to tie Isaac on an altar and take his life as a sacrifice to God, it must have broken Abraham's heart. However, he loved God and he did his best to obey Him.

Abraham took his young son up on a mountain, tied him up and lay him on the altar. Don't you think there were tears streaming down his cheeks as he raised the knife to take his son's life? Before he stabbed the knife into his boy, God, in His grace, stopped him. He saw that Abraham loved Him more than anything, even more than his long-awaited son.

Couldn't God know that before Isaac was put on that altar? Couldn't He look at Abraham's heart and see how much the old man loved Him? Yes, God could have done that. But, by playing the scenario out to the end … Abraham knew it, too. And, so did Isaac. Nothing can be more important than God. Nothing and no one.

God asked Abraham to do something incredible – to give up his most precious possession. Abraham held nothing back. Is there something you're holding back from God? Is there something that occupies first place in your heart instead of God?

The Impossible!

The Lord said to Joshua, "I have given you Jericho, its king, and all its strong warriors. You and your fighting men should march around the town once a day for six days … On the seventh day you are to march around the town seven times, with the priests blowing the horns … Then the walls of the town will collapse, and the people can charge straight into the town."

JOSHUA 6:2-5

God promised the Israelites that they would have their own land. They had been walking around in the wilderness for 40 years and it was finally time for them to enter the Promised Land. They had to capture the powerful city of Jericho. It had a mighty army and it was surrounded by high, thick walls. Could Joshua's little army defeat them?

God's plan was to help the Israelites defeat the army of Jericho without even having a battle. God said, "March around the city once a day for six days in silence. On the seventh day, blow the rams' horns and shout. The big walls of the city will fall and you can capture it."

God, in His grace, helped Joshua do the impossible in an impossible way. When God gave Joshua the plan, perhaps he wondered how this was going to work but when God wants something to happen, He will make it happen!

When difficult situations develop in your life and you can't imagine how they can possibly be resolved, don't give up. Trust God! He has a plan and He will see it through!

Are there things happening in your life now that you would like God's help with? Do they seem impossibly difficult? Do you trust God's strength, power, creativity and plan?

God's Rescue

Moses told the people, "Don't be afraid.
Just stand still and watch the LORD rescue you today ...
The LORD Himself will fight for you. Just stay calm."
EXODUS 14:13-14

God helped Moses lead the Israelites out of slavery in Egypt. They were free! But then Pharaoh and his army chased after them. The Israelites were backed up against the Red Sea and the Egyptian army was bearing down on them. The people were understandably frightened and they complained to Moses. "Why didn't you just leave us in Egypt?" they shouted. Imagine thousands of scared men and women shouting and screaming at Moses.

Moses' response is classic (and important), "Stand still and watch." In the middle of their panic, Moses tells them to stand still. He told them to be calm.

Sometimes when you're frightened and need God's help, you just need to stop running, stop panicking, stop crying. Just stop. Be still and see what God will do to rescue you. His help may come in the form of a miracle like parting the waters of a sea, or He may solve your problem in a very normal way. Either way, just wait for Him to do what He's going to do. He will always fight for you.

It may be key to be still and stay calm so that you can see what God will do. How good are you at waiting in stillness and calmness to see how God will rescue you?

Jesus' Birth Announcement

That night there were shepherds staying in the fields nearby, guarding their flocks of sheep. Suddenly, an angel of the Lord appeared among them, and the radiance of the Lord's glory surrounded them. They were terrified, but the angel reassured them. "Don't be afraid!" he said. "I bring you good news that will bring great joy to all people. The Savior – yes, the Messiah, the Lord – has been born today in Bethlehem, the city of David!"

LUKE 2:8-11

Jesus is God's own Son. He's the royalty of heaven. So when He was born as a human baby, His birth could have been announced to kings and princes or at least to the religious leaders of the day but that's not who God gave the birth announcement to. God, in His grace, went to the common man; shepherds watching their flocks out in a field, and they were the first to know that this special baby had been born.

Jesus didn't come to earth just for the powerful or mighty. He came for every person regardless of their status in life. If the birth announcement had been made to a king then the attitude would have been that He came for the powerful, not for the common man.

Jesus came for you. It doesn't matter if you're a CEO, a stay-at-home mom, a student. Your status doesn't matter in the least. All you need to know is that He loves you and His grace forgives your sins. He is your Savior. He came for you.

What does it mean to you that Jesus' birth was announced to the shepherds and not to kings? Does His birth bring joy to you?

Praying Friends

Suddenly, there was a bright light in the cell,
and an angel of the Lord stood before Peter.
The angel struck him on the side to awaken him and said,
"Quick! Get up!" And the chains fell off his wrists.
Then the angel told him, "Get dressed and put on your sandals."
And he did. "Now put on your coat and follow me," the angel ordered.
ACTS 12:7-8

King Herod had killed the Apostle James, and that brutal act made crowds of people so happy that he also put Peter in prison. He planned a trial after Passover and probably would kill Peter, too. But Herod didn't consider what God could do. Peter's Christian friends met together and prayed passionately for Peter's safety.

While they were praying an angel appeared in Peter's prison cell, told him to get up and to follow him out of the jail. Peter did even though he had been chained to four guards and locked in a cell in the center of the jail. His chains fell off and the prison door opened. Peter walked out of the prison without a guard saying a word!

When God wants something to happen, it will happen. In His grace, God wanted Peter's freedom. So God motivated the Christians to pray for their friend.

No situation can be considered hopeless when God is involved. When you have difficulties, pray. Believe that God hears and will answer. Pray and then watch to see what God will do.

When have you joined with others to pray for a specific
crisis? How did God respond to your prayers?

God's Grace Takes You All the Way

Elijah the prophet walked up to the altar and prayed,
"O LORD, God of Abraham, Isaac, and Jacob, prove today that
You are God in Israel and that I am Your servant. Prove that
I have done all this at Your command. O LORD, answer me!
Answer me so these people will know that You, O LORD,
are God and that You have brought them back to Yourself."
1 KINGS 18:36-37

Elijah was standing alone against 450 prophets of Baal. They had set a contest to see which of their gods could send fire from heaven to burn up an animal offering. The prophets of Baal went first, begging their god to act. He didn't. Then Elijah, doused the animal on his altar with water, lots of water. When he called on God to send down fire, God sent it immediately and burned up the bull and dried up all the water around the altar. God is God!

Elijah was God's prophet and God sent him to this contest to prove to the people who gathered to watch that He was God and Baal was not. It could have been frightening for Elijah since he was alone. But, he knew God would come through. He had seen Him do it before. God will never send you into a battle or situation where His grace will not protect you.

When God tells you to do something, obey Him and believe that He will guide and protect you through to the end.

Has God taken you to a project or ministry where you felt ill-equipped? Did He give you what you needed to do the job? How did you see His grace in the process?

Hunger Pains

Then the LORD said to Moses, "Look, I'm going to rain down food from heaven for you. Each day the people can go out and pick up as much food as they need for that day. I will test them in this to see whether or not they will follow My instructions."
EXODUS 16:4

The Israelites were first-class complainers. They had been slaves in Egypt for years, all the while begging God to rescue them. In His grace, He answered their prayer by sending Moses to lead them to freedom. He did some very impressive miracles to convince Pharaoh to let them go. He protected them numerous times on their journey. He led them with His presence in a pillar of cloud and fire. But still, each time something didn't go their way, they complained.

Now they were whining to Moses because they were hungry. So, God rained down food from heaven for them. He met their need because He loved them.

God's care is not just for your spiritual needs. He also cares about the daily needs you face. He cares if you're hungry, cold, sad, lonely or whatever you're feeling, He cares. He may not meet your need with a supernatural rainstorm of food, but He will take care of you in some way – either through a friend or a ministry or perhaps just holding you close through the pain of what you're facing.

Have you talked with God about a practical
life need you have? How did He answer?

Words of Healing

"I can't, Sir," the sick man said, "for I have no one
to put me into the pool when the water bubbles up.
Someone else always gets there ahead of me."
Jesus told him, "Stand up, pick up your mat, and walk!"
JOHN 5:7-8

Crowds of sick people lay near the Pool of Bethesda. When the water bubbled up, the first person in the water was healed. Jesus saw a man there who had been lame for over 30 years. He asked the man if he wanted to get well and the man said that he did but he could never get to the pool in time. Someone always beat him to the water. Jesus' response was simply, "Stand up. Pick up your mat and walk." The man obeyed … and he walked home that day for the first time in over 30 years!

Jesus didn't touch the lame man. He didn't say any magic phrases. He just told the man to get up and walk. Power flowed from Jesus so strongly that His words could heal sick people and bring dead people back to life. Compassion flowed from Jesus when He saw someone sick or hurting, He felt for them and wanted to help. Grace flowed from Jesus and He often helped.

Jesus sees your needs too, and He cares about your pain and your need. Listen to Him, He will tell you what to do. Obey Him and He will help you.

There is amazing power in Jesus' words. Where do you find His words today? Yes, in Scripture. Do you commit His words to memory so you can recall them when you are in need? What's your favorite verse about God's love?

Your Heart Attitude

Then Samson put his hands on the two center pillars that held up the temple. Pushing against them with both hands, he prayed, "Let me die with the Philistines." And the temple crashed down on the Philistine rulers and all the people. So he killed more people when he died than he had during his entire lifetime.

JUDGES 16:29-30

Samson accomplished more in his death than he did in his life. He was set apart as a special servant of God but he didn't always make good choices in his life. Still he was known as the strongest man in the world. Samson was captured by the Philistines through another of his bad choices. They gouged his eyes out and made fun of him. But Samson's heart still yearned to serve God. Even though he was blind and chained, Samson asked God for one more chance to serve Him.

God, in His grace, honored Samson's request and gave him back his strength so he could push down the pillars of the room, collapsing the ceiling and killing all inside, including himself. Samson killed God's enemies with his one last request.

Whatever you've done in your life – whether you've obeyed God or not – if your heart truly desires to serve Him, tell Him. Ask Him for one more chance as Samson did. In His grace, He will give you more opportunities to serve Him. God sees your heart and rewards you by the desires of your heart.

What's the attitude of your heart?
Is your desire to serve Him? Even though you've
disobeyed God, He will use you. Are you ready?

A Young Girl's Service

Naaman and his entire party went back to find the man of God.
They stood before him, and Naaman said,
"Now I know that there is no God in all the world except
in Israel. So please accept a gift from your servant."
2 KINGS 5:15

Naaman was the commander of the king's army. He was an important man, but he had leprosy. His wife's servant, a young Jewish girl who was a slave, wanted him to go see God's prophet, Elisha. She knew that through God's almighty power he could heal Naaman of the dreaded disease.

Finally Naaman was convinced to go see Elisha. He was stubborn so when he didn't get personal attention from the prophet, he was offended. However, eventually, Naaman did what Elisha told him to do and his leprosy was healed!

Did you notice that it was a young slave girl who was instrumental in directing Naaman to go see Elisha? A young girl who was a slave. She had a great idea and Naaman listened to her!

God has work for everyone. It doesn't matter if you're young or old. Wise or simple. Famous or average. He has a purpose for every person. How is God using you? What are you able to do for His Kingdom?

God has work for every person. What has
He directed you to do? How have you
been able to serve Him in the past?

Be Ready

As for Philip, an angel of the Lord said to him, "Go south down the desert road that runs from Jerusalem to Gaza."
ACTS 8:26

An angel told Philip where to go. It made no sense. It was illogical. Philip had to turn around and run the opposite direction but he obeyed. Because he obeyed, Philip had the chance to explain the Scripture to a government official who then wanted to immediately be baptized. Philip baptized him then God whisked Philip away. But Philip's immediate obedience when God called allowed him to be a part of another man believing in Christ.

Obeying even when it makes no sense can give you the opportunity to be used by God in an amazing way. When God directs, don't argue, just obey. It may make no sense at the moment but God knows what He is doing and you could have the opportunity to tell someone else about God's love and care.

Be ready to obey God with a submitted heart that is always ready to share what you know of Scripture and the Christian life. You never know when God will give you opportunities to serve Him. Be ready to do something unexpected. Be ready to take a chance.

If you had the chance to explain Scripture right now, could you do it? Are you prepared to share your faith?

Multiplied Blessings

This is what the LORD, the God of Israel, says: There will always be flour and olive oil left in your containers until the time when the LORD sends rain and the crops grow again!
1 KINGS 17:14

There was a terrible drought in the land and Elijah was hungry. God told him to go to Zarephath where a widow would give him food. Elijah obeyed but when he got to the town, the widow told him she didn't have enough food to share with him. She only had enough flour and oil to make one small loaf of bread and after that she and her son would die of starvation.

But Elijah trusted God. He knew God had directed him to this woman so he said, "Go ahead and make bread for you and your son but first make a small loaf for me. God says that there will be enough flour and olive oil for you and your son to survive until this drought is over."

The woman trusted Elijah because he was God's prophet. She made bread for him and sure enough, from that moment on her flour and oil never ran out! God, in His grace, blessed her because she served Elijah.

Serving others is not always easy. You may think you're sharing your last bit of food or money or energy. But, God sees you serving and He will, through His grace, multiply your blessings so your needs are continually met.

Has God blessed you for sharing with others? How?
Has He encouraged you to be generous with others?

Great Sin and Great Forgiveness

"I tell you, her sins – and they are many –
have been forgiven, so she has shown Me much love.
But a person who is forgiven little shows only little love."
Then Jesus said to the woman, "Your sins are forgiven."
LUKE 7:47-48

A sinful woman came to Jesus while He was having dinner at the home of a religious leader. The woman had a jar filled with very expensive perfume. She knelt down by Jesus and poured the perfume on His feet. Then she wiped His feet dry with her hair. The religious leader was upset that Jesus was letting an immoral woman touch Him.

But Jesus used this experience to teach the religious leader that a person who has sinned a little is only forgiven for a little. But a woman who has sinned a lot is forgiven for much and that makes her gratitude run deep and true. She willingly gave her love and worship to Jesus and He forgave her sins then and there.

Be honest with yourself before God by admitting your own sinfulness. Recognizing how much Jesus has forgiven you should touch your heart and give you a sense of gratitude like you've never known before. As you grasp the magnitude of God's forgiveness and grace thank Him for His gracious love.

What were you like before Christ saved you? Has He forgiven you for great sin? Does gratitude flow from your heart for His graciousness? Do you speak your gratitude to Him?

Childlike Trust

Then Jesus called for the children and said to the disciples,
"Let the children come to Me. Don't stop them!
For the Kingdom of God belongs to those who are like these children.
I tell you the truth, anyone who doesn't receive
the Kingdom of God like a child will never enter it."
LUKE 18:16-17

The old adage that children should be seen but not heard didn't fly with Jesus. His disciples tried to keep the kids away from Him so that He could deal with "more important" people. But Jesus opened their eyes to a very important fact. The children were closer to God's Kingdom than any of the "important" people.

Children have open, tender hearts that so easily trust and believe. They are less likely to criticize and be judgmental. They are less self-centered and usually very concerned about others. Jesus' comments that everyone must be like a child to receive God's Kingdom is telling. As people mature they become more cynical and the drive to succeed makes them push others down so they are personally lifted up. There's not much love in that.

Trusting God with a submitted, humble heart means you trust His grace-filled love, you believe Him without question and you follow His leading without fighting. Sometimes it feels like blind trust; well, it is, except you know He will never let you down. There's a lot of love in that kind of trust and that brings a lot of joy to your heart.

Where does your faith land on the childlike-adult spectrum? Have you learned to trust more completely as you've matured? Do you love more freely? Are you submitted more fully?

Jesus Understands

Jesus, full of the Holy Spirit, returned from the Jordan River.
He was led by the Spirit in the wilderness, where He
was tempted by the devil for forty days. Jesus ate
nothing all that time and became very hungry.

LUKE 4:1-2

You've probably had the experience of battling against a strong temptation, something that continually pulled at you, calling your name and mocking you to pay attention. It's a struggle to push it away. You can distract yourself with the other things of life; the people around you, a job, hobbies … whatever.

Jesus was alone in the wilderness facing off against Satan for 40 days! He had no support system around Him except His relationship with His Father. He had no distractions except the Scripture He had in His own heart.

Satan tempted Him with His physical comfort, power and authority, and His own physical life. Jesus experienced powerful temptation with three categories that Satan uses against people all the time.

Jesus understands the battles you fight because, by His grace to understand, He went through them, too. He fought Satan back by using the Word of God. That confirms how important it is to read Scripture, but not only read it, commit it to memory. You never know when you're going to need it.

Is there one particular thing that Satan continually tempts you with? He knows where you are weakest. How do you fight him off? Does Scripture help?

The Greatest

"Many who are the greatest now will be least important then,
and those who seem least important now will be the greatest then."
MATTHEW 19:30

What was Jesus talking about when He referred to the "greatest?"
Who does it make you think of? Government officials who control
your country's laws and standards? It can feel that your one little vote
doesn't have much impact on what they decide. You're at their mercy.
Maybe you think of those who lead the company you work for. You're
subject to their rules. Perhaps it's even church leaders with whom you
don't always agree. Maybe you think of the people around you, family
or friends who are powerful people.

If any of those "greatest" people you think about don't have hearts
submitted to God then they are great only in their own minds, not
God's. Someday things will be evened out and by God's grace, those
whose hearts are submitted to Him, those who serve Him, those who
love and care for others – they will be the greatest.

Submit your heart to God and love Him with all your heart.
Accept His will for your life. Love those around you even more than you
love yourself. Be God focused first and others focused next. By not
being concerned with being the greatest, you become the
greatest in God's Kingdom.

Do you concern yourself with being "great"
or are you submitted to God and focused on
loving Him and others. What part of that do
you need to work on improving in your life?

A Spiritual Continuum

So to keep me from becoming proud, I was given
a thorn in my flesh, a messenger from Satan to torment
me and keep me from becoming proud.

2 CORINTHIANS 12:7

A humble heart is important to God. Paul spent his life preaching about God. Much of the New Testament is Paul's writings. You might think that God would protect this man so that his ministry could flourish even more.

However, you may be able to see in Paul's writing that he was a powerful man who was used to having authority. That power could easily slide into pride if Paul wasn't careful. God helped keep Paul humble with something Paul called a thorn in the flesh. No one knows for sure what that was, but it served to remind Paul that God is God and Paul wasn't.

God will help you with keeping your heart humble if necessary. He will do that because He loves you and to serve Him you must have a humble heart that is submitted to Him. It's necessary to love Him in order to submit to Him. It's necessary to submit to Him in order to trust Him. There is a continuum in your spiritual journey and because of God's grace-filled love for you, He will help you move along in loving, submitting and trusting Him so that your arrogant heart doesn't push Him out of the way.

Do you struggle sometimes with having a
submitted heart? Is pride an issue for you?
How has God reminded you that He is God and you're not?

Praise in the Hard Times

NOV
28

Therefore, let us offer through Jesus a continual sacrifice
of praise to God, proclaiming our allegiance to His name.
And don't forget to do good and to share with those in
need. These are the sacrifices that please God.
HEBREWS 13:15-16

Praise God! Praise God through Jesus and because of Jesus' sacrificial death and the forgiveness and grace that act affords you. What does it mean to offer a sacrifice of praise? Shouldn't praise be joyful and positive? Sure ... sometimes.

But what about when life is hard? Do you praise God in the hard times? Praise Him when the medical test reveals bad news. Praise Him when the job is lost. Praise Him when a loved one dies. Praise Him when a relationship breaks. Praise Him when the money runs out. Praise Him in the storms of life. If you enjoy and praise Him in the good times, shouldn't you also accept and praise Him in the hard times? After all, it is in the hard times that He can most reveal to you His strength and support, His love and care. Praise Him in the classroom of struggle. Praise Him for the lessons learned.

At the same time, God says to shift your focus off yourself and your problems and help those around you who are struggling with their own needs. Don't think only of yourself, helping others will encourage you to look outward and upward, not always at yourself.

Are you able to praise through your pain?
Do you see God's lessons in the hard times?
How are you doing at looking outward and upward
and not always at your own struggles?

Useless Praise

Away with your noisy hymns of praise! I will not listen to the music of your harps. Instead, I want to see a mighty flood of justice, an endless river of righteous living.
AMOS 5:23-24

Oh boy. So you go to church each week and sing songs of praise to God. You lift your hands, close your eyes and plant a look of worship on your face. Maybe you even mean it at that moment in time.

But God wants more. He wants honesty. He wants sincerity. He wants consistency. Of course, God loves your praise but not if your life doesn't reflect who He is.

Before you lift your hands in praise, examine your heart. Have you given God your heart? Is it submitted to His will? Are you following God's commands so that others see your love for Him and your concern for them? Do the secrets of your heart – known only to you and God – show a desire to obey Him and not your own will?

It's easy to project a spiritual image to those around you but the condition of your heart is the real you. If your heart is stubbornly refusing to let God be God, then work on that, ask Him to cleanse your heart and help you with humility and trust. Then lift your hands in praise and sing your heart out!

Is your praise for show or honest worship? Only you and God know the true condition of your heart. Do you need to confess some things and ask His help in cleaning up your heart?

Everything You Need

By His divine power, God has given us everything we
need for living a godly life. We have received all of this
by coming to know Him, the one who called us to Himself
by means of His marvelous glory and excellence.
2 PETER 1:3

When you purchase a kit to make something you get everything you
need to create the final product. It's all in there. It makes your creation
a bit more effortless and success a bit easier.

Praise God, when you accept Jesus as your Savior you get everything
you need to successfully live a godly life. That's God's amazing grace
in action! God loves you. You don't deserve His salvation or forgiveness. You did nothing to earn it but He gives it because of His love.
What's in this godly life package? Scripture. By studying His Word you
learn His character and that you can trust Him with every aspect of your
life. His Words instruct you in life, challenge you to stay close to Him,
help you fight temptation and encourage you in your faith.

The Holy Spirit lives in your heart to hold your thoughts and behaviors
accountable, to encourage you and remind you that God is present, to
pray for you when you can't find the words, to teach you about your God.

These, along with teachers, ministers and friends and the
powerful gift of prayer that make up the package God immediately gives you when you accept Christ as Savior.

Do you sometimes try to make a life of faith more
difficult than it should be? Are you using all the tools
God gave you? How is your faith walk growing?

December

Growing Grace

"But I say, love your enemies! Pray for those who persecute you!"
MATTHEW 5:44

You've experienced God's amazing grace not just daily but moment-by-moment as He not only forgives your sins but forgets them and just keeps on loving you. He forgives you even when you knowingly and intentionally disobey His commands. That's His grace.

Are you able to offer that same grace to those who wrong you? What about those who knowingly and intentionally persecute you? Those who come after you with the goal of taking you down, emotionally, psychologically, spiritually or in your career?

Forgiving isn't easy in the best of situations but when it is a personal attack it's even more difficult. The challenge is that Jesus instructed you to forgive your enemies. Not only to forgive them but to pray for them! Why did He ask you to do this? Because, loving your enemies enough to pray for their wellbeing and spiritual growth is God's love in action. It shows not only that God's love is deeply present in your heart, but that you are submitted to His love so you can pass it on, even to those who hurt you. Forgive them, forget what they've done, pray for them. How? Only with God's love, grace and strength flowing through your submitted heart.

Do you need to forgive someone? Start by asking God to help you forgive. Actually pray for that person - a simple prayer at first for them to have a good day. Let God grow grace in your heart.

Trust Muscle

Can anything ever separate us from Christ's love?
Does it mean He no longer loves us if we have trouble
or calamity, or are persecuted, or hungry, or destitute,
or in danger, or threatened with death? No, despite all these things,
overwhelming victory is ours through Christ, who loved us.
ROMANS 8:35, 37

Asking Christ into your life does not mean an easy road from that moment on. In fact, it may mean more trouble, some simply because you claim Christ, some as the natural outcome of life in a fallen world, some because there will be powerful lessons to learn. But regardless of what comes, none of it means Christ has stopped loving you. Nothing can ever make that happen. So, why do you have to go through these difficult times? Because it's how you strengthen your trust-in-God muscles. When a person starts exercising to strengthen muscles it takes the hard work of using that muscle over and over. It makes the muscle sore. No pain, no gain is often the motto.

When you're learning to trust God with bigger issues, your trust is developed by exercising it. Sometimes that means going through tough situations and staying close to God. He wants you to grow stronger in your faith. That goal is more important than your momentary comfort and ease.

Remember you're not alone. Christ is still with you, loving you, strengthening you and celebrating all you're learning about trusting Him.

Have you ever felt abandoned by God when you were facing a trial?
As you look back, did you learn from the trial? Can you see how
God was with you through it? Has your faith grown because of it?

Crippling Fear

I lay down and slept, yet I woke up in safety,
for the LORD was watching over me.
PSALM 3:5

Fear is crippling. When fear is consuming your heart it's impossible to think about anything else except what you fear is going to happen. Fear wakes you in the middle of the night, playing over scenarios in your mind of "what ifs." Those thoughts prevent you from going back to sleep.

Rest doesn't happen when you're afraid. Fear makes you stop eating or eat nonstop. It keeps you from being concerned about others or engaging in their lives. You can't think about anything else.

However, when you give your fear to God, things get better. Give it to Him – just tell Him that you know you can't fix this. You know He can see what's scaring you and He knows what will actually happen. Ask Him to free you from fear.

Admittedly you will have to do this over and over because Satan knows he can trip you up with fear and pull you away from God. So, each time that fear pops into your mind, stop it. Tell God, "I know You have this. I'm not going to let it consume me. You handle this God."

Then, lie down and sleep in peace. God is watching over you.

Is there some fear consuming you right now?
Have you given it to God? Then, did you
grab it back? Give it to Him again as often
as you must to gain freedom from fear.

Everything You Need

"Don't worry about these things, saying, 'What will we eat?
What will we drink? What will we wear?' These things dominate
the thoughts of unbelievers, but your heavenly Father already
knows all your needs. Seek the Kingdom of God above all else,
and live righteously, and He will give you everything you need."
MATTHEW 6:31-33

Trust doesn't happen automatically, at least not at a deep level. When you first invite Christ into your life, you're excited and feel that you can take on the whole world because He is with you, strengthening, guiding and providing. But you soon realize that trust begins on one level and then grows deeper and deeper as you see God's grace in providing for you and your faith matures.

Unfortunately, there are also times, even for a more mature believer, of worry and fear. There are times when everything ahead of you is foggy and murky. You just can't see how things could possibly turn out well. There's certainly no way that you can make that happen. So, you worry. Sometimes that worry is about basic things like food and clothing. Sometimes it's about really big things.

God reminds you that He already knows everything you need so there's not really anything you need to worry about there. The only thing you need to do is focus on knowing Him and living for Him. He will take care of everything else.

Worry is such a tough topic. It's difficult not to be worried about
something or another. What do you worry about? Have you
prayed about it? Do you believe God is working on it?

In the World,
Not of the World

You adulterers! Don't you realize that friendship with the world makes you an enemy of God? I say it again: If you want to be a friend of the world, you make yourself an enemy of God. Do you think the Scriptures have no meaning? They say that God is passionate that the Spirit He has placed within us should be faithful to Him.

JAMES 4:4-5

Whoa! This is pretty strong language. If you try to live the way the world says is right instead of obeying God, you're cheating on Him like an adulterer. That's nothing to take lightly. OK, look at the facts: God saved you by His grace through the sacrifice of His Son. He forgives your sin and His Spirit lives in you. In essence, you belong to Him. So take your faith walk seriously. Don't try to live like you did before sometimes – like when you're with your non-believing friends, then live like a Christian when you're with your Christian friends. You're either all in with God or you're not in at all.

The Christian life is a journey that you begin as a baby and through study, prayer and experience your faith grows stronger. Only if you make the effort and do not intentionally sabotage your growth by friendship with the world. Scripture teaches you should be "in the world" but not "of the world." That means you live here, sure. But you shouldn't believe or behave like those who do not know God.

Honesty time. Is there some part of your pre-Christian life that you're trying to hold on to? Is there some behavior that you slide back into when you're with those friends?

Strength in Numbers

But you, dear friends, must build each other up in your
most holy faith, pray in the power of the Holy Spirit,
and await the mercy of our Lord Jesus Christ,
who will bring you eternal life. In this way,
you will keep yourselves safe in God's love.
JUDE 1:20-21

God in His wisdom and grace provided you with Christian brothers and sisters who can play an important role in your faith walk. God is all you need, but He also knows that sometimes you need someone who can hold your hand, give you a hug, pray with you, laugh with you, cry with you.

A good Christian friend or spouse will hold you accountable by challenging you if your decisions seem to waver from the teachings of Scripture. You can do the same for him or her. Together you pray for one another and for situations God places on your hearts. There is strength in the power of Christians praying together. Christians are to encourage one another, in their faith, ministry and life. Don't waste time by tearing each other down. Remember you are both saved by grace. You are both working for the Kingdom. You are both members of God's family. Help each other stay strong and grow stronger.

Thank God if you have a spouse or a friend you can do this with. It's a gift from Him.

Do you have a Christian friend or spouse with whom you
have this kind of close relationship? How do you encourage
one another? How do you help each other stay strong?

Be Careful What You Say

Among all the parts of the body, the tongue is
a flame of fire. It is a whole world of wickedness,
corrupting your entire body. It can set your whole
life on fire, for it is set on fire by hell itself.
JAMES 3:6

Perhaps you said the childhood chant, "Sticks and stones may break my bones but words will never hurt me." Cute, but not true. Words do so much damage. If you let your mind float back to your younger days can you still recall something unkind or downright mean that was said to you or about you, even years ago?

Someone has said that one unkind word outweighs ten kind ones. Tender self-images absorb the negative and don't believe the positive.

Here's the thing, in a fit of anger or frustration you can say some pretty cruel things to someone. Then, when you calm down you apologize and say you didn't really mean it. However, the damage is done. Those unkind words will lie on that person's heart for a long time and damage is done to her self-perception that can take a very long time to heal.

Your words matter. They hurt others or lift them up. They discourage or encourage. Your words should reflect the fact that the Holy Spirit lives in you. They should show that you know you've received God's grace and you wish to pass it along to others.

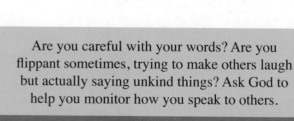

Are you careful with your words? Are you
flippant sometimes, trying to make others laugh
but actually saying unkind things? Ask God to
help you monitor how you speak to others.

Your Safe Fortress

I wait quietly before God, for my victory
comes from Him. He alone is my rock and my
salvation, my fortress where I will never be shaken.
PSALM 62:1-2

You do need a fortress to hide in sometimes, don't you? A place where your cares are kept at bay. Your enemies can't get close to you. A place where you have no worries. You can snuggle down with a soft, fuzzy blanket and know that you're safe.

There's only one place where you can be that protected and that's with God.

How does He become your rock; your fortress? It happens because you trust Him to protect you. There's no doubt in your mind that He loves you and has your best interests in His plan. So, you love Him, you give Him your heart and life. Then, when hard things come or you're frightened and alone, you turn to Him, shutting out the rest of the world. Keep your eyes focused on Him because He promises to be your safe place.

There will be times when you're concerned because that's the way God made you. You care about loved ones, your health, terrible things happening in the world. Concern is OK. But when that concern slides over to worry, run to God. Trust Him with the concern and rest in Him.

How does God become your fortress? What do you visualize as you hide in Him? How does He make you feel comforted and protected?

Living for Christ

Let the message about Christ, in all its richness fill your lives. Teach and counsel each other with all the wisdom He gives. Sing psalms and hymns and spiritual songs to God with thankful hearts.

COLOSSIANS 3:16

You've accepted Jesus as your Savior. You believe what Scripture teaches about Him. You believe His words. In order to grow deeper in your faith in Him, let His teachings sink down deep in your heart. Let it make a difference in how you live, what you speak, how you think.

Spend time in Scripture reading about Him. Get to know Him through His own Words. Let Christ's teachings make you a brand new person. By His grace He fills you with His wisdom, learned from His Word, so that you can counsel others in their Christian lives. Pay attention to the Holy Spirit guiding your words as you teach and counsel others. Be careful that the counsel you give is from His wisdom and not your own opinions or desires. Be extremely careful with this responsibility of helping others.

Don't forget to praise God! Sing your praise loudly with a heart that is exploding in thankfulness for His love and grace. Praise Him every day! Let the whole world know that you give God credit and praise for all you have and all you are. It's all a gift to you from Him. Celebrate!

Honesty time, how much time do you spend reading the Bible? How often do you meditate on what you read there? How are Christ's words sinking into your heart?

Your Helper

*Since we are living by the Spirit, let us follow the
Spirit's leading in every part of our lives. Let us not become
conceited, or provoke one another, or be jealous of one another.*
GALATIANS 5:25-26

When you became a Christian, God's gift of grace to you was the Holy Spirit. What a wonderful gift! He helps you understand what Scripture teaches by helping it make sense in your heart. He gives you twinges of conscience when you aren't fully obeying. He helps you get back on the right track when you're straying away from obeying God. He is your mentor, coach and leader in every way.

So, if you're serious about growing stronger in your Christian walk; if you want to become mature in your faith: pay attention to the Spirit! When He tells you to straighten up, listen to Him. When He guides you to do something, obey Him. When He challenges you to turn from a certain behavior, attitude or thought, do it. If you're not going to pay any attention to the Holy Spirit, why have Him in your heart? He's there to help you.

Don't get conceited about that or bossy with others because you have the Spirit, so do they. You're part of the same family and you have the same goals. Get along with one another and work together as a team.

How does the Holy Spirit make Himself known to you? When was a time that you knew He was holding you accountable or challenging you? Did you pay attention? What happened?

Super Power

I also pray that you will understand the incredible
greatness of God's power for us who believe Him.
This is the same mighty power that raised Christ
from the dead and seated Him in the place of honor
at God's right hand in the heavenly realms.
EPHESIANS 1:19-20

God's grace to you began with the world He made for you. Then of course you know His grace of saving you and forgiving your sin. But, beyond that His grace makes available to you His incredible, extravagant, amazing power!

There's nothing He can't do. There is no enemy He can't defeat. There's no problem He can't solve. Look, His power raised Christ from the dead! That power is for you. What do you need? Ask Him. What do you want God to do for you? Ask Him.

Have you recognized all that's available to you? Do you only read about God's power or do you access it in your life? Your life can be so much more when you do. Your trust in God makes His power available to give you energy and strength to face every day. His power will grow your faith and your ministry for Him!

Study God's Word so you can understand His power and learn how to allow it to guide your life and be useful to you in your service to Him.

Do you think about God's power and how even one
little bit of it can change everything for you? How can
you enjoy more of His power in your life and work?

Deep Roots

DEC
12

I pray that from His glorious, unlimited resources
He will empower you with inner strength through His Spirit.
Then Christ will make His home in your hearts as you trust in Him.
Your roots will grow down into God's love and keep you strong.
EPHESIANS 3:16-17

You will be empowered – filled with strength and perseverance – from the limitless resources God owns. There's nothing you can't do because you have God's Spirit living in you and He is God's power, wisdom and strength.

When you first accepted Christ you no doubt embraced your faith with energy and excitement. But, now as you grow more mature, you understand more about Christ and about living for Him. So, He is even more at home in your heart.

Paul prays for you that your roots will go down deep into God's love. Think about that. Think of a tall tree, blowing and buffeted in the wind. Sometimes it seems to nearly be bent double by the wind's power but it doesn't break and it doesn't pull out of the ground because its roots have gone down deep. Its roots hold it firm. By God's grace, your roots in Him will hold you firm in the storms that come along in your life.

Take time to study God's Word and to pray so that you grow closer and closer to Him. Open your heart to trust Him more and more so your roots can go deep!

Your roots settled deep in God's love means you love Him
and trust Him completely. Can you say that's true for you?
How can you grow your roots deeper in Him?

A Pleasing Aroma

Imitate God, therefore, in everything you do,
because you are His dear children. Live a life filled with love,
following the example of Christ. He loved us and offered
Himself as a sacrifice for us, a pleasing aroma to God.
EPHESIANS 5:1-2

You've accepted Christ and by God's grace your sins are forgiven. What's next? How does your life change because Jesus is in it? How do you learn to live for Him?

Because of God's grace He gave you the Bible which is filled with stories showing you how God worked with people, how Jesus interacted with people and all He taught and the miracles of compassion He did.

Scripture tells you what God wants you to know about relating to others, loving them, treating them with respect. But, it's not just a bunch of rules. It's not just a list of dos and dont's. The Bible actually shows you God.

God wants you to imitate Him, copy His behavior. Copy Him as you learn so that His standards sink into your heart. Begin with loving others, as Christ did. He sacrificially loved. Of course that's evident because He died for your sins. But, He also loved sacrificially when He was on earth by giving His time and energy, even when He was tired or hungry, to help others. He cared about all He met. Imitate Jesus and you, too, will be a pleasing aroma to God.

How do others see Christ in you?
How do you imitate the way Christ lived?

Spiritual Gifts

> There are different kinds of spiritual gifts, but the same Spirit
> is the source of them all. There are different kinds of service,
> but we serve the same Lord. God works in different ways,
> but it is the same God who does the work in all of us.
> 1 CORINTHIANS 12:4-6

When you accepted Christ, He gave you a spiritual gift. He does that for everyone who accepts Jesus. It may be a talent or ability that you had before becoming a Christian but God enhances it or opens your eyes to the possibilities of how you can use it for Him. Don't expect to wake up one morning and be a concert pianist if you've never had a lesson. Just pay attention to the things you enjoy doing and that you get positive comments from others about. That could easily be the gift God wants you to use for Him.

Every person has a gift to be used for God. All the gifts are from His Holy Spirit but they are all different. Some are uniquely different, some are slightly different. Some are out front, ministering to the masses. Some are humble caring for the poor. Some are teaching children, some are social. Some are writing. Some are simply being a friend, sharing conversation over cups of coffee.

All gifts are being used for the same purpose – serving God. So, yes, your gift is different from others. But, it's necessary. It's useful. It's for God's Kingdom.

What do you consider to be your spiritual gift? How do you use it for the Lord? How have you worked at developing and growing it to be even more useful?

DEC
15

The Greatest Thing

Three things will last forever – faith, hope, and love –
and the greatest of these is love.
1 CORINTHIANS 13:13

Why are some people so hard to love? There are those people who just rub you the wrong way. Each word they speak is annoying and they speak often!

Those people who make everything about them. No matter what the conversation is or who's talking, they interrupt and bring everything back to them. There are those people who think they know more than anyone else and they loudly and firmly give their opinions, dismissing anyone else's ideas. Yes, those people are hard to love. Does God really expect you to love those people? Is it really that important?

God says there are three things that will last forever. Your faith, which God gave you by His grace, will go into eternity with you because of the Lord you worship. Hope which is the promise of heaven with God forever – your eternal reward. And the greatest is love.

Love for God and from God that is greater than any other love. But, don't discount that Jesus said often to love others. Love is what sets you apart from those who don't know Christ. So, if there's someone you have trouble loving, ask God to help you. Let Him love through you.

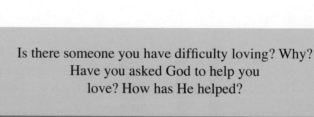

Is there someone you have difficulty loving? Why?
Have you asked God to help you
love? How has He helped?

God's Protection

In times of trouble, may the LORD answer your cry.
May the name of the God of Jacob keep you safe from all harm.
PSALM 20:1

Where do you go when life gets messy? Do you cry out to God when you have trouble? Is He the first place you go? Or do you try to handle things yourself for a while?

If you go to God, that means you trust Him and you have let go of control of your own life. You trust Him to guide your steps and direct your life. Your heart is submitted to Him and you're willing to go wherever His plan takes you.

Life will have problems – that's part of living. But you have God watching over you and protecting you.

Don't be afraid. Call on God. He will hear you. He will answer. He will keep you safe from harm. That's His grace in action.

As you're going through difficult things and continually calling on Him for strength and protection, your faith in Him will grow stronger. That's the good thing that comes from problems.

Call on God to help you and then watch and see how He will guide and protect you!

God promises to protect you, though that doesn't mean He stops your problems. How have you seen His protection?

All-Day Praise

It is good to give thanks to the LORD,
to sing praises to the Most High.
It is good to proclaim Your unfailing love in the morning,
Your faithfulness in the evening,

PSALM 92:1-2

How do you start your day? Do you sing praises to God before you even get out of bed? Is your first thought to thank Him for a good night of rest and the new day ahead?

Start your day by telling God how much you love Him and by thinking about how much He loves you. What a great way to begin your day – with love! That starts your day with joy and security in your place in God's family.

Throughout the day, continue thanking Him for His guidance. Ask His direction and advice in the things you face throughout the day. Notice His blessings and thank Him for them as you do. Make your praise a constant throughout the day.

Before you close your eyes at night, thank God for His faithfulness to you. You were not alone for one moment in the day. Thank Him for the specific ways you saw His presence and the definite ways you experienced His guidance.

Thank Him for watching over you as you sleep and keeping you safe. Because of all He does you can sleep in peace.

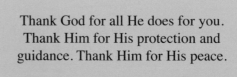

Thank God for all He does for you.
Thank Him for His protection and
guidance. Thank Him for His peace.

Grace for Dorcas

There was a believer in Joppa named Tabitha
(which in Greek is Dorcas). She was always doing
kind things for others and helping the poor.

ACTS 9:36

Dorcas was a nice person. She made clothes for the poor widows. She gave of her life to help others. Many people loved her so when she got sick and died her friends were very sad. They would miss her generosity and kindness. Dorcas' friends sent for Peter. They believed that he could bring their friend back by God's power. Peter came. He heard all the wonderful stories about Dorcas. Then, with God's power and by God's grace, he raised Dorcas back to life and restored her to her friends.

You never know what God's response will be to your work for Him. His grace restored Dorcas to life. But on the other side of that He also restored a good and helpful friend to the women of Joppa.

How do you serve others? Are you generous with your time and money? Do you notice people around you who are in need? Does your heart hurt for them? Are you willing to do whatever God directs you to do?

What about your friends? Do you notice when they are doing nice things for others? Do you thank God for their generosity? Praise God for all who serve Him and serve others.

Do you serve others? If God places someone on your heart, do you respond by doing what He wants? Do you notice those in need around you?

Step of Faith

Jesus immediately reached out and grabbed him.
"You have so little faith," Jesus said. "Why did you doubt Me?"
MATTHEW 14:31

Jesus was walking across the top of the lake walking on water to get to His disciples who were crossing the lake in a boat. A big storm had blown up and the disciples were scared. Then they saw Jesus walking toward them through the storm. They thought He was a ghost. They were scared!

But then, Peter realized it was Jesus and he cried, "Let me come to You." Jesus said, "Come." So Peter locked his eyes on Jesus and jumped out of the boat and walked on water. Peter walked on water!

But then Peter noticed the waves and the wind and he took his eyes off Jesus. Right away he sank into the water. When he cried for help, Jesus reached out and pulled Peter up. He was sad that Peter's faith had doubted Him. Peter would have been safe if he had kept his eyes on Jesus and trusted Him.

In His grace, Jesus rescued Peter from the water. He will rescue you, too, when your faith stumbles. Take a risk because you trust Him. Take a step of faith but keep your eyes on Jesus!

Have you ever taken a step of faith?
Were you afraid? Did you keep your eyes
on Jesus? How did He protect you?

One Sheep

"In the same way, it is not My heavenly Father's will
that even one of these little ones should perish."
MATTHEW 18:12

In three little verses Jesus shared how important you are to God. He said that if a shepherd had 100 sheep and even one wandered away that shepherd would leave the other 99 alone and go searching for his one lost sheep.

Isn't that amazing? He still has 99 sheep. But he's willing to leave them all alone while he searches through the hills for his one lost sheep. That one sheep matters to him as much as the other 99.

Jesus said that this is just how God feels about even one person leaving this earth without knowing Him. One person. That could be you. God's desire is that every single person who has ever lived or ever will live should know Him.

God will pursue all people by giving chance after chance for them to meet Him. It's not a one chance only situation. He doesn't give up. He will bring repeated opportunities for individuals to meet Him through people and their stories.

Perhaps you will be one of those opportunities for someone. Perhaps by sharing your gift and your testimony you will open the door for someone to accept Jesus!

Doesn't it make you feel special that God cares that much about you? How did He pursue you? How has He used you to share His love with others?

Servant Heart

"Whoever wants to be a leader among you must be your servant, and whoever wants to be first among you must become your slave. For even the Son of Man came not to be served but to serve others and to give His life as a ransom for many."
MATTHEW 20:26-28

The mother of two of Jesus' disciples came to Him with the amazing request that her boys be allowed to sit on either side of Him in heaven. That would be quite a place of honor. Jesus turned to the two men and told them they had no idea what they were asking. The other ten disciples heard the conversation and they were upset that the first two might get more recognition than them.

That's when Jesus pointed out that in order to be a leader you have to be a servant. A true leader serves his people. He doesn't lift himself above them. What the boys were trying to do was be more important than anyone else, to be special, to be above the masses. But that isn't leadership at all.

This is important – your job as a child of God is to take the position of a servant, a slave. Serve others, don't try to be above them. Show them God's grace by doing the things that no one else wants to do for them. Do the jobs that are behind the scenes. Don't expect people to serve you. Share God's love by letting others see your love through serving and helping.

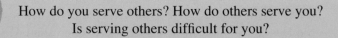

How do you serve others? How do others serve you?
Is serving others difficult for you?

Unexpected Protection

Paul's nephew – his sister's son – heard
of their plan and went to the fortress and told Paul.
ACTS 23:16

A bunch of Jews decided they were going to kill Paul. They were angry about his teachings about Jesus. He had been imprisoned several times but now they made a plot to ambush him and kill him. They got the authorities to order that Paul be brought before the high council and they would ambush him along the way. Forty men vowed not to eat or drink anything until Paul was dead.

But, Paul's young nephew heard about the plot. He went to visit Paul in prison and warned him of the plot. Paul had him tell the commander not to take Paul that way.

The young boy saved Paul's life. But he didn't do it on his own. God, in His grace, used that boy to protect Paul. God always has a plan and protection can come from anywhere.

There may be times when you are part of the plan that saves someone else. There may be times when you are saved or protected by someone. There will be times when you don't even know God has protected you. That's His grace, always watching out for you.

It's probably a good thing that you don't know all the times God protects you. It would be scary to know how often you're in danger. But, when has He protected you? How did He do it? Thank Him!

Willing Sacrifice

"Abba, Father," He cried out, "everything is possible for You.
Please take this cup of suffering away from Me.
Yet I want Your will to be done, not Mine."
MARK 14:36

Jesus knew who He was. He knew why He came to earth. He was part of the plan. But now He was in the Garden of Gethsemane, just prior to His betrayal and arrest. He knew what was coming. He even knew who of His friends would betray Him.

Now, three of His closest friends were sleeping a little ways from Him. They were supposed to be praying but they kept falling asleep. He was alone and He knew what was ahead for Him.

Jesus' prayer here is telling. He asked God to stop things, change the plan, do something else. However, He was willing to do what God knew was best. God's will not His will. The grace of Jesus' sacrifice seems even greater when you think about it here.

It reminds you that salvation wasn't free for Him. It cost Him pain and suffering. It cost Him His life.

Jesus' submission to God's will in this prayer is beautiful. Does it make your heart fill with gratitude? It should because it shows you how much He loves you. He willingly went through torture and crucifixion because He loves you.

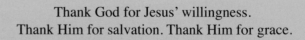

Thank God for Jesus' willingness.
Thank Him for salvation. Thank Him for grace.

Promise Kept

There was a man in Jerusalem named Simeon.
He was righteous and devout and was eagerly
waiting for the Messiah to come and rescue Israel.
The Holy Spirit was upon him and had revealed to him
that he would not die until he had seen the Lord's Messiah.
That day the Spirit led him to the Temple.
So when Mary and Joseph came to present the baby Jesus
to the Lord as the law required, Simeon was there.
LUKE 2:25-28

God kept a promise to Simeon. The Spirit had told Simeon that he wouldn't die until he had seen the Messiah. Then the Spirit led him to the temple on the exact day that Mary and Joseph brought their infant son to be dedicated. Simeon saw the baby and God opened his heart to know that this child was the Messiah!

Simeon must have been a dedicated servant of God with the Spirit living in him because he obeyed the Spirit to go to the temple and he recognized the child right away.

God's grace applies even to things like allowing a grown man to see a specific infant at a specific time because that was part of His promise. When God makes a promise you can be certain that He will keep it. His grace extends to more than salvation and forgiveness, it fulfills promises, too. You can trust Him to keep His promises.

Which of God's promises are you holding on to?
Do you believe He will keep His promises?
Have you seen Him keep some already?

Humble Servant

John answered their questions by saying,
"I baptize you with water; but someone is
coming soon who is greater than I am – so
much greater that I'm not even worthy to be His
slave and untie the straps of His sandals. He will
baptize you with the Holy Spirit and with fire."
LUKE 3:16

John knew what his job was. He was getting the people ready to hear Jesus' teachings. He wasn't the main attraction, but he was advertising it.

Some of John's disciples may have wished that he was more important than Jesus but John didn't feel that way. He knew from the beginning that Jesus was coming and that He was more important and more powerful than John and he was just fine with that.

John had a humble spirit. He knew what his job was and he was happy to do it. He didn't have to be number one. He never tried to be. He gladly stepped aside when Jesus came.

Humility in God's service is important. A humble person knows what her job is and she does it with gladness. A humble person is happy to let someone else take center stage. She doesn't need to passive-aggressively push others aside. She knows that God's work is a team effort and every job is important to Him.

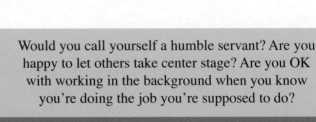

Would you call yourself a humble servant? Are you happy to let others take center stage? Are you OK with working in the background when you know you're doing the job you're supposed to do?

Faith of Friends

Four men arrived carrying a paralyzed man on a mat. They
couldn't bring him to Jesus because of the crowd, so they dug a
hole through the roof above His head. Then they lowered the man
on his mat, right down in front of Jesus. Seeing their faith, Jesus
said to the paralyzed man, "My child, your sins are forgiven."
MARK 2:3-5

These four men were really good friends to the paralyzed man. They
carried him on a mat to a crowded house. When they couldn't get
in to see Jesus, they didn't give up. The believed Jesus could help
their friend. So they dug a hole in the roof of the house and lowered
the mat down right in front of Jesus. They disrupted the room full
of people. They stopped Jesus' teaching. They didn't care because
they wanted Jesus to help their friend and they believed He could.
Jesus saw the faith of the four men and because of their faith, He
healed their friend! Amazing.

Faith that carries a friend on a mat. Faith that tries to push into a
crowded house. Faith that digs a hole in the roof. Faith that disrupts
Jesus' teaching. That's faith. They believed He could heal. They believed He would. He did.

Jesus pays attention to faith. He honors it. Maybe you don't carry
a friend on a mat to Jesus. But do you carry her in prayer to Him? Do
you believe He can help? Do you believe He will?

It's a privilege to be able to pray for a friend.
When you tell someone you will pray for her,
do you? Do you pray believing God will answer?

Not Average at All

"What is the price of five sparrows – two copper coins?
Yet God does not forget a single one of them.
And the very hairs on your head are all numbered.
So don't be afraid; you are more valuable
to God than a whole flock of sparrows."
LUKE 12:6-7

Do you ever feel that you're nothing special? Oh sure, you know that God loves you. He says He does. But, you feel like you've never done anything big for Him. Your testimony of salvation isn't dramatic. You feel that you are … average.

There's nothing wrong with average. Look around at nature – you can't get much more average than a sparrow. They are everywhere. In Bible times they were one of the cheapest things to buy for sacrifices. Even if they were a dime a dozen, God doesn't forget a single sparrow. He knows where each one is every moment.

Not only that but He keeps track of how many hairs are on your head. That must mean you're pretty special to Him. You may be average by the world's opinion but to God, you are someone very special. He loves you. He saved you. He forgives you. He has a job for you to do. He has reserved a spot in His heaven for you. Average? Not in God's eyes!

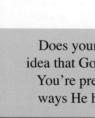

Does your self-image need a boost? Does the idea that God counts the hairs on your head help? You're pretty special to Him. List some of the ways He has blessed you. You matter to Him.

Loving Others

We love each other because He loved us first.
1 JOHN 4:19

Love is a wonderful thing. Life wouldn't be very pleasant if we didn't feel loved. It would be pretty bland if we had no one to love. Of course not everyone has a spouse, but there are family members to love and friends and even pets that make life so much richer.

The Originator of love is God. He even described Himself as love – God is love. It began with Him even before He first created anything. It's His character so He was love before He made the first person to love. But then He made Adam and Eve and loved them. He loves all of their descendants – that's you.

God gave you the ability to love, too. Your first love must be Him. No one should be more important to you than He is. The more you love God the more He teaches you about love. That gives you the ability to love others.

Can people love who don't know God? Sure. But, love with God in it is fuller, deeper and richer than any other love. Loving other Christians gives you a bond that no other love can understand. It's a love for eternity.

How strong is your love for God? Is He Number One for you? How is your love for others? Do you find your love to be stronger and richer because God is in it?

The Culmination of Grace

Then I saw a new heaven and a new earth,
for the old heaven and the old earth had disappeared.
And the sea was also gone. And I saw the holy city, the
new Jerusalem, coming down from God out of heaven
like a bride beautifully dressed for her husband.
REVELATION 21:1-2

This is part of the description John gave of heaven. It is the ultimate gift of God's grace. Yes, you have salvation. You will have experienced God's forgiveness a multitude of times by the time you get to see heaven yourself. God's grace will have guided and blessed you every day of your earthly life. But the culmination is here. You are allowed, by God's grace, to enter His heaven. You will be a resident there forever. In His presence. With His angels. With your loved ones, even the ones who died a long time ago.

Satan will be no more. There will be no more evil or sin. There will be no sadness, only joy. You will be in the presence of your Savior! John tells us that it's a beautiful place with streets of gold and alabaster buildings and pearl gates and walls made of gems. But you know, none of that will really matter because you'll be with Jesus and He will shine brighter than anything else! Everyone there will focus on worshipping Him. Peace and joy forever. Praise God for the gift of heaven!

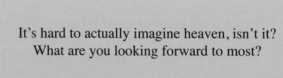

It's hard to actually imagine heaven, isn't it?
What are you looking forward to most?

Be a Witness

"You will receive power when the Holy Spirit
comes upon you. And you will be My witnesses,
telling people about Me everywhere – in Jerusalem,
throughout Judea, in Samaria, and to the ends of the earth."
ACTS 1:8

No one lives forever. This earthly life ends for all of us. God is not willing that anyone should leave this earth without having the opportunity to hear about His love and make their choice about accepting Jesus. That choice means the difference between eternity in hell or heaven. It also means the difference between a life filled with God's guidance and love or a life without Him.

But how will people hear if you don't share? When the Holy Spirit was given, this challenge was also give that God's children are to be His witnesses throughout the entire world. Just because you don't go to a foreign country doesn't mean you aren't a witness. Tell your neighbors, coworkers, family. Let them know about God's love.

If you don't know how or you're afraid to speak your faith, ask God to show you how. Ask Him to give you opportunities to live your faith in front of them by showing love and grace. Ask Him for conversations that naturally lead to a chance to share your faith.

God wants them to know. He will help you in the work. His grace saved you. His grace will help you.

Are you courageous about sharing your faith? Do you know people who don't know Christ? Do you believe that He will come soon and opportunities will be lost for them to choose Him?

Come Quickly, Jesus!

He who is the faithful witness to all these things says,
"Yes, I am coming soon!" Amen! Come, Lord Jesus!
May the grace of the Lord Jesus be with God's holy people.
REVELATION 22:20-21

From the time Jesus started teaching on earth, He told people that He would go back to heaven and get a place ready for them. Then He would come back and get His children and take them to heaven with Him to live forever.

Ever since Jesus returned to heaven, people have been waiting for His second coming. Some have predicted dates but they weren't right. Jesus said that no one would know the hour or the day that He would come back. Only the Father knows. That means you have to be ready at any moment. Don't get lazy about obeying Him. There won't be time to change much about your life when He appears. It will happen quickly and without warning. Be ready.

The more evil this world becomes the more you anticipate Jesus' return. He will take you to heaven where there's no evil at all.

Be intentional about obeying God. Be serious about sharing His message of love with others so they can choose to accept Jesus. Be encouraging with your friends and family to help them grow deeper in their faith. Be so in love with Jesus that you can speak this prayer and mean it, "Come, Lord Jesus!"

Are you eagerly waiting for Jesus to return?
Are you ready? Have you shared His love with
others so they can anticipate Him, too?

THE
SHIP'S
REVENGE